About this book

The remarkable array of women's activists and leaders from different parts of the world assembled for the dialogue in this volume are deeply concerned at the recent emergence of various trends that may threaten the ongoing work of women's movements in advancing gender equality, women's human rights and sustainable human development. These phenomena include the multifarious impacts of globalization and neoliberal economics, developments in biotechnology, the neo-conservative backlash against women's rights, monopolistic ownership patterns over information technologies that exclude women, fundamentalisms of various kinds and the rise of identity politics that subordinate or marginalize women's issues, and the increase in violent conflict and war.

The contributors to this volume are united in seeing a pressing need for women's movements to evaluate the methods they have used until now, with a view to making their political work more effective in future. They try to identify current issues and trends in the world. They think through how these may impact on women and the work of women's movements. And they identify how women should prepare for them, and what strategies they should prioritize, in order to protect and advance their agenda.

With as deliberately diverse a group of women thinkers as this, there is inevitably a thought-provokingly diverse range of views about how women ought to respond if they are not to be pushed on to the defensive, but instead regain the initiative and be more proactive across the wide range of issues that bear particularly on one half of humanity.

AWID

The Association for Women's Rights in Development (AWID) is an international membership organization, headquartered in Toronto, Canada, with almost 6,000 members in over 100 countries, primarily in the global South. Set up in 1982, AWID has been working to bring about policy, institutional and individual change that will improve the lives of women and girls everywhere. AWID does this by sharing strategic information and creating critical spaces for organizing and strategizing. AWID is one of the few organizations to play the role of facilitator and provocateur amongst gender equality advocates at the global level.

Mama Cash

Mama Cash is an independent women's foundation based in Amsterdam. Mama Cash strives for a peaceful and just world where women are free to make their own choices and decisions. To this end Mama Cash mobilizes resources and financially supports women's groups that initiate ground-breaking, taboo-breaking and often risky initiatives centred around bodily integrity, art, culture and media, economic justice, peace and security and leadership and participation. Mama Cash believes that social transformation involves forward-looking strategic thinking as well as great courage and creativity. Mama Cash, founded in 1983, is the oldest international women's fund in the world, and has raised over €20 million and supported more than 5,000 women's groups globally.

JOANNA KERR, ELLEN SPRENGER
AND ALISON SYMINGTON | editors

The future of women's rights

Global visions and strategies

Zed Books
LONDON | NEW YORK

published in association with

The Association for Women's
Rights in Development (AWID)

Mama Cash

The future of women's rights: global visions and strategies was first published by Zed Books Ltd, 7 Cynthia Street, London N1 9JF, UK and Room 400, 175 Fifth Avenue, New York, NY 10010, USA in 2004.

Second impression, 2005
www.zedbooks.co.uk

published in association with:

The Association for Women's Rights in Development (AWID), 96 Spadina Avenue, Suite 401, Toronto, Ontario, Canada M5V 2J6 <www.awid.org>

Mama Cash, 1e Helmersstraat 17, PO Box 15686, 1001 ND Amsterdam, The Netherlands <www.mamacash.nl>

Cover designed by Lee Robinson/Ad Lib Designs
Set in FF Arnhem and Futura Bold by Ewan Smith, London
Index: ed.emery@britishlibrary.net
Printed and bound in Malta by Gutenberg Press Ltd

Distributed in the USA exclusively by Palgrave Macmillan, a division of St Martin's Press, LLC, 175 Fifth Avenue, New York, NY 10010.

A catalogue record for this book is available from the British Library.
US CIP data are available from the Library of Congress.

ISBN 1 84277 458 1 cased
ISBN 1 84277 459 x limp

Contents

Acknowledgements

This book grew out of a two-year collaborative project between the Association for Women's Rights in Development (AWID) and Mama Cash. Many people contributed to the project during that time and this book would not have been possible without their enthusiasm, creativity and dedication. To each of them we are indebted.

First of all, we extend our gratitude to all of the authors who contributed their ideas to this collection and to the women who generously donated their time to be interviewed for this project. Furthermore, we acknowledge the contributions made by the participants in the interactive workshops which were part of this project. This critical engagement was vital to both the processes and the products of this project.

We also wish to thank the staff of Mama Cash and of AWID who have been so supportive throughout the production of this volume. In particular, we thank Nancy Jouwe and Astrid Aafjes of Mama Cash for their insights and comments, and Klaartje Spijkers for her administrative support. Special thanks also go to Lisa Phipps of AWID for her detailed copy-editing of several of the chapters, and to Carmen Reinoso and Klaartje Spijkers (of Mama Cash) and Shareen Gokal (of AWID) for facilitating the workshop at the Feminist Encuentro in Costa Rica, November 2003.

Special thanks are also due to Rhonda Leeson, who conducted the interviews and lent her research and editorial assistance to the completion of the manuscript, to Erin Leigh who compiled the interview transcripts into chapters for the collection, and to Paul Perret who administered the survey of the AWID membership and compiled the data for analysis. We also thank Nicole Lisa who translated two of the chapters from their original Spanish into English. These contributions were invaluable to the completion of the manuscript and enhanced the breadth of analysis included herein.

This project was made possible by the generous financial support of Cordaid. We also acknowledge Novib, Oxfam Netherlands for their financial contribution, and for organizing the Gender Policy Review Workshop in November 2001, during which the idea for this project was born.

We would be remiss not to thank Robert Molteno of Zed Books for his enthusiastic support and flexibility with this project. It has been a pleasure to work with him and also with Anna Hardman. We are most pleased to have the book published by Zed Books, a publisher committed to international feminism and social transformation.

Finally, to the countless hundreds who have given us ideas and inspiration along the way, we hope this book supports your great work and provokes new ideas. We look forward to engaging in many more future-oriented strategic thinking sessions with you in the years to come.

The Editors

1 | Introduction: the future of women's rights

ALISON SYMINGTON AND ELLEN SPRENGER

The year is 2033 ...

Three decades into this new millennium, we find ourselves on a transformed planet. Over the past thirty years the world has changed substantially, in terms of the environment and climate, populations, geopolitics and socioeconomic levels. Who would have known, that water – not oil – would become the most sought-after commodity in the world and that wars would break out between water have and water have-not nations? Or that China, barely a player on the world stage in the latter part of the twentieth century, would transform global trading patterns with its hundreds of millions of low-paid workers? Today, fortunately, we have cures for HIV/AIDS, malaria, all cancers, Ebola and tuberculosis; but remember how long it took, and how many millions of tragic deaths, before healthcare came to be seen as a fundamental human right rather than a costly service and profit-generating sector.

The prolific scientific innovation of past decades has played havoc with our humanity and our rights. For example, 25 per cent of parents now use genetic modification procedures to guarantee blue-eyed, pale-skinned children, artificial wombs have become a hot commodity, and a nimble-fingered woman who needs very little sleep has been successfully cloned. Our legal systems are barely keeping pace with the implications of such developments in terms of reproductive rights, patent protections, labour standards and distributive justice. Multilateralism and the United Nations were revived after that bleak period when the United States (at that time the most powerful country in the world) perceived the rest of the world to be its enemy. Age-old struggles over beliefs and religion have remained major influences in much of the world, however, to the continuing detriment of women.

In these thirty years then, there have been laudable achievements as well as major setbacks. The struggle has not been an easy one, but women's movements have indeed shaped the world we now live in. Feminist leaders have formed powerful political parties, moved into key positions in all international institutions, and have been able to define, debate and broadcast the new 'spirituality' based on universal human rights – irrespective of sex, religion, caste, class, sexuality, ability or race. Feminists forged alliances across all identities and social movements. We built political and economic agendas that the majority of government departments, international institutions and businesses could no longer ignore. We fought back from the local level right up to the World Trade Organization to ensure that every woman, man and child had clean, accessible water, adequate shelter and a nutritious diet.

With heart, soul, humour, passion, wisdom and energy, women's rights have been defined and defended across this planet. And we continue to be leaders in movements to advance the equal rights of all as ever new challenges arise.[1]

The current juncture: devising strategies and visions for the future

When feminists gather today, whether it be in a community group around a kitchen table or under a tree, or as delegates at a major international conference, the discussion often turns into a reflection on our own work. Questions are posed about the efficacy of the strategies we are employing, about new issues and trends that may have an impact on our work to advance gender equality, and about new opportunities for activism, collaboration and alliance-building. At times there is a sense of urgency and trepidation, and an acute awareness of the struggles of the past and uncertainty about the future. But there is also an optimism which accompanies this growing willingness critically to assess our own work. So while there is a growing backlash against women's rights, at the same time there is also a renewed vigour to act collectively, decisively and effectively. Today, aware of the crisis situations we currently face and the inevitable obstacles that we will have to overcome in the next five, ten, even twenty-five years, when feminists gather we discuss how to act more strategically, where to put our efforts, and how to shape the future in order to transform women's reality in a positive way. This collective critical thinking is the motivation behind this book.

The central questions of this project are: *What emerging trends and future developments will have an impact on the rights of women?*; and *What are the best strategies with which to respond to these issues?* While these questions could be relevant to any civil society movement at any moment in history, the current challenges in advancing women's rights and gender equality indicate that we are at a critical time in the struggle for gender equality and women's human rights.

There is no denying that we are witnessing, and indeed living, global crises. Increased militarization and armed conflict, devastating terror attacks and a 'global alliance against terrorism' which breeds fear and hatred, the spreading HIV/AIDS pandemic, environmental degradation, the widening gap between resource rich and resource poor, and ethnic and religious extremism/fundamentalisms, are all symptoms of the situation we are facing around the globe. All over the world, most people continue to be socialized according to values based on domination and violence, rather than diversity and respect. Moreover, militarization, terrorism and religious extremism are closely associated with increasing levels of violence against women. The violation of women's rights, therefore, is located at the heart of the current crisis.[2]

These factors produce a sense of urgency. We are losing ground. Despite all of the work we have done and progress we have made, women as a category and as individuals continue to be devalued, discriminated against and abused. We find ourselves in a position of sliding back and having to defend the gains we have made, even refighting battles previously won. So while there is increasing recognition that 'another world is possible',[3] much of our energy is currently taken up by responding to developments and other people's agendas, either in reacting to their impact on women's rights or in lobbying to ensure that women's rights issues are included. The challenge therefore is to be proactive and articulate our own agendas.

Feminist movements are, in fact, some of the largest, most dynamic social forces in the world. We have been active in movements for peace, we have achieved legal equality in many countries, we have developed an extensive jurisprudence on women's human rights, and we have risen to positions of power within our communities, governments, corporations and various institutions. Yet we find ourselves at a critical juncture, where global challenges mean that we have to be even more proactive, more effective, and more innovative. Collectively and individually, therefore, we must ask ourselves, how is social transformation brought about? What are the most important driving forces of change? How can we engage with these forces in order to bring about more just societies? And how can we remain committed to collective action to improve the status of women, yet reject simple solutions and universal assumptions that will not help to bring our visions of a just future to fruition? These pressing questions and the belief that alternative feminist visions can be realized are at the heart of this project.

The 'Facing the Future' project

This book is the result of a joint project of the Association for Women's Rights in Development (AWID) and Mama Cash, referred to as 'Facing the Future'.[4] The project is focused on identifying and analysing issues, processes and events in their early stages and anticipating their potential impacts on women's rights and gender equality in the coming years. The rationale for the project has been quite clear from the beginning: the world is changing at an ever-accelerating pace. While it is impossible to predict the future, it is possible to identify trends at very early stages. Future-oriented thinking, therefore, has been employed throughout the project as a means to revitalize and refocus our movements and ourselves.

The project has been one of collaboration, consultation, dialogue and writing. Feminist leaders living and working in different parts of the world were invited to prepare papers addressing three questions: (i) What are the most important emerging trends and future developments that are, or will, have an impact on the rights of women?; (ii) How do these trends and developments relate to the strategies used by women's movements?; and (iii) In the light of these trends, what strategies should women's movements prioritize? These questions were also explored at three interactive workshops presented at major international gatherings in 2002 and 2003[5] and several interviews were conducted with provocative, strategic feminist thinkers to probe some of the issues raised from different perspectives. Finally, in May 2003, a survey of AWID's members was conducted, including questions ranging from 'In five to ten years time, what do you think the most important challenge will be for gender equality work globally?' to 'If you had unlimited resources, what would be the most important strategy that you would pursue to promote gender equality globally?' By facilitating open discussion and inviting widespread input on change processes and critical issues that either support or undermine women's rights, the project set out to provoke and inspire. This book is a compilation of this project. It is our hope that it will contribute to the further development of transformative, proactive and future-oriented strategies that ultimately lead us to a more just global society.

Challenges and opportunities: key issues for gender equality and women's rights

To be at the heart of global transformation, feminists need visions of alternative futures and of transformative processes by which we can bring about a more just, more equal world. And while Utopias are interesting and useful in their own right, developing strategies for engagement requires that our visions be grounded in reality. A logical starting point in this exercise, therefore, is to identify the key issues that are now, and/or will be in the near future, affecting women's enjoyment of their human rights. As the editors of this volume, we therefore take advantage of this moment to reflect on some of the key threats, challenges and opportunities facing feminist agendas and to consider the implications of these issues for action strategies.

Health and education As is reflected in the chapters that follow, women's access to 'the basics', including education and health, remains a fundamental issue for women's equality throughout the world. Our approach seems to have expanded somewhat, however, from fighting for access to services, to fighting for quality services and accountability. Our analysis also has shifted in that we now more frequently focus on education and health in relation to their role in contributing to women's empowerment or to broader problems such as the spread of HIV/AIDS among young women, the spread of misogynist value systems through conservative faith-based education and corporate sponsorship of education, and the implications of the privatization of service provision through economies. Until quality, universal access and accountability are guaranteed for all basic services, we can expect that these issues will remain central foci of our movements and also will remain key strategies for empowering women to respond to all of the other issues and challenges we face in bringing about global transformation.

Economic restructuring and globalization Another set of issues that have featured heavily through this project and recur in the chapters that follow are issues associated with neoliberal globalization and economic restructuring. With the emergence and acceleration of these developments, issues were placed on the agenda of women's movements which previously had little perceived importance, including investors' rights, currency exchange regulation, trade liberalization and the accountability of international financial institutions. The shifting boundaries between the public and the private spheres and between the state and the market undermine many assumptions and 'tried and tested' methods of feminist activism, forcing us to re-evaluate our sites of engagement and our strategies.

Geopolitical relations The role of geopolitical relations and shifting 'balances of power' is another theme which has important implications for the future of women's rights as well as global security. In the Cold War era, it seemed that a 'balance of power' existed which was somewhat predictable and constant. Since 1989, however, new global players have emerged and different power struggles have dominated, leaving us with less certainty and more turmoil. Many questions emerge as a result of these shifts and uncertainties. For example, what is the role of China, the world's most populated country, and how will China use its power in the years to come if it continues to become more economically integrated with the rest of the world? Are coalitions of Southern countries able to counteract the military and economic power of the United States and, increasingly, the European Union? Moreover, how will the 'superpower' character of the United States and the European Union evolve in the coming years? In relation to all of these types of geopolitical questions, we need to consider our priorities as women's movements in relation to the centres of power and amplify our role in maintaining focus on the driving forces of global politics and exposing the truth behind issues.

Shifting populations Patterns in demography, migration and life expectancy are also shifting and will likely lead to human capacity and economic problems with global ramifications. For example, in countries of the global North, life expectancy has doubled in the twentieth century and this growth trend continues. Populations in the global North, therefore, are said to be 'greying'. Meanwhile, the HIV/AIDS epidemic and other disease outbreaks could devastate adult populations in certain parts of the world, especially regions of the global South. What impact will these tendencies have on population compositions, economic development, migration policies and citizenship models in the years to come? How will women in particular be affected by these transformations?

New technologies A related issue area is that of new technologies. Very few women's organizations currently focus on the implications of scientific research and technological development, yet these issues could become one of the most important influences on women's rights in the coming decades. From biotechnology, to surveillance and communications technologies, and agricultural technologies to medical research, women's health, their bodies and their labour are deeply affected by the availability and development of new technologies. While some represent impressive advancements that can benefit women, there is great anxiety about the possible consequences of many others. The questions (and answers) are not clear-cut. Establishing frameworks for understanding these developments and also for demanding transparency and accountability in their production and distribution will be increasingly urgent challenges facing gender equality advocates as private corporations roll out further discoveries and products.

The natural environment Another area of issues, which has been with us for decades and continues to demand attention, is that of our natural environment. In recent years we have seen environmental resources increasingly being treated as private commodities rather than as community resources or global commons. With increasing pressures on our environment to support the growing global population with its intensified activity, competition for control of resources and environmental damages are ever more insidious and dangerous. Consider the issue of water, for example.

We see demand increasing as reserves are shrinking, and private control of water and water distribution are on the rise. Currently, 1.2 billion people in the world do not have access to safe drinking water; it was projected at the Third UN Water Conference that by 2050 this number may increase to anywhere from 2 to 7 billion people without access. Consider other resources as well, such as forest, flora and fauna, fossil fuels and our atmosphere. Pollution, privatization, competition for scarce resources and increasing pressures from high-impact activities are causing similar tensions in these areas as well, and women around the world are affected diversely, but mostly adversely, by these developments. How can we most effectively deal with these issues for the future? How can we promote sustainability and equity with respect to safe drinking water and other resources? How can we build on positive developments such as sustainable energy sources and international regulatory schemes?

Fundamentalisms Another phenomenon that characterizes our times and is critical to the future of women's human rights is the rise of conservative and religious fundamentalist forces. Today, conservative movements and religious fundamentalists are the most vocal groups opposing women's rights in the United Nations, European Union, national governments and also within many local communities. In particular, they are resisting any advances in women's political, economic and cultural rights, including the right to own property, to inherit and to dress as one wishes, and also access to contraceptives, abortion and sexual and reproductive rights. Many of these groups are well funded and retain professional lobbyists. Many are also brutally violent, murdering women in the name of morality, honour and religion.

In the last decade, the fundamentalist or extremist advocates within the major world religions, including Buddhism, Christianity, Confucianism, Hinduism, Islam, Judaism and Sikhism, have grown more powerful and become increasingly dedicated to preserving religious traditions which they believe to be threatened by 'modern life'. At the same time, progressive faith-based groups are gaining momentum in their work to reform religious doctrines, provide alternatives to extremism, and build cultures around a belief in democracy, freedom of speech, non-violence and universal human rights.

Towards the future: strategies and visions for feminist engagement

While it is important to describe accurately and to understand the major current issues outlined above, as women's rights advocates our concern goes beyond reporting into planning, engaging and indeed attempting to shape the future. So we may look at current global challenges, as well as where and how we have been successful in advancing women's rights, and consider what we could have foreseen years ago and how our actions have had an impact on how things have turned out. There are many lessons to be learned from such an exercise.

Similarly, we can look ahead, considering how different actors may exert an influence on emerging trends, and anticipate possible opportunities, threats and new concerns, and strategize accordingly. So, for example, which countries or institutions are moving into positions of greater influence in the international system? Who may challenge them and who may become their allies? How will their history, culture and political systems position them on issues of international cooperation, economic policy and disputes?

Similarly, what scientific research is being conducted now and what potential developments will emerge under the control of corporations, universities or government-sponsored research institutes in the coming decade? Will scientific innovations in areas such as medicine, agriculture, communications and transportation offer new opportunities and freedoms to women, and, if so, which women, where, and at what cost? On which exhaustible resources are we currently dependent? How are they being protected or overused? What renewable resources could we be using in their place and can the political will be fostered to bring about their widespread use?

Likewise, what will be the role of popular culture and media and how can we best use these channels for drawing people in? How can we better market our movements and how will we be able to mobilize resources for our work? And, linked to all these questions: with whom can we best forge alliances for this work?

These are the types of questions we need to be asking. The extent to which we are able to claim spaces and influence key driving forces of change depends on the quality of our analysis, our ability to respond quickly, and our capacity for innovative and cooperative actions. We need to think creatively, strategically and collectively while at the same time recognizing plurality and a multiplicity of priorities.

In thinking strategically, we should not overlook the internal questions facing women's groups and feminist movements throughout the world. Fostering and maintaining feminist leadership, for example, and finding the necessary funding to keep our organizations functioning, are ever-present issues that continually require new strategies and new energies. What does it mean to be a feminist today? What is the connection between theory and practice, between our thinking and our doing? How can we link the many different locations of feminist theorizing and activism? Where should we focus our advocacy in order to best achieve transformation: towards legal institutions, United Nations mechanisms, international financial institutions, private corporations, or community structures, for example? Building alliances with other progressive movements is another prerequisite to achieving our goals. The opportunities for constructive and dynamic engagement are many; it is our ability to identify key driving forces and strategic opportunities that will largely determine our level of success. This book is one tool in the process.

The contributors to this volume This collection does not represent any one feminism or put forth a unified vision of the future. It includes a diversity of perspectives and proposals from women of different generations, from different locations, with different experiences. What connects the work of these authors is a shared commitment to addressing inequality and injustice as well as a belief in acting strategically, proactively and purposefully. Each looks at current issues and emerging trends that impact on women's rights and then turns to future-oriented strategies for addressing these challenges.

The first contribution to the collection, 'From "opposing" to "proposing": finding proactive global strategies for feminist futures' by Joanna Kerr (Chapter 2), identifies several key issue areas and forecasts how they will play out in future years. The issues she focuses on are: trade liberalization and investment policy; technological development; militarization and armed conflict; religious, cultural and ethnic extremism, and the HIV/AIDS pandemic. Considering the potential future impacts of these issues on the rights of women, she presents possible approaches we can take to advance the women's rights agenda in the years to come, including working with the convergence of development and human rights activism, moving women into seats of power, achieving institutional changes, putting theories of diversity into practice, and building our movements and alliances. She thereby sets out a vision built upon hope for the future as well as the preliminary steps we need to take to move in that direction.

In her contribution, Bisi Adeleye-Fayemi (Chapter 3) discusses the challenges currently facing African feminism, including poverty, globalization, armed conflict, political exclusion and citizenship, and the continuing failures, indeed roll-back, in terms of guaranteeing women's basic rights. In the light of these issues, she emphasizes using feminist analysis and claiming feminist spaces, thereby maintaining the political edge of the movement. She argues that the global feminist movement should see its task as one of continually creating new, transformatory identities of women from which new strategies and visions will emerge. In this respect, using the avenues opened up by globalization is an opportunity for the movement to rebuild, renew and revitalize itself.

In the contribution by Mahnaz Afkhami (Chapter 4), we are introduced to some of the key debates around culture, rights and globalization. She places women's individual rights of choice at the centre of feminist discourse. With a keen sense of history and attention to transformations associated with globalization, she makes connections between the policies and trends characterizing our world today, including technological development, privatization, religious zeal and terrorism. She interrogates cultural relativism and development, drawing lessons for feminist activity from her analysis, concluding with an action agenda for practical feminist mobilization into the future.

When asked for her analysis of the most pressing issues for women's rights and the best strategies for dealing with these issues, Josefa (Gigi) Francisco focused on US unilateralism and international institutions. In the interview included in this volume (Chapter 5), she urges us to make demands of ourselves and of women's movements, proposing a political reconstruction of social movements through strategic dialogue, reflection and deliberate action. She proposes joining with other social movements and engaging in tactical planning together, as well as bringing more young women into leadership roles within the women's movement.

In Chapter 6, Deepa Dhanraj, Geetanjali Misra and Srilatha Batliwala explore how increasing poverty, escalating conflicts and militarization, and the rise of fundamentalist movements, are eroding women's rights in the South Asian region. Noting the political context and hence the urgency of the situation of women in South Asia, they assert that women's movements must take the lead in transforming global social movements. Central to their strategy is the importance of creating movements led by grassroots women who are able to mobilize marginalized people around a progressive agenda. Furthermore, they suggest that we re-examine our feminist analytical frameworks, strengthen the movement by supporting the emergence of strong grassroots organizations, and build fluid and open learning movements that are genuinely open to change.

In her contribution, Sarah Bracke (Chapter 7) interrogates the contradictions and complexities of late global capitalism for contemporary feminism. She argues that feminist perspectives and struggles need to be informed by the contradictions within and between the lives of women, focusing in particular on neoliberalism and the position of Europe. Her analysis of feminist activism and theorizing in Europe and the juxtaposition of equality gains made in the twentieth century with the deterioration of many women's lives in recent decades, leads her to encourage the (re)politicization of women's movements and to prioritize alliance building.

Ana Criquillion (Chapter 8) uses lessons learnt from our successes and failures in the past as a basis for her analysis of present challenges and future-oriented strategies. Noting the challenge of diversity, including inequities among women and the different experiences women have of the processes of globalization, she explores issues of women's political participation, popular culture and the media, fundamentalisms and macroeconomic policies. She argues in favour of intensifying our efforts in areas where feminist movements have had success, including in building organizations, influencing public policy and using television and film to reach broad audiences.

Neoliberal globalization is also identified by Alda Facio in Chapter 9 as the major challenge for feminist movements at this time. She argues that globalization has made most women worse off, cut at the heart of feminist politics, imposed a homogenous culture and fragmented our movements. According to her, feminist movements have gone off course and become complacent in recent years. In order to confront globalization effectively we will need to rebuild a movement that is able to confront both the old issues associated with patriarchy and the new issues associated with neoliberal globalization. A key strategy for her is developing a feminist spirituality and consciousness, where human reproduction is valued and we work together in a spirit of love, friendship, pleasure, sisterhood and mutual support.

Vanessa Griffen (Chapter 10) questions whether the actions and strategies currently used by women's groups are sufficient to bring about the type of transformative change we desire. She prioritizes critical assessments of our movements and focuses her contribution on the types of analysis which we will need to develop in order to bring about gender equality in the future. Her chapter looks specifically at the need for a feminist analysis of security and defence policy, a much more concerted effort to challenge global media and information technologies, the need to repoliticize gender equality work, and reasons why engaging through mechanisms of the United Nations may not be strategic. In terms of international advocacy work, she encourages links between the local and the global, as well as reasserting a collective feminist identity and commitment.

Sisonke Msimang's contribution (Chapter 11) focuses on the interconnected issues of HIV/AIDS and economic globalization and their impact on the rights of women and girls. She identifies constructing power bases that are not oppressive and further developing feminist theory around identities as challenges for young feminists today. In terms of strategies for the future, she outlines a commitment to transparency, building bridges between local and global activism, developing activist citizenship, scaling up advocacy efforts and using human rights frameworks as areas where we should be directing our energies.

In reflecting on appropriate strategies for achieving women's rights globally and in post-socialist countries, Anastasia Posadskaya-Vanderbeck notes the tactical choices which we must be making in these difficult times in order to counteract military proliferation, poverty, fundamentalisms and the so-called 'war on terror'. In Chapter 12 she expresses concern that when we critically assess our past strategies we often completely reject them and try to replace them with something novel. In her opinion, it is premature to turn away from battles such as gender mainstreaming, addressing violence against women and realizing reproductive rights. On the other hand, she suggests that sometimes we do need to create new and different mechanisms, such as the current need for alternative processes for using human rights instruments outside the United Nations' reporting mechanisms. She advocates more collective thinking and brainstorming to maintain the movement and respond to new challenges.

In the final chapter of this collection, Rhonda Leeson reports on the findings from a survey of a diverse group of gender equality advocates from AWID's membership, based throughout the world. The questionnaire asked respondents to identify both the most pressing issues and the best strategies for achieving women's rights in the next five to ten years. As reported in Chapter 13, the most common responses on priority issues related to the areas of the empowerment of women, economics and financial resources, and education. In terms of strategies, the most frequently cited approaches were education and advocacy campaigns, and global networking. The results of this survey are compared and contrasted with the ideas of the contributors to this collection, providing a rich and comprehensive discussion of possibilities, challenges and global perspectives into the future.

Moving together into the future of women's rights

Shaping the future requires that we take active steps to develop processes and activities that bring about structural change. By looking to the complex past of feminist movements throughout the world, analysing our present context, and putting forth visions and strategies, we are moving together into the future. As such, we are a movement in a process of continual reflection and reinvention, figuring out how to bring about the future that we collectively desire.

This is not to say that our strategies will be universal or our visions will all be shared. Instead, it is a call to be using the most effective and appropriate means for different contexts and circumstances, based on constant reflection, re-evaluation, dialogue and recognition that our lives are interconnected and we need to work in solidarity in order to make a difference.

As the chapters that follow make clear, the fight which the next generation faces is in many respects different from that of previous generations and women's movements. New issues will emerge, new actors will surface and new strategies and tactics will unfold. By posing critical questions, the authors and editors of this book hope to contribute to the realization of a transformed, just and feminist future.

Notes

1 Excerpt from a multimedia presentation developed by Joanna Kerr and Ellen Sprenger, September 2003.

2 See P. Antrobus (2002) 'Feminism as Transformational Politics: Towards Possibilities for Another World', *Development*, 45 (2): 46–52.

3 'Another World is Possible' is the slogan of the World Social Forum.

4 The project had its origins in a Gender Policy Review workshop hosted by Novib Oxfam Netherlands, 1–2 November 2001 in The Hague where Joanna Kerr presented a paper on trends in gender equality work around the world. As executive directors of international women's organizations, Joanna Kerr (of the Association for Women's Rights and Development) and Ellen Sprenger (of Mama Cash, fund for women) saw the importance of forward thinking, both for women's movements globally as well as for their own organizations.

5 The workshops took place during AWID's Ninth International Forum on Women's Rights in Development (Mexico, October 2002), Encuentro Feminista latinoamericano y del Caribe (Costa Rica, November 2002) and the World Social Forum (Brazil, January 2003).

2 | From 'opposing' to 'proposing': finding proactive global strategies for feminist futures

JOANNA KERR

If we could only look into a crystal ball and see the future, we could then identify what new challenges will face us, and, with the benefit of hindsight, what paths we should have taken. If as feminists we had known thirty years ago about the spread of HIV/AIDS, the effects of the World Trade Organization, or the power of CNN compared to the United Nations, it is quite likely that our strategies for gender equality would have been different.

I do not consider myself a 'futurist', a label ascribed to one who specializes partly in trend analysis and partly in science fiction. Instead, as a 'strategist', I recognize the value of looking forward to anticipate new threats and opportunities with the prospect of acting proactively. To date, women's movements, like so many social movements, have been largely reactive to a relentless catalogue of discrimination and rights violations related to violence, education, healthcare, reproduction, citizenship and economic well-being, just to name a few. Gender equality advocates in different parts of the world have been able to redress some gender imbalances, but our strategies have not been effective enough to sustain progress for women. Can our ultimate aim of eradicating gender discrimination – along with discrimination based on race, class, religion, ethnicity, ability, sexuality or age – be attained using the tools, analysis and forms of resistance with which we have worked so hard thus far, or is it time to consider different scenarios and alternative approaches to take on new global and seemingly intractable barriers to the achievement of human rights for all?

This paper examines several major current trends and extrapolates what they might mean to the pursuit of gender equality in the future. From militarization to globalization, a fast-changing global terrain is dictating new challenges and ways of approaching the women's rights agenda. Against this shifting backdrop for gender equality work, this paper also examines how we might transform, deepen or accelerate our current strategies towards women's empowerment. If we are to be ready for the undoubted challenges ahead, new analyses and means for change will inevitably be required. This chapter intends to reveal some of these key obstacles as well as hopeful approaches that could bring about systemic change to benefit both women and men globally.

First, a caveat. A chapter of this nature will, inevitably, present both generalizations and subjective views. It is impossible to portray a clear picture of the dynamism of gender equality work simply because of the fact that the women's movement has never been one singular movement but rather movements, multiple and diverse, each operating and based in different realities, with its own local struggles and challenges. Similarly, activists and practitioners rarely document new ideas, trends or future scenarios: these are the subjects of animated discussions or personal e-mails. As such, the majority of the substance for this chapter is derived from such engagements.[1] Alongside the thoughtful contributions from other practitioners and analysts in this volume, it is hoped that a menu of strategic insights and action plans can be derived for consideration by women's organizations and movements around the world.

Extrapolating from major global trends

Mortgaging our futures? trade liberalization, investment and privatization There are major economic forces at play today that will redefine our futures. What some refer to as 'corporate-led globalization' includes efforts to liberalize trade, open markets and deregulate industries, and constitutes the dominant economic strategy pursued by governments and transnational corporations all over the world. In many instances, these economic trends are not recent; in fact, privatization, trade liberalization or economic integration can be seen as extensions of earlier processes of colonization and structural adjustment. What makes them different now is how the development industry, embodied in international agencies such as the World Bank or bilateral agencies such as the US Agency for International Development, perceives trade as the development agenda so that human and other social development goals must be pursued through markets. And what makes these economic trends so significant for the future is their irrevocability (trade rules that cannot be changed once they have been agreed to, for example), the speed at which they are being implemented, their worldwide reach, as well as the extreme effects that they are having, and will have, on women's lives. From affecting the flexibility of employment to the quality of healthcare, from the use of technology to secure livelihoods, globalization is radically transforming both the issues women's movements will be addressing and the strategies they will use to address them.

Take water, for example. Many trend watchers name the lack of access to water as a looming crisis.[2] According to the United Nations, global demand for water is doubling every twenty years so that by 2025 demand will actually considerably overtake supply.[3] Since in most developing countries women are responsible for water management and water transport, and a person needs a minimum of 20 litres of water a day to meet basic health and hygiene needs,[4] the availability of water will inevitably become a women's rights issue.[5] Supply issues are being further confounded by the privatization of water services. In fact, World Bank and IMF debt relief and loans have increasingly become conditional on the privatization of 'inefficient' state-run enterprises such as hospitals, water and sanitation companies. When water goes private, it is usually controlled and sold to the poor by a small number of primarily American or European transnational corporations at a much higher cost than prior to privatization. Some say, therefore, that if privatization of essential services continues at the current rate, the essence of life will become unaffordable to most women and men living in poverty.

As this example shows, women must now and in the foreseeable future engage with supra-national actors including international financial institutions and private sector corporations (whereas in the past, the primary sites of struggle for women's movements were the household, the workplace, and the state). 'Think locally, act globally' is becoming the more appropriate mantra.[6] For example, economic reforms have allowed capital to flow much more easily across national boundaries than in the past. Women have therefore needed to understand how this affects their employment opportunities and the structure of their local economies. They have experienced and come to understand governments' strategies of low wage growth as built upon gender inequality and the exploitation of women's labour.[7] Also, because globalization has often required the roll-back of state social protections for formal and informal workers, the sick or elderly and the environment, gender analysts and activists in different regions are finding themselves facing the same issues of additional reproductive burdens, increasing insecurities, environmental degradation, and widening disparities between the privileged and the most vulnerable. In terms of strategies, because international financial institutions, trade regulating bodies and transnational corporations now dictate policies that would formerly have been within the purview of the state, more and more gender equality work is shifting to focus on influencing global actors in addition to, or instead of making demands on the state, a shift which requires new tactics and an understanding of economic values and language.[8]

Taking on this agenda will require a conceptual and ideological shift; we will need to move beyond mainstream gender and economic approaches towards more holistic and political strategies. Currently, in most development circles the 'women in development approach' (WID) is most common, characterized by a focus on welfare, economic self-reliance, efficiency, equality and empowerment, and having evolved over time to focus more on relations between men and women and working towards the goal of equitable, sustainable development. Common to this strand are microcredit and gender mainstreaming projects that focus on enhancing economic opportunities and providing protections in the face of vulnerabilities. What is so problematic with the majority of these approaches is that change is seen in terms of technical fixes as opposed to longer, more systemic power and structural shifts.

Economic justice approaches, on the other hand, are quite distinct, having developed out of socialist feminist and liberation movements. Economic justice approaches more commonly tackle the multidimensional causes of women's poverty and disempowerment and focus on the policies of international financial institutions, including the World Bank, the International Monetary Fund and regional development banks, the global trading regime including international and regional trade agreements, and larger questions of gender and economic processes. This analysis is situated within a framework of a critique of North–South relations and the neoliberal economic agenda, and also attempts to take account of the gender, class and race dimensions of social and political relations in a holistic way.[9]

While a large part of feminist analysis related to globalization still focuses on impacts, there is a growing consensus that feminists must concentrate on the much tougher agenda of developing viable alternative economic models for the future. Gender equality advocates working within the World Social Forum movements, for example, are attempting to influence their progressive male colleagues to show that 'another world is possible' only when gender equality is part of the overall alternative vision.[10] Meanwhile, feminist economists seek to redefine economic models and the dominant neoliberal economic policy framework through strategic alliances with mainstream economists, research and advocacy. A prospective vision of an alternative economic paradigm would be pluralistic (that is, there is no 'one-size-fits-all' strategy model for development), be geared to human well-being rather than market access, be informed by politics and social differences, incorporate the cost of human reproduction, and would allow for citizens and their governments to determine the pace and path of development.[11] In sum, a future with economic justice will require a system of economic democracy from the local to global level.

The future of technology Globalization and increased corporate control have also brought about transformations in technologies at a speed that none of us could have predicted. Within the gender and development and women's rights communities, ICTs (information and communication technologies) have been heralded as a boon for creating alliances and coalitions across great distances. Email and the internet have made it possible to plan campaigns and share data almost immediately, wherever there is access. On-line education tools on issues as far-ranging as peace-building, human rights and small business skills have made it possible to provide training for women who have asked for it in some of the most remote areas of the world.[12] At the same time, the communication revolution and increased corporate control of the media are leaving behind or marginalizing many women and further strengthening the hegemony of the English language (and one particular worldview), so issues of access and a 'digital divide' will be of growing concern to the women's movement. Moreover, policy debates related to the future control of information sharing, the media and communication technologies have until now not been considered gender issues, but more gender advocates are now recognizing the importance of influencing this field.

The production of new reproductive technologies, such as a controversial anti-fertility vaccine or genetically manipulated future offspring, as well as new bioengineered organisms such as genetically modified foods, by corporations is raising new and very complex issues with regard to women's safety and bodily integrity. With new advances in genetics, technology can now 'happen' inside the body. Testing is most often conducted on women in the South or Eastern Europe where fewer enforceable civil and regulatory protections exist. While this work is still in its infancy, as social justice and scientific communities come to grips with the implications and ethics of these new technologies, a small but growing number of gender equality advocates are ringing the alarm bell and naming new technologies as central concerns to the human rights of future generations.[13]

Advances in human genetics beyond those relating to reproductive technologies have been largely neglected by the feminist community. Even more difficult technologies, such as biotechnology, neuroscience, robotics, military and surveillance technologies, and nanotechnology, such as mechanical antibodies, are quickly coming into our reality and our markets. The implications of these new technologies are profound and far-reaching and are inextricably linked to other forces at play in the world today, including globalization, economic change and militarization. Thus far, decisions about these technologies have been left largely to the private sector, without even basic government assessment. The scale and scope of these technological advances will inevitably create a whole new range of problems for women's rights in terms of invading women's bodies, undermining women's safety and limiting control over our food and environment. Because of existing inequalities, new technologies will be designed to benefit the rich and powerful. As long as economic and social injustice exists, 'technological justice' will elude us or, even worse, huge technological gaps will be created at the expense of poor women.

Despite the urgency to become informed and take action to prevent life-altering cloning technologies or the proliferation of dangerous military technologies, few gender equality advocates are engaged in these issues. The reasons for this are unclear, but can be inferred. Perhaps technology issues are perceived as purely 'Western' or, alternatively, as too remote to deal with given other immediate priorities. Lack of engagement could also be a result of the relatively fewer women and, more specifically, feminists engaged in science and technology as compared to men. In any case, it will be critical in the coming years not to be complacent so as to address these questions head on while there is still time to take a measured and careful look at the techno-world in front of us.

Facing the new global conflict and militarization A third major trend and force that will have an impact on the future of women's rights is militarization. Since 11 September 2001, militarization has only grown more potent and alarming in terms of what it implies for any future with peace. Most feminists argue that ongoing military interventions will only exacerbate violence and insecurity instead of fostering security on our planet. In terms of gender equality, women 'know how a male-centred, militaristic culture utilizes women in conflicts for power – from the reliance on women's labour to maintain fatherless families and rebuild war-torn nations, to loss of public services and economic and social rights when resources are diverted, to the prostitutes around military bases to the abuse of women within the military to rape of women in war'.[14]

Gender equality proponents also know that women are not only victims of war and conflict; they can also be militant fighters themselves, complicit in allowing the conflict to flourish, or central to peace negotiations. These roles of women, as well as sophisticated social and gender analyses, are usually ignored by the international community thus making current programmes related to peace-building, peace-making or post-conflict reconstruction at best ineffective, and at worst more damaging to the lives of women.[15] Similarly, humanitarian and development agencies seem continually to reproduce their prior mistakes, from Kosovo to Afghanistan to Iraq. To start, therefore, we need to be prioritizing women's and men's needs in each phase pre- and post-conflict. To this end, UN Security Council Resolution 1325 (2000) on women and peace is an important tool, but one that needs to be utilized carefully, for the resolution itself reproduces protectionist language. We need to be clear that peace-building protects women's rights, not women themselves.[16]

In terms of developing ways and means of ending this most disturbing phase of global unrest characterized by successive US-led military interventions, we need greater clarity about the linkages between patriarchy, the broader effects of globalization, increased militarization and religious extremism. So much violence on this planet is born of increasing gaps between rich and poor as a result of current (un)development strategies, where religious (cultural or ethnic) leaders exploit resentment against the 'haves' or the 'West' to mobilize the marginalized from Pakistan or Gujarat to Sierra Leone and the Balkans. We are also now seeing Northern governments turn inwards and prioritize domestic security, shutting borders and becoming increasingly socially and economically exclusive.[17] It is clear that the current global disorder emanates from a crisis in leadership – a leadership that has allowed suffering to exist, as well as hatred to thrive. Whether it is hate against abortion providers, 'welfare mothers', immigrants, a particular ethnic group, religion, nationality or race, our leaders have allowed it to flourish often for political and, more often, economic gain.

A future of peace, most importantly, will require a major shift in resources away from military 'solutions' towards poverty eradication, social transformation, natural resource management and justice. (Just imagine: according to Oxfam International the monies spent in 2003 by the US military for the attack on Iraq could have more than fully wiped away the debts of all African countries and provided HIV/AIDS treatment for the continent.)[18] Without these resources, conflict simmers below the surface, only to boil over when political leaders or so-called terrorists do or say something to turn up the heat. More challenging still, this work ahead requires us to both name and stop the internalization of hatred of 'the other'.[19] Families and societies breed discrimination, contempt and distrust of difference. Change, inevitably, will require feminists to focus on the personal, transforming violent patriarchal and militaristic values and approaches in our cultures into those of respect, diversity and tolerance, one child at a time. Education and socialization, therefore (yes, back to the basics), have never been more appropriate or proactive.

The rise in religious, cultural and ethnic extremisms In this world of growing conflict and economic insecurity, religious movements have found fertile ground in which to grow. Some of these movements speak to the current crisis of modernity in that progress has not provided for people's material or spiritual needs.[20] This rising trend should be taken very seriously by any women's rights proponent. Throughout the world, religion is being used, in addition to ethnicity or culture, to gain and mobilize political power and exert social control. In particular, many religious leaders seek to control gender identities and roles. In the US 'bible belt', women are denied any sexual or sexuality education. Pakistan, Iran and Nigeria are just a few places where Islamic religious leaders condemn women to death on accusations of adultery. Rape and torture of Muslim women has happened recently in Gujarat as a product of Hindus asserting their power, which has actually been supported by the state. Whether Christian, Hindu, Jewish, Buddhist or Muslim, political religious movements are taking women's lives, denying or undermining women's education, decision-making, ownership of resources and mobility, and especially controlling women's sexuality.

In fact, the struggle over women's sexuality will inevitably be political and contentious for the foreseeable future. According to the Special Rapporteur on Violence Against Women, one of the greatest causes of violence against women is the regulation of female sexuality.[21] Feminists recognize that since feminist advocacy for sexual and reproductive rights made significant achievements at the 1994 Cairo Conference on Population and Development, there has been a dramatically strengthened conservative backlash at the United Nations, led by the Christian 'right' along with the Muslim fundamentalists. Under the Bush administration, key resources have been stripped away from legitimate causes if they happen to do anything remotely close to abortion counselling. From Mexico to Poland, women's reproductive rights are being chipped away in the name of 'God's word'.

Women's groups around the world, therefore, are increasingly concerned about the ways in which extremist religious, cultural and ethnic forces have been gaining ground. With their networks, financial resources and close ties to political power, many feminists see these political/religious movements as a formidable foe that will require an immense amount of advocacy, consciousness-raising, resources and political power to stand up to.

Many feminists recognize that a multipronged strategy to countering the power of fundamentalist groups is necessary. Secular spaces need to defended and expanded.[22] Women's rights advocates will have to challenge governments who fund religious schools or impose religious practice and education, while defending individuals and women's organizations against attacks by fundamentalists.[23] Similarly, Catholics for a Free Choice are leading a major campaign that has received widespread support to change the Roman Catholic Church's status at the UN from its current almost 'state' ranking to the status of a non-governmental organization, in order radically to weaken its voice and political power at the UN; power that has particularly undermined the rights of women and girls.[24] In addition, many recommend 'insider–outsider approaches', whereby gender equality advocates would build alliances with progressive religious organizations, interpreting religious texts from feminist perspectives. Finally, and perhaps most importantly, organizations such as Women Living Under Muslim Laws demand that we focus on reclaiming women's identities and spirituality as means towards empowerment and greater control over their lives. Religion should never mean women lose their freedom of expression or 'right to dream'.[25]

In any case, as religious (as well as ethnic or cultural) extremisms intensify around the world, greater emphasis on understanding them, acting against them and developing alternative approaches to counter them, will likely become a more central priority to gender equality work in the coming years. Furthermore, it will become even more critical for women's movements, as described below, to make the links between poverty and neoliberalism, religious extremisms and militarization. Challenging the core conditions that breed and encourage extremisms – such as lack of real democracy, ignorance, corruption and, of course, poverty and economic marginalization – by effectively offering an alternative vision and leadership to the one being proposed by extremists, will be essential in the long-run.

Seeing HIV/AIDS as a human rights issue alongside other women's health needs Given the overwhelming magnitude of the AIDS crisis and its impact on women, this issue has finally been acknowledged as a priority in the gender and development and women's rights community worldwide. Up until very recently, however, unless one was living in Southern Africa, the impact of HIV/AIDS on women was hardly an issue of urgency and much less a critical factor for the future. Slowly, policy-makers, funders and activists in the North, South and Eastern Europe are recognizing that, if trends continue, the next ten years will see communities well beyond Africa ravaged by the virus as teachers, farmers, parents, bureaucrats and other key social and economic actors tragically disappear.

According to the UN Secretary-General Kofi Annan, 50 per cent of those with HIV/AIDS are female yet only one-third of countries have policies to ensure women have access to prevention or care.[26] Up until now, the issue has largely been taken up as a medical crisis, while the gender aspects and links with poverty and globalization have received little attention. Future work will therefore depend on the pandemic being addressed in terms of human development, human security and human rights. AIDS is both a cause of poverty or deepening poverty, and a result of the effects of poverty and social and economic inequalities. Furthermore, the fact that women are biologically, economically and socially/culturally more at risk must figure into any viable responses. Young women, in particular, are more vulnerable because of their relative lack of control over their bodies, of access to information, and of self-confidence in demanding protection.[27]

The AIDS crisis has also created additional health and human rights problems for women, unrelated to their HIV status. For instance, trafficking in girls and women and increased forced prostitution have become major symptoms of this pandemic as in some societies virgins are regarded as cures for AIDS, and are often shunned by families, ending up as sex-workers with no other choices. Meanwhile, studies show that women are avoiding HIV-testing for fear of violent reactions from their partners.[28] More priority in the future, therefore, will have to be given to HIV/AIDS as both a human rights and a women's empowerment issue. Unless more take the position that the scope of human rights must be fully extended to economic security, this crisis cannot be resolved.[29]

This being said, however, women's movements need to remain vigilant so that the focus on HIV/AIDS does not divert financial and research resources away from other major women's health problems. Holistic responses to the care and prevention of malaria, tuberculosis, nutrient deficiencies, breast cancer and heart disease will continue to be just a few of the critical priorities for women's healthy futures. The international health and development community tends to focus on the 'flavour of the day' and highlight one problem in isolation, often to the neglect of funding and political attention for other significant diseases and their causes. Governments and other funders will first need to be convinced that women's health needs are presently underfunded, with the exception of maternal health, which many mainstream agencies see as an apolitical way to do gender work or a means of supporting population control. More importantly, we will need comprehensive strategies that tackle all the causes and consequences of women's health issues going beyond a medical perspective to a human rights and economic justice perspective if women's rights are to be a reality in the future.

From the 'what' to the 'how': finding ways to be more strategic and proactive

How does change happen? This is a simple question with no straightforward answers. For many of us, women's rights objectives are debated and theorized as categories of issues. So health problems, violence, education and political representation, for example, are the core issues that dominate much of our theory and analysis. In contrast, we spend far fewer resources assessing, evaluating, researching or developing better strategies. When development agencies force women's groups who receive their funding to focus on 'methods to achieve results', they are often met with resistance.

Many feel the pressure to produce outputs, from posters to workshops which are only short-term tools on the path to equality. Social transformation takes time. Instead of bending to this pressure, women's groups and movements need to see the value of strategy analysis and of being a 'learning movement'.[30] The way forward, therefore, will require us thoroughly to interrogate this question of how change happens. In part, this next section takes on this challenge and considers where we should invest in proactive strategic actions.

Converging the best of development and human rights approaches

Throughout the 1990s, in the UN conference processes, and in the burgeoning of new organizations and initiatives working for gender equality, two communities and approaches were particularly visible: one associated with women's human rights and another working from a gender and development perspective. These two streams of the women's movement both have knowledge and experience to contribute, although they often have not worked together. They have distinct terminology, different experts, specialized methodologies, separate agencies, and ultimately they target different institutional actors. Over the years, this persistent divide has resulted in unnecessary duplication of efforts, as well as approaches that lack holistic understanding.

More recently, however, we have witnessed the paths of development and human rights converging, in particular around issues related to globalization. Development actors increasingly recognize the link between laws and institutions that influence women's status on the one hand, and the outcomes of development schemes and programmes on the other. At the same time, women's rights activists and legal practitioners are focusing more on economic and social well-being, cultural practices and traditions, and state economic policy. As the UNDP's *Human Development Report 2000* noted, human rights and human development share a common vision and purpose, which is to secure the freedom, well-being and dignity of all people everywhere.[31]

Development practitioners and agencies from Oxfam to UNICEF are recognizing the benefits, for example, of using a rights-based approach over a gender mainstreaming approach. In his famous book, *Development as Freedom*, Amartya Sen puts forward a compelling rationale for adopting a rights approach so that our attention is focused simultaneously on the freedoms that make development possible and on the freedoms that constitute the ultimate objective of development.[32] In other words, human rights must be both a means and an end to development. As many of us have found, so many gender mainstreaming initiatives have not borne fruit because of inadequate analytical skills, lack of political commitment to substantive equality (instead, a commitment to abstract and often depoliticized notions of 'gender') and inadequate funding. In many cases, while 'women' as a category have become visible, steps have not been made towards their equality. A rights approach, some argue, helps to avoid such pitfalls by keeping the end output – guaranteed rights for all – in constant focus. Women become rights-holders, rather than passive recipients. A rights agenda provides standards by which to measure success and ties results to objectives and procedures. Similarly, since rights are legally enforceable obligations, moral arguments for justice can become legal ones.

On the other hand, development approaches offer strong analytical and methodological tools for understanding and shaping the effects of economic forces. In addition, with a longer history of incorporating gender analysis, particularly with the influence of feminisms from the global South, the development field has been a powerful force in global women's movements, organizing and presenting alternatives to the status quo. In general, development approaches have been more broadly focused, more participatory, more contextualized and more inclusive than human rights approaches.[33] In particular, feminist economic justice approaches to development, described earlier, provide a more political and transformative agenda to gender equality in the context of globalization.

Increasingly, there are warnings about mainstream development agency attention towards rights-based approaches.[34] Unfortunately, we have all too often seen important conceptual or theoretical approaches transformed or co-opted by the development industry with less than stellar results: gender and development, gender mainstreaming and participation are just three obvious examples. With this new rush to 'the flavour of the month', critics warn that rights-based approaches, as they are being pursued, create new problems. On one hand, some see that lawyers will become a new layer of interlocutors between women as rights-holders and the policy-makers or legislators meant to bring about change. Some Southern feminists feel that 'rights-based development' is just the latest Western paradigm now being imposed on the South, that, with its bias towards individual choice, actually undermines community development imperatives. Finally, given the fact that human rights accountability systems are still relatively weak, particularly those that apply to economic and social rights, and harder to apply to non-signatories of instruments, such as multinational companies or international financial institutions, investing in them now could seem a less than efficacious strategy.

The key for the future, then, is to maximize the strengths and minimize the weaknesses in all approaches to gender equality. Interdisciplinary, holistic and collaborative strategies that build on what has worked and are informed by potential risks will be more effective. History shows that when we have defined the problems of women in narrow ways and then attempt to remedy them using a limited number of tools, change is rarely long-term or systemic. Inevitably, women's movements will have to stop working in thematic and institutional silos. Achieving peace, equality and well-being will require political and economic strategies that build on many different approaches and analyses – from human rights, development, political economy, popular education and so on – that are the most appropriate for that context.

Out of the margins and into the seats of power Looking forward, we can anticipate two other important, and paradoxical, trends: decentralization of decision-making from national to local levels, and at the same time strengthened international institutions, such as the World Trade Organization, whose policies can come into conflict with those of national governments. At the local level, many countries, especially in South Asia, have witnessed a trend towards decentralization of power, functions, responsibility and accountability to grassroots communities while women have won constitutional rights to one-third of the seats in India and Bangladesh.[35] Meanwhile, regional and international institutions that dictate global economic reforms are heavily influencing decisions at the national level, through coercion, cooption or cooperation, depending on the economic and ideological agenda of the government in power. Power is not devolving away from the state as many think: governments still play major roles in the directions of global economic and political reforms. Governments decide what recommendations they take from international institutions, with, of course, the richer countries having a greater say than others.[36]

So what does this imply in terms of strategy? It seems that many gender equality advocates have a love–hate relationship with institutions of power. Future strategies depend on more of us resolving this complicated rapport and becoming clearer on how best to work both *outside* institutions and with allies on the *inside*.

From the outside, our message has been and will continue to be clear: we demand accountability of institutions from the village to the World Trade Organization for promises made towards gender equality. Women need to play a strong role in transforming the current crisis in democracy. Only when organizations and processes of power and decision-making are held to account for women's rights will equality ever be a reality. This means that we will first need to pay much greater attention to the influence of decision-making processes as well as to accountability and transparency of governance structures at local, national and international levels. Second, it is even more critical that women do not just squeeze their issues into the margins of the agendas of powerful institutions, but instead actually articulate what those agendas should be. Policy change does not come about when women simply advocate the inclusion of 'a gender perspective'. Third, clear visions and priorities should be put forward when the political space is open enough and women demonstrate sufficient clout.[37] All too often, women's demands have been ignored when women's groups have been invited into policy spaces, such as the Poverty Reduction Strategy Paper processes. As a group of advocacy specialists note: 'Simply participating to take advantage of an opportunity to engage with powerful institutions is insufficient without aiming to ultimately transform existing power relations.'[38]

With regard to working from the inside, a glance at the Nordic countries will show that women's strong representation tends to translate into more equitable policies and programmes. Entering institutions of decision-making is therefore a critical strategy for social change and women's rights generally. Beyond these Northern countries, however, women have not transformed institutions of power that successfully. Here, a few statistics are needed for illustration. Today women worldwide hold only 15 per cent of seats in national parliaments.[39] Moreover, women constitute only a dismal 2.2 and 5.5 per cent of the IMF's and World Bank's boards of governors respectively.[40] Even where reserved seats exist, for example in South Asia, women are finding it very hard to have a political voice because local patriarchies resist most changes sought by women and in some cases challenge them outright in hostile or violent ways.[41]

So can feminists enter into powerful institutions without being co-opted? Do more women want to dare to get their hands dirty in party politics? Will gender equality advocates be able to stand up to strong local patriarchies within district governments, village councils and the like? Clearly, more of us will need to learn how. If we think that change will come about by working inside only less powerful institutions such as the UN Commission on the Status of Women, where we are most welcome, we are certainly deluded. For those on the inside to be able to make changes, it will be necessary to support them effectively from the outside: it is not an either-or strategy but one that is strategically symbiotic.

Nothing will happen without institutional change Related to these tensions with power described above, a significant number of gender and development and women's rights proponents have turned their focus to organizational and institutional change issues. After years of promoting gender equality through organizations using gender training methods, gender policies and other bureaucratic tools, these actors now claim that equality will depend more on changing the structures of organizations and, most importantly, the institutions, or rules of the game, that embody them.[42] According to Rao and Kelleher, these hidden rules determine 'how resources are allocated and how tasks, responsibilities and value are assigned. In other words, the rules determine who gets what, who does what, and who decides.'[43]

These insights have already brought about important changes. For instance, much effort has gone into advocating better organizational 'infrastructures' to ensure that equality objectives are met. Examples include strong national machineries for women, a gender focal-point and procedures in mainstream development or policy organizations, and the formulation of gender-responsive budgets. These changes to established organizations, however, have manifested relatively little positive change because the underlying cultural and political norms within them have not been tackled, namely power relations, attitudes and political commitment. Similarly, the struggle for voice, resources and rights depends on changing the broader institutional norms. As a simple example, while Bangladeshi women might have gained access to decision-making in local government through seat quotas, change will not come about until their husbands let them attend meetings.

This brings us to gender mainstreaming. Some critics believe that because of mainstreaming efforts the basic organizational shifts that were a necessary starting-point, and were successfully achieved in many bilateral or multilateral agencies and NGOs, are actually withering away. Mainstreaming has effectively made gender equality work so technical, apolitical and geared simply to making visible 'both women and men', that it has lost its original intention of tackling discrimination. The unfortunate story now goes something like this: everyone is doing 'gender work' because it has been mainstreamed; there should not be a special programme for women if we are mainstreaming gender as that only ghettoizes them; and/or we can integrate 'gender' into our projects but mainstreaming has little to do with our organizations.

It seems, therefore, that we need to redouble efforts and work simultaneously on changing how organizations function and on the cultural, political and other underlying power relations that undermine paths to gender equality. This means tackling the complex and deep problems behind gender inequality, including addressing power head-on, namely classism, racism and sexism, and issues that have hitherto been perceived of as in the private realm, such as the work–family divide and cultural traditions.

For many of us, the first step will be to start with ourselves. We need to reorient our own organizations and make them more effective both in terms of impact and sustainability. Without a doubt, throughout the world, women's organizations are relatively weak given the lack of economic and political priority given to gender equality work. Questions of sustainability and funding, balancing work and personal life, measuring results and monitoring and evaluation are therefore constant challenges. In attempting to stay on top of these priorities, we too fall into the trap of becoming too bureaucratic and depoliticized. So alongside this basic planning and organizing, our organizations need to embody the rules and norms which we are trying to put in place in our communities and countries by working from values of anti-oppression, sustainability, transparency and participation.

For many, the next step will be to understand what institutional change really means, and then work on the more difficult task of how to make it happen.[44] This means going beyond influencing traditional power, such as in the courts, parliaments or CEOs' offices, in order to change the unwritten rules upon which patriarchy flourishes. This is the ultimate challenge for the future: making the achievement of women's rights not just a political project but a successful method to identify and transform hidden power and the rules of the game that stand in the way of social, cultural and economic transformation.

Getting beyond 'the other': taking on diversity in theory and practice If things continue in the way they are going, the future holds a world with dangerous divisions between the rich and poor, religions, ethnicities, races, age groups and even genders. Even women's movements are replicating social divisions caused by patriarchy and its forces of corporate-led globalization and militarization. As many have noted, a key weakness within gender equality work has been the inability to address effectively the diversity of women's identities based upon class, religion, race, ethnicity, age, caste, sexuality, ability and location, and hence those with less privilege have ended up becoming further marginalized.

Simply naming racism or classism is insufficient as an effective strategy. A current trend, therefore, is the development of new conceptual frameworks as well as methodologies to understand the implications of diversity as well as the construction of power and privilege.[45] Many groups are working with the concept of intersectionality as an essential means to understand and tackle women's subordination in all its forms. Intersectionality can also be a powerful tool for making the simultaneous interaction of discriminations visible. The notion of intersectionality has its roots in

Third World feminism and feminist theory but truly came to the forefront of feminist practice at the 2001 Durban World Conference against Racism, Racial Discrimination, Xenophobia, and Related Intolerances (WCAR).

In terms of actually using this concept in practice, the expert group meeting on racial discrimination and gender, in the lead-up to the Durban summit, recommended a three-part method of, first, collecting disaggregated data; second, undertaking a contextual analysis by documenting the impacts of a problem that result from converging identities; and, third, evaluating policies and programmes for their ability to tackle problems arising from intersecting forms of discrimination.[46] This analysis is particularly important within human rights where there exists a constant tension between respect for diversity and the demand for universality. As Charlotte Bunch suggests, however, we 'must respond to this debate by emphasizing that all women have a universal right to the enjoyment of all human rights, but this does not mean that all women's experiences, strategies or choices in affirming their human rights are or need to be identical'.[47]

The coming decades need to be informed by the rich and sophisticated analyses by (predominantly) Third World feminists on intersecting discriminations and how to overcome them. White, middle-class Northern feminists have an even greater responsibility to understand and apply this analysis *daily*. This specifically means ensuring that the most disadvantaged women have a voice, space and priority in our work. It also means that women's rights cannot be generalized and priorities cannot be determined according to a white, middle-class lens. For all women's rights advocates, it is also about using our privilege in strategic ways instead of trying to hide it. Identity is relative and so at any given moment we can associate with one part of our identity that wields more power (experience, ability, heterosexuality, whiteness or economic status, for example) instead of working from parts of our identities from where we face discrimination.[48] We can connect our oppressions in order to be more holistic in the fight for human rights for all. In the same way, we can connect our privilege and use this power in transformative, visionary ways.

The need to widen the circle and strengthen our alliances In the last decade, it has become increasingly apparent that the involvement of younger generations in women's rights, development and social justice work is an absolute necessity. Many activists and professionals are reaching the last stretches of their careers, making it essential to foster the transfer of knowledge between generations and regions in order to sustain and build upon efforts to date. Similarly, the movement needs to benefit further from the new ideas, energy, strategies and visions that young women provide.

Women's rights issues of today and tomorrow – resulting from increased economic integration, the 'digital divide', the new genetics, or globalized images of 'perfect' young women through Western media – are different from those of a generation ago. Moreover, the rights issues of adolescents have received limited research and policy attention, yet interventions at this stage of life are critical for addressing gender inequality.[49]

Although younger women are needed, so many are finding it difficult to find their voice, let alone employment, in the fields of human rights and gender and development. While many are eager to take on new challenges, they receive insufficient support, information and opportunity. In the same way, the generation gap illustrates the lack of appreciation of the contributions and experience of the women who have brought us thus far. There is a critical need, therefore, to build a stronger movement, whereby younger leaders are empowered to take on the new complex challenges and understand the systemic linkages of gender inequality while explicitly recognizing that they 'stand on the shoulders' of the feminist leaders of past decades.[50]

Parallel to efforts to develop a more intergenerational movement and focus to women's rights, a growing number of researchers, activists and practitioners are encouraging stronger alliances with progressive men. Work in the past several years on men's roles and masculinities has slowly influenced gender and development work in order to give significance and legitimacy to feminist men, that is, those men who 'support the cause'.[51] There are the 'big boys' who create spaces where feminists can get access to decision-makers, resources and strategic information. My own work around economic justice agendas has shown that women and men can work together on the basis of competency, forming issue-based and/or temporary coalitions. This is where we are opportunistic as feminists.[52]

While indeed this is a growing trend, some would argue that building alliances with men is still at a nascent stage. At the same time, however, it will be critical to avoid certain pitfalls of working with the 'wrong men'. We want to work only with those men who recognize that equality work requires sensitivity and the ability to be effective, while not taking up a lot of space.[53] Several feminist women speak of the dangers of working with men who don't know their 'place' and end up hijacking women's organizations or action.[54] Feminists also want to work with men who see women's rights in the context of fundamental global change – not merely as micro- or marginal issues. On the other hand, many feminist men criticize women's organizations for holding on to gender equality work by referring to 'our feminism and you men' and thereby diminishing opportunities for common agendas.[55] For the future, then, strategic thinking and trust on all sides will be required in order to create genuine partnerships within the movement for gender equality.

The third trend, an on-going struggle, relates to how best to link gender equality work at the macro- and microlevel. That is, how can we truly ensure that we are forging solutions and positions from the grassroots up? SEWA (India's Self-Employed Women's Association), for example, takes a pragmatic view of policy shifts by asking the most basic question: How will this affect our membership? In this way, SEWA has supported certain kinds of trade liberalization that increase work for poor Indian women, and has opposed other aspects of free trade when it does the opposite.[56] The more the gender equality community puts the interests of the poorest at the centre and then links these interests with macro- or global policies, the more effective our solutions will be in that they will be based on reality, instead of merely on rhetoric or ideology.

This challenge also speaks of the critical links between NGOs and social movements and how they need to be enhanced in order for social movements to grow. To those who are not part of either movements or NGOs, these two communities are often conflated. But they are not the same by any means and work from very different places with different strengths and weaknesses. The World Social Forum process (WSF) is a vivid example of the connections and differences between NGOs and movements. The WSF brings together a collection of movements, including peace, women and landless peasants, among others, that are dynamic and political, representing very diverse interests from the grassroots up. Their flexibility, openness and power of numbers are their strengths. NGOs are organizations with distinct members, agendas and accountability requirements to funders and other bureaucracies. Their strength is their structure, ability to organize and to deliver on certain goals. Women's movements include NGOs as well as individuals and groups who are committed to ending gender discrimination. NGOs, on the other hand, do not represent movements. As such, as NGOs, movements or individuals with a mission, we need to forge dynamic, supportive and strong relationships. Furthermore, our efforts need to be more concerted, more holistic and more collective. This is a time for forging new and stronger alliances with all progressive movements in order to strengthen us overall, diminish our isolation and demonstrate an obvious and alternative form of global transformative leadership.

'Marketing' feminism In truth, so much of our vision and analysis is seen as relevant to a broader mass. While there are a few exceptions, women's rights agendas are not grabbing mass attention. In many parts of the world, there is a negative stigma associated with feminism: some say, for example,

it is too angry and anti-male, it is about victims and complaints, or, worse, it is irrelevant. This image problem inhibits our successes. Instead, this rich work and these movements need to be seen for their risk, creativity, humour and energy. We need to broaden the movements by attracting new allies from all sectors, ages and identities. A key answer, then, lies in us doing a better job in 'marketing' feminism to a variety of audiences – through popular culture for some, or sophisticated policy research for others. Feminism needs to have as positive a brand image as environmentalism, such as 'Feminism is Fun: Join the Party for Global Justice and Peace'. Our inspiring visions *are* about a just society, true democracy, peace and freedom. Quite simply, we need to bottle these visions and sell them as *hope*.

Feminist futures: some conclusions

This chapter has explored many critical and enormous issues for the future. From patriarchy to growing neoconservatism, the old forces that have dogged our efforts for social transformation will continue in the decades to come, but in mutated forms. More venture capitalists, robots, guns, religious zealots and diseases will work against our human rights and security. Fortunately, we, as women's movements and organizations, are becoming more concerned with the need to understand how change happens, to take the best of learning and approaches from all disciplines, to assess strategic opportunities, use power and privilege, cooperate and form strategic alliances, and be proactive, future-oriented and not afraid to take risks. Strategies and alternatives exist. Going forward at this time of intense global turmoil, then, we need a surfeit of hope and inspiration. That, and the knowledge that feminists a hundred years ago could never have dreamed of the successes so many of us enjoy today. Just imagine how feminists in the twenty-second century will celebrate our achievements.

Notes

1 In particular, I appreciate the conversations with AWID's international board members, Marilyn Waring (visiting scholar), the staff of AWID and Mama Cash, as well as conversations in Brazil, Mexico, South Africa and New York with scores of feminists grappling with the future.

2 Polaris Institute (2003) 'Global Water Grab: How Corporations are Planning to Take Control of Local Water Services', pamplet series (Ottawa: Polaris Institute).

3 Ibid.

4 G. Howard and J. Bartram (2003) *Domestic Water Quantity, Service and Health*, WHO/SDE/WSH/03.02 (Geneva: WHO).

5 A. E. Obanda (2003) 'Women and Water Privatization'. See <www.whrnet.org/docs/issue-water.html>

6 In many conferences and conversations I have heard this twist on the popular slogan attributed to many different people; the author therefore remains unknown.

7 Third World Network Africa (2003) 'Trade and Investment in Africa: Gender and the Role of the State', GERA Programme Policy Brief: Governance (Accra: Third World Network Africa).

8 See J. Kerr (1999) 'Responding to Globalization: Can Feminists Transform Development?', in M. Porter and E. Judd (eds), *Feminists Doing Development* (London: Zed Books).

9 See any statement by the Women's International Coalition for Economic Justice.

10 'Another World is Possible' is the slogan of the World Social Forum, which has now spurned regional and national social fora. Their momentum has grown significantly in the few years of their existence, given the strong resistance to current forms of globalization as well as US-led military attacks.

11 Discussions at the First Annual Conference for Development Change, Antigua, Guatemala, 28–30 July 2003.

12 See on-going programmes of the Women's Learning Partnership headquartered in Washington, DC, the International Women's Tribune Center, New York, or the Association for Progressive Communications, working virtually everywhere.

13 Personal communication with Ann Elisabeth Samson, 2003.

14 Women's International Coalition for Economic Justice, *Statement on Iraq and War*. See <www.wicej.addr.com/antiwar.html> (accessed 25 March 2003).

15 A. El Jack (2003) *Gender and Armed Conflict, Overview Report*, BRIDGE (part of cutting-edge pack on Gender and Armed Conflict) (Brighton: Institute of Development Studies).

16 Personal communication with Sunila Abeysekera, Sri Lankan women's rights and peace activist and researcher.

17 WIDE (January 2003) *WIDE Bulletin. Europe Moving to the Right: Where Lie the Alternatives for Transnational Feminism?* (Brussels: Women In Development Europe).

18 From Oxfam's trade campaign posters leading up to the 2003 Cancun WTO Ministerial.

19 See Women Living Under Muslim Laws (1997) *Plan of Action* (Dhaka) <www.wluml.org>

20 N. Yuval-Davis (January 2003) 'Neo-liberalism, Militarism and Zenophobia: Some Implications for the Gendered Politics of Belonging' (see note 17), p. 7.

21 United Nations High Commissioner for Human Rights, Integration of the Human Rights of Women and the Gender Perspective Violence Against Women. Item 12(a), Statement by Ms Radhika Coomaraswamy, Special Rapporteur on Violence Against Women, Its Causes and Consequences, Commission on Human Rights, 59th Session, 9 April 2003.

22 Personal communication with Farida Shaheed from Shirkat Gah.

23 See Women Against Fundamentalism at <http://www.gn.apc.org/waf/>

24 See <http://www.seechange.org/> for details of this international campaign.

25 See <www.wluml.org>

26 Secretary-General's address to the plenary session of the General Assembly on the follow-up to the Declaration of Commitment on HIV/AIDS, New York, 22 September 2003.

27 UNIFEM and the Association for Women's Rights in Development (2002) *ACT NOW! A Resource Guide for Young Women on HIV/AIDS* (New York UNIFEM).

28 S. Maman et al. (2001) 'HIV and Partner Violence', *Horizons* (Washington, DC: Population Council). This study was carried out during the 1990s with families in Dar es Salaam, Tanzania.

29 WHO (June 2000) 'Human Rights, Women and HIV/AIDS', Fact Sheet 247 (Geneva: World Health Organization).

30 Dhanraj, Misra and Batliwala, this volume, Chapter 6.

31 United Nations Development Program (2000) *Human Development Report 2000* (New York: UNDP).

32 A. Sen (1999) *Development as Freedom* (New York: Knopf).

33 For instance, while a legal rights approach to land inheritance might focus on the impediment to women's ability to inherit land contained in religious personal law, a development approach might address family/household structures, women's organizations and small groups, the community administrative and market institutions, the political system, culture and the legal system.

34 Personal communication with Dzodzi Tsikata, Ghanaian academic and activist.

35 See Institute for Development Studies (2001) 'Gender and Participation', *Development and Gender in Brief*, 9 (August).

36 I thank Marilyn Waring for reinforcing this point in a personal communication.

37 Action Aid, Institute for Development Studies-Participation Group and Just Associates (2003) *Making Change Happen: Advocacy and Citizen Participation Pamphlet* (London: Action Aid), p. 2.

38 Ibid.

39 See <http://www.ipu.org/wmn-e/world.htm>

40 WEDO. (2002) 'The Numbers Speak for Themselves', Fact Sheet <www.wedo.org/ffd/representation.htm>

41 N. Uddyog (2001) 'Improving Women's Access to Justice, Bangladesh', *Annual Report: Year One. July 2000 to 2001* (Nagorik Uddyog and Oneworld Action). On a visit to Pakistan in December 2002, I learned that a local council woman was stripped naked and paraded through the streets for her political actions disapproved of by the local elites.

42 See, for example, M. Macdonald, E. Sprenger and I. Dubel (1997) *Gender and Organizational Change: Bridging the Gap between Policy and Practice* (Amsterdam: Royal Tropical Institute); A. Rao, D. Kelleher and R. Stuart (1999)

Gender at Work (Bloomfield CT: Kumarian); S. Cummings, M. Valk and H. Van Dam (2000) *Institutionalizing Gender Equality: Commitment, Policy and Practice* (Netherlands: Royal Tropical Institute and Oxfam GB); A. M. Goetz (1997) *Getting Institutions Rights for Women in Development* (London: Zed Books); N. Kabeer (1994) *Reversed Realities: Gender Hierarchies in Development Thought* (London: Verso).

43 A. Rao and D. Kelleher (2002) 'Unravelling Institutionalized Gender Inequality', Occasional Paper 8 (Toronto: Association for Women's Rights in Development).

44 For example, an international collaboration has recently been formed, known as Gender at Work, with CIVICUS, AWID, the Women's Learning Partnership and UNIFEM as a South–North knowledge-building network to facilitate institutional transformation for gender equality. See <www.genderatwork.org>

45 See, for example, R. Raj (ed.) in collaboration with C. Bunch and E. Nazombe (2002) *Women at the Intersection: Indivisible Rights, Identities, and Oppressions* (Brunswick, NJ: Center for Women's Global Leadership); R. Marks (2000) *Gender Race, and Class Dynamics in Post-Apartheid South Africa* (Boston, MA: Center for Gender in Organizations, SIMMONS Graduate School Management); E. Holvino (2001) *Complicating Gender: The Simultaneity of Race, Gender and Class in Organization Change(ing)* (Boston, MA: Center for Gender in Organizations, SIMMONS Graduate School Management).

46 The full report, written by Kimberle Crenshaw, can be found at <http://www.un.org/womenwatch/daw/csw/genrac/report.htm>

47 C. Bunch (2001) 'Why the WCAR is Critical to Women's Human Rights Advocacy', Presentation at a panel held during the Commission on the Status of Women.

48 Mallika Dutt shared this concept at the AWID Forum. See M. Verma (2003) 'A Question of Identity: Intersectionality and the Women's Movement', in *Reinventing Globalization: Highlights of AWID's 2002 International Forum on Women's Rights in Development* (Toronto: Association for Women's Rights in Development), pp. 15–17.

49 See the International Center for Research on Women, Strategic Plan for 2001 to 2005.

50 I thank Peggy Antrobus for sharing a speech, 'Feminism as a Transformational Politics: Women's Leadership Now', given at St Mary's University, Halifax, on 21 September 2001, which discusses this issue of intergenerational strategies.

51 See, for example, Institute in Development Studies (2000) 'Do Men Matter? New Horizons in Gender and Development', *Insights*, 35 (December), or the long list of books recently published on masculinities: see <www.sagepub.co.uk> for a clear example of this. Similarly, male violence against women movements are emerging in communities from South Africa to Nicaragua to Canada. Despite this, with a few exceptions, men are seldom explicitly referred to in gender policy documents.

52 I thank Ellen Sprenger for this characterization – a very useful way to understand our strategies of working with men.

53 Personal communication with David Kelleher.

54 B. Adeleyi-Fayemi, this volume, Chapter 3.

55 Just Associates and AWID (2003) 'Dialogue for Building Movement Solidarity for Economic Justice, Peace, and Women's Rights', *Report from the World Social Forum, 2003*. See <www.justassociates.org>

56 See R. Kanbur (2001) 'Economic Policy, Distribution and Poverty: The Nature of the Disagreements', at <http://www.people.cornell.edu/pages/sk145> I thank Aruna Rao for this point and example.

3 | Creating a new world with new visions: African feminism and trends in the global women's movement

BISI ADELEYE-FAYEMI

Many profound challenges face the global women's movements today, from globalization to HIV/AIDS; some of these issues are old, but some have taken on new faces. In the meantime, the leadership, agents and movements working for change are also under attack. In this respect, it is critical that we reflect on what we have accomplished, what we have yet to bring about and the context in which we work. This chapter starts by considering the specific context of African feminism and the global trends, issues and influences which are defining African women's movements. It then looks at the impacts this context has on feminist organizing, and how strategic African feminist spaces are under attack. Finally, it turns to the international scene and considers the global women's movement more generally, putting forward strategies that could lead to a revitalized, effective and inclusive movement. By linking the local to the global, feminists can understand the contemporary world we are facing and put forth new visions for our movement and our world.

The current context of African feminism: the challenges we face

The 'glocalization' of poverty Over the past twenty-five years, consciousness has been raised on issues affecting women all over the world, at both macro- and microlevels. In spite of this increased awareness, the material conditions of women have not necessarily improved; quality of life has continued to deteriorate for both men and women in most of the developing world. Global phenomena such as the debt crises, structural adjustment policies and increased militarization and communal violence have continued to widen the gap between most Western nations and developing regions. What is a 'regional' or national perspective or issue, therefore, is a result of global trends, while global events have direct and immediate local consequences.

In discussing African regional issues and global trends, an important phenomenon to note is what has been referred to as 'glocalization'.[1] The first time I used the term 'glocalization' in a paper, it came back to me from the editors corrected to 'globalization'. I politely informed them that glocalization was in fact not a typographical error but a specific contemporary experience of interplay between the local and the global. In other words, events and processes at the global level affect women's situation at the local level at the same time as women's local activities affect global processes.

One of the most obvious global trends of recent times has been the rapid globalization of the economy and its attendant structures. Globalization favours the deregulation of markets, free trade and privatization. It involves the movement of capital 'at the speed of light' and the formation of 'quasi-governments' in the form of multinational financial institutions such as the World Trade Organization, World Bank and International Monetary Fund. While this economic globalization takes place at an intangible global level, it plays out in actual places and is manifested concretely in the lives of real people.

The implementation of economic policies, including structural adjustment programmes, trade liberalization and the privatization of education and health services has compounded the feminization of poverty, for example. Global economic trends take local form in terms of loss of livelihoods, unemployment, trafficking in women, street children and a total rupturing of the social fabric that binds communities together. Moreover, when international policies and economic transactions cause local economic crises, women are affected in different ways from men and, in most cases, they suffer more.

The African region has fared particularly badly over the past two decades and women in Africa have borne the brunt of the continent's misfortunes. Consider, for example, that approximately 44 per cent of Africa's population, the majority of whom are women, are currently living below the poverty line of US $39 per month.[2] Furthermore, women continue to lack access to resources such as land, capital, technology, water and adequate food. The majority of women in Africa continue to live in conditions of economic underdevelopment and social marginalization.[3] These local realities certainly shape feminism within Africa and also shape and reshape global trends.

So as some parts of the world grow fantastically rich and most parts grow desperately poorer, we need to ask questions about the true meaning of globalization. Does it mean we all exist in a 'global village' where a few get to have all the comforts and riches on the basis of their geographical location and race, while the rest literally clean their toilets? Or does it mean seizing opportunities to ensure equal access to the benefits of trade and investment, and to fairness, equity and justice?

Conflict and militarization These days, teenagers in the United States have come up with an expression for anything outdated or out of sync with the times. They say 'That is so September 10th'. For on 11 September, these youths, and of course most of their parents, had an excruciatingly painful awakening to the horrors of war, senseless destruction and despair. Yet, for millions of people around the world for whom conflict and communal violence have been a way of life for many years, the only thing that was different about 11 September was that they got to watch a real-life Hollywood blockbuster for free on TV. Millions have been killed in wars, conflicts, genocides and communal violence in recent years. Many states in the poorer parts of the world, with massive encouragement from the West, spend more on militarization than on education, health and food security combined.

With 'advances' in military technology, it is possible to obliterate an entire community from the air without sending in any ground troops. This has created the illusion that the ways in which wars are waged has changed. This change is touted as a new and positive trend in 'civilized' war-mongering. The impact of war and conflict remains high, however, in terms of massive violations of human rights, disruption of services and the diversion of already scarce resources to sustain the war effort. The impact on ordinary people is devastating, particularly on women and children. Conflict has increased the feminization of poverty, with women losing their own livelihoods, and the support of fathers, husbands and sons. Landmines and small arms abound during and after periods of conflict, and an entire generation of child soldiers exists in many conflict areas. People still suffer and still die. So, in fact, nothing has really changed in the way wars are fought or won.

Over the past fifteen years, millions of Africans have lost their lives in wars and genocide, and many more have become refugees. Twenty-three armed conflicts are currently raging on the African continent.[4] These conflicts have placed tremendous burdens on women who suffer displacement, loss of families and livelihoods, various forms of intense, gender-based violence, and the responsibility of sustaining entire communities. Women and children from countries such as Liberia, Rwanda, Sudan, Sierra Leone, Democratic Republic of the Congo, Burundi and Somalia have spent the last decade living under unbelievably difficult circumstances. The irony is that the donor community is developing new proposals to support 'failed states', and making immense investments to restore countries in conflict while, in many cases, having for decades financially supported the build-up of arms or politically supported undemocratic leaders in the region.

Exclusion from politics and full citizenship One critical area which African feminists have analysed extensively is the experiences of African women with the state and the exclusion of women from full citizenship. Women were active in liberation struggles that provided them with an entry point into political and social activism in several African countries, including Namibia, Zimbabwe, Eritrea, Kenya, South Africa, Mozambique, Uganda and Guinea-Bissau. But after the liberation struggle, what happened to the women? In many instances the constitutions that emerged following independence effectively wrote women out of existence as citizens.

Many African constitutions are now being questioned and renegotiated as a result of feminist activism. These constitutions do not recognize women as full citizens in that they deny women the right to transfer citizenship to another person, which is a basic right of modern citizenship. *Bona fide* citizens have the right and legal capacity to confer their citizenship on their children or a foreign spouse, for example. Millions of African women are therefore not full citizens of the very countries for which they fought and risked their lives to build. A related issue is that of land ownership, a right of citizenship which is also denied to most women in Africa.

Women are underrepresented in most levels of government worldwide, and Africa is no exception. Concern was raised about this issue in the Beijing Declaration and Platform for Action, for example, and United Nations Economic and Social Council (ECOSOC) set a specific target for women to hold 50 per cent of managerial and decision-making posts by year 2000.[5] African governments have also made specific commitments on this issue. For example, several countries and political parties created quota systems and affirmative action programmes and reserve 25–50 per cent of elective seats at national and local levels, as well as other appointive positions, for women. As a result some countries such as South Africa (29.3 per cent), Mozambique (25.2 per cent), Seychelles (23.5 per cent) Uganda (21 per cent) and Namibia (22.2 per cent) now have significantly higher levels of women's representation in national assemblies and other positions of power and decision-making.[6]

Despite these advances, gaining access to mainstream decision-making and political power for African women remains a challenge. In the first place, millions of women are illiterate. Those who are literate have to contend with the difficult process of seeking the support of husbands, family and friends, and acceptance from party colleagues. They have to mobilize the necessary campaign finances and endure the harsh realities of political campaigns in Africa that can break the toughest of women. Those who are elected tend to find it very difficult to work within the established structures, which can be hostile to the empowerment and equality of women.

The implications of women being excluded from full citizenship and political decision-making are serious. If women do not have a voice in key decisions which affect their lives, their capacity for full development and equality is severely limited. In contrast, women's involvement in decision-making contributes to redefining political priorities, placing issues on the political agenda which address women's gender-specific concerns, values and experiences, and provides new perspectives on mainstream political issues. Without the active participation of women and the inclusion of their perspectives at all levels of decision-making, the goals of equality, development and peace cannot be achieved.[7] The exclusion of women and the denial of their full citizenship rights, therefore, shape feminism within Africa and are fundamental areas of struggle for women all over the continent.

New politics and religion, without basic rights Africa has the lowest literacy rate in the world at only 50 per cent. The majority of the illiterate are women, and they live in rural areas with limited access to clean water, good transportation, adequate food, land, credit facilities and healthcare. The continent has one of the highest maternal and infant mortality rates in the world and decreased health spending and privatization of healthcare systems have had a grave impact on the health of women and girls. Furthermore, the HIV/AIDS pandemic has exacerbated the already vulnerable status of women's health. Of the six countries globally with the highest number of HIV/AIDS-infected people, five are in Africa: Botswana's infection rate is 18 per cent, Zimbabwe 17.4 per cent, Zambia 17.1 per cent, Malawi 13.6 per cent and South Africa 11.4 per cent.[8] Women are more vulnerable to infection due to biological, social and economic reasons, and have less negotiating power with partners. They also spend a great deal of their time and resources caring for other family members who are sick.

African women face discrimination in all spheres of life. Violence against women is still a major crisis, religious and cultural fundamentalisms are on the increase, discriminatory laws still control women's lives and bodies, and harmful traditional practices persist. Negative stereotypes and attitudes prevent many women from realizing their full potential and making the contributions towards their communities that they would really wish to.

In many parts of Africa, as elsewhere in the world, there is a backlash against women's rights and a roll-back of gains previously made. Three high-profile cases involving the interpretation and application of Sharia law in Northern Nigeria, with scores of such cases still pending, have raised concerns about the conceptualization of women's personhood.[9] At the beginning of the twenty-first century, women in Nigeria, one of the most powerful countries in Africa, are faced with being stoned to death as a result of the heavy politicization of religion. How has it come to pass that we are now faced with the possibility of women being stoned to death in a country which is espousing 'a New Partnership for African Development'?[10]

The use of organized religion to control women's bodies and lives is not the exclusive reserve of one religion. A disturbing trend in many African countries is the emergence of hundreds of ultra-conservative evangelical establishments. Feminist work is under serious threat because of the large numbers of women we are losing to these institutions. Many are providing jobs, education (even up to university level), food and shelter. In so doing, they are building a very large constituency.

The once unique African urban experience has become a nightmare for young, successful women who have the confidence to live on their own, a new trend in many African cities. They have become targets for violent attacks, including sexual assaults in the presence of family members. The motivation for these attacks may be that they have dared to claim a public space or to punish the men in their lives for their successes.

Reclaiming feminism and feminist spaces to take on global challenges

As the section above clearly illustrates, the challenges to ensure gender equality and rights for African women are enormous. We need to be asking ourselves hard questions such as: What are we really up against? Do we really understand what is going on in the world today, or only what our governments and the media want us to understand? Where do our loyalties and energies lie? How is patriarchy evolving in response to our gains? Once we do understand what is happening, are we prepared to do what it takes to transform the world? Do we have the conceptual, human, material and financial resources to effect this change?

So where does the leadership for change come from? In my view, it will come from the feminist movement. I would like to speak of a 'feminist movement' and not just a 'women's movement' because, inasmuch as we can use the women's movement to mobilize around specific issues and address ourselves to a plethora of strategies at various levels, we still need a feminist analysis of the world in which we live. We need continually to go back and sharpen our feminist analytical tools.

The feminist movement, for feminists of all persuasions, is a political and ideological space. This space is made up of the many individuals, organizations, associations and entities that constitute the feminist movement; it is made up of our friendships, networks, bonds, organizations and our individual and collective feminist energies. It is a space for feminists to claim and to use. We use this space to mobilize around our feminist principles, to hone our analytical skills and to seek, and sometimes find, answers to our many questions. What makes the space work is faith: that is, the belief that this space is needed to make our lives better and easier. This faith is manifested in our processes of self-discovery, our hopes, our dreams, our aspirations, and our yearning for more knowledge and revelations. The two – space and faith – are interdependent. We need our space as feminists in order to walk the road together and we need the faith that will keep us together in good and in bad times.[11]

At local, national, regional and global levels, we have worked hard to create feminist spaces and discourses. The gains for women embodied in the Convention on the Elimination of All Forms of Discrimination Against Women, the Vienna Declaration on Human Rights, the Beijing Platform for Action and other international agreements came out of many hard years of feminist struggle all over the world. These movements have grown and evolved and the voices of poor, marginalized women have been a part of them. These feminist spaces, however, are at risk; they are at risk of being hijacked by 'friendly' and 'unfriendly' forces and of ultimately becoming obsolete.

One of the key challenges I see facing the women's movement globally and the feminist movement in particular is the need to maintain the focus on the specificity of women's oppression, their rights and their needs. Within the African context, it is becoming increasingly difficult to sustain space for feminist activism because most states are hostile to women's rights issues. While the laws and constitutions of the countries say one thing, the politicians and opinion leaders say and do something else. State actors, in fact, usually undermine the very important work of lobbying for legal reforms and constitutional amendments that could raise the status of women. The media, political parties, trade unions and other civil society groups do not genuinely understand why a feminist movement is needed. In this environment, it is an increasingly difficult challenge to garner attention for women's specific issues.

Another key challenge is that the women who are in leadership positions in government structures and other strategic institutions lack either the consciousness or clout to push a progressive agenda for women. These women sometimes become a liability to the feminist movement because of their reactionary positions at worst, or conservative positions at best. For example, a very common strategy is for them to work with or hold up as an example rural grassroots women who have no gender analysis. They are held up as the 'real women' instead of articulate, middle-class women, who are mainly urban-based. This strategy serves to erode any political women's rights efforts because the rural women are not able to represent women's strategic interests. At the same time, the self-esteem and energies of feminists are undermined by making them continuously apologetic for whatever privileges they are perceived to have.

Yet another key challenge facing feminists in the global women's movement is a lack of conceptual clarity within the movement itself. A trend I have noted with great concern in recent years is the depoliticization of feminism and feminist politics as a result of gender and development language and praxis. At a conference I was attending in 1998, for example, a woman stood up proudly to announce, 'I have moved beyond feminism to gender'. In this strange analysis, the struggle for the specificity of women's rights and needs is rendered obsolete and replaced with a new politics which 'empowers both men and women', although without questioning the context or who is doing the empowering. It is precisely because 'gender' has been simplistically analysed in this way that many women in the movement describe themselves as 'gender activists' and not 'feminist activists'. Gender is safe, while feminism is threatening. Gender can be accommodated and tolerated by the status quo, while feminism challenges it. As a result, the feminist spaces we have tried to create for ourselves are in danger of being 'genderized'.

Many women ask, 'What does it matter what we call ourselves? As long as we are all fighting for women's rights, isn't that what matters?' For me, this is not good enough. The work of fighting for women's rights is as deeply political as the process of naming. Choosing to call oneself a feminist is a clear statement of ideology. We need feminist analysis because if we do not have an adequate theory of the oppression of women, we will lack the analytical tools to develop appropriate strategies of resistance. We will end up working only on symptoms and not on root causes.

Finally, the participation of men in women's movements is another challenge to sustaining our feminist space. We have been asking, and have been asked, questions such as, 'Why are we not talking to men and working in partnership with them?' It has been noted that there are men who are feminists and are deeply committed to supporting the feminist movement and that having progressive men on board as allies early on can help protect the work that women do in marginalized communities. There is a belief that after years of gender mainstreaming, men have been 'left behind' and they now need to be 'carried along'.

As feminist activists, we all have to work with men, build personal and professional partnerships with them, and seek them out as allies. Increasingly, men in our communities are stepping forward to provide moral and financial support for our movements. We must be cautious, however. Does this new trend imply that feminist spaces have to be surrendered to men or carved up so that men can have a 50 per cent stake? Does including men imply employing them to run women's organizations, men editing women's magazines, speaking on behalf of women and counselling women suffering from abuse? Does it imply tolerating the company of men who philander, or those who batter their partners physically and emotionally in private while seeking to be our allies in public? Moreover, are these men that we are 'carrying along' prepared to give up the powers and privileges that patriarchy confers on them?

This is an issue that we need to think about carefully: some of us have lost our feminist spaces to men. In places where women are still developing the tools they need for self-expression and self-discovery, insisting that they let men into those spaces without a clear strategy is a recipe for disaster. While it is important that we work with men, we need to have a strategy about how and why we want to work with them.

New identities and globalized visions

Many debates among feminists in Africa revolve around issues of 'culture' and 'identity'. For example, what is African culture and what constitutes an African identity? Moreover, who defines them? These two terms are used by some African scholars, practitioners and politicians in reference to vital elements of our humanity which were lost through many years of exploitation, brutalization and dislocation. These concepts, however, mean very different things in the day-to-day lives of African women.

Within the context of an African culture defined and interpreted by patriarchal values, a woman is a second-class citizen, her labour is unremunerated, her body is available and disposable, her rights are subject to validation and violation, and her daughters will share her fate. She is socialized into sustaining the very structures that will oppress her throughout her life. There will be some rewards that come with compliance, and also punishment for rebellion. This, in essence, is her identity.

African feminists point out that definitions of 'Africanness' cannot be constructed outside the personhood of African women. This conceptual framework also applies to our global feminist movement; we should see our task as continuously creating new, transformatory identities for women. New strategies and new visions will emerge through the process of creating and re-creating our own identities.

In spite of its many curses, globalization does bring with it some key opportunities that the women's movement can take advantage of and which can be used to create new identities. One example is the increased demand for democratization processes and a broadening of the spectrum of guaranteed rights for women, men and peoples all over the world. These aspects of globalization can strengthen the women's movement in the following ways.

Universal human rights guarantees An identity that women can now take advantage of is that of 'global citizen' with internationally protected human rights in parallel to their national citizenship and nationally protected rights. National citizenship is enriched through the coexistence of a global one, which provides recourse to regional and international legal instruments, mechanisms and universally accepted principles of justice and human rights.

In all of our countries, organizations are working on mobilization and awareness-raising around women's rights, such as violence against women and harmful traditional practices. They work with women in very poor communities, in both rural and urban areas, on changing structures, beliefs and attitudes. They use the language of human rights and appeal to universal values of justice and equality. This is a process of re-creating identities and redefining a personhood for women which has been opened up by processes of globalization.

New avenues for state accountability Emerging international norms of democracy and human rights have presented novel possibilities for engagement with the state. New demands for accountability and representation have brought about decentralization programmes, political representation, affirmative action, gender mainstreaming and calls for legal and constitutional reform, for example. Women have been active advocates in these sites of engagement. In nations such as South Africa and Uganda, women's movements have won the inclusion of constitutional provisions on the protection and promotion of women's rights, including quotas and affirmative action.

Women not only are taking advantage of new opportunities to engage with their state, they are recognizing that for their work to be effective they must be represented in government. There has been a deliberate shift towards fighting for access to decision-making positions and also towards strengthening women's leadership within hostile, patriarchal structures. A good example in this regard is the Women's Budget Initiative, which was spearheaded in Africa by women in the South African parliament and is now being taken on board in other African countries. Through these new means of engagement with the state, women's movements are again redefining and re-creating the identities of women in Africa.[12]

Opportunities for women to shape policies in post-conflict countries As the international community has focused its attention on agendas for reconstructing war-torn societies and countries in political transition, new roles for women in shaping policies and priorities are emerging. We are witnessing a general refocusing on how, where and by whom power structures are defined and the re-creation of human agency in actors such as women's organizations, trade unions and human rights organizations.

Over the past ten years at least, civil society organizations have kept countries running when they had virtually collapsed, such as Sierra Leone, Liberia, Rwanda and Somalia. Women in particular have formed broad-based peace movements and called for new values with respect to defining communal relationships and state–civil-society relations. Such values include accountability, transparency, anti-corruption and inclusiveness as crucial elements of good governance. With the understanding that no society can rejuvenate itself without the active participation of women, reconstruction and nation-building processes are serving to reaffirm and re-create the roles of women in their societies as well as at the international level.

Refocusing women's movements

One key lesson that we have learned as a global women's movement is the value of multidimensional thinking and activism. Our issues are always interrelated and mutually reinforcing. Understanding the influences and trends described so far in this chapter, it becomes clear that feminist organizing must respond to these new realities and challenges, always conscious of how the 'new issues' are related to the 'old issues' and how challenges in one region or sector are interconnected with other issues.

The vital strength of the global women's movement is that it is made up of numerous local women's movements, but this has also been its weakness: there are too many preachers with the same message. In proposing a strategic direction, therefore, rather than dwelling on the need for 'division of labour' strategies which could imply that each region, organization or network map out a piece of turf and guard it jealously, I would like to suggest strategically building a movement that has crucial elements within it for its survival. As Bella Abzug once said: 'to live to get the whole job done, great movements must reinvent themselves. To sustain themselves, movements must not only grow: they must change. This is not only because times inevitably change. It is because we ourselves have changed the times. Thus, we must react in part to our own history.'[13]

How, then, can we consolidate our gains and make use of the opportunities that now exist to reinvent our movement? What follows are my personal recommendations of strategic priorities for the global women's movement and local women's movements all over the world, in light of the global trends and emerging issues which we face.

Repoliticize the movement The feminist movement worldwide should now concentrate on confronting global structures and systems. In order to engage critically with the global patriarchal structures responsible for women's lack of personhood, we need more feminists, not just women in decision-making positions. The time has come for us to face the fact that if the women's movement is aiming to struggle against all forms of patriarchal oppression, then it has to be feminists and their allies who do this. It is an inherently political struggle. The criterion for being in the women's movement can no longer be mere biology. We need *feminists* with power.

We need feminists as public advocates, politicians and law-makers, in the corporate sector and in social movements. If we are to see any lasting changes in the lives of women this century, if we are to see a change in our politics and economies, if we are to have lasting peace in our communities, we will need a feminist conceptualization of power and governance. This great transformation will not be achieved, I am reluctant to accept, solely by putting feminist women in power; we have to take risks and promote 'feminist' men as well. We also have to remember that the battle is not won simply by getting feminists into positions of power; we all have to do what we can to support them and keep them in their positions, and we also have to hold them accountable.

Develop new feminist knowledge The global feminist movement has made very good progress in the creation of knowledge. Feminism has thrived in the academies in the North, at least in part because feminists in these countries have been able to acquire the necessary spaces and resources. This success has unfortunately led to intellectual hegemonies: the sisters in the North are the ones with the academic institutions, women's/feminist studies programmes, fellowships, research grants, technology and access to international publishing. Thus they appropriate the knowledge bases of women in the South, resulting in an intellectual dichotomy whereby the women from the North are regarded as the thinkers and scholars and the women from the South are the practitioners, with, of course, more value and respect attached to the former. How many Western feminist writers on Africa refer to the works of African women? How many books on 'international feminism' include contributions from African feminist scholars and activists? There has been a very effective silencing of other women's voices and experiences.[14]

The sole responsibility for redressing this imbalance does not rest in the North, however. We feminists in the global South should also challenge ourselves to devote time, space and energies to writing our own stories and to theorizing. We have to scale up our contributions to the rich debates on feminist theory and practice that are going on throughout the world. A very important area of work for us should be thoughtfully and consistently to document our experiences as women's movements. Only when all voices are being heard will we be able to talk of a truly global feminism.

Strengthen feminist institutions Feminist organizations today are somewhat different from what they were at their inception many years ago. Feminist spaces must be capable of evolution in order to survive. Feminist organizational development requires significantly more research and attention because it is a substantial challenge to assess the implications of marrying conventional organizational development theory and practice with the experiences of feminist organizational leadership. Building and sustaining our institutions, however, are critical to the movement and we must not neglect this foundational aspect of our work.

Frequently, feminist organizations have been premised on principles of non-hierarchy, collective work and collective responsibility. They have also been highly dependent on volunteers. These structures, however, do not necessarily support the institutional capacity to sustain long-term activities. While some might argue that so-called professionalism ruins social movements because it adds a dollar price to people's commitment, we need to also be realistic and accept that for movements to survive they need to grow and evolve. Commitment, good-will and volunteerism are vital, but they are no longer enough to sustain women's organizations.

A related issue is the fact that, as a result of ideological differences, donor involvement and poor employment opportunities, among other factors, civil society organizations tend to proliferate. Many organizations, therefore, carry out work that is not necessarily adding value and which is not part of an overall strategy for transformation. This tends to encourage cynicism, suspicion and a lack of respect for non-governmental organizations on the part of potential beneficiaries, donors and governments. It gives opponents an easy opportunity to discredit civil society institutions. Building and sustaining effective feminist institutions should be a collective priority for the global feminist movement in the immediate future.

Acquire money of our own Feminist organizations need to acquire their own resources in order to consolidate and sustain their legacies. Too many organizations operate on shoestring budgets and are both donor-dependent and donor-driven. We can not afford for our movement to be at the mercy of donor funding, without mechanisms for sustained institutional development or independence. We cannot truly own our own agendas if we do not have our own resources.

Thankfully, there is now an emerging global feminist philanthropic movement and 'women's funds' in all parts of the world, with varying levels of resources and at different stages of growth and development.[15] What these funds all have in common is the desire to place resources at the disposal of the feminist movement. One major challenge ahead will be to convince ourselves and other women of the need to invest in our own sisters by donating to these funds.

Managing our diversity We have now had many debates on diversity and the politics of identity and race within our movement. Feminists from the global South, as well as many Northern feminists, have actively critiqued the lack of an intersectional analysis in our work, including the issue of racism within the global women's movement itself. While we would like to think that we have worked on this and that it is no longer an 'issue', it has not been fully resolved. As feminists from both the North and South, we have to continue learning to redefine the ways in which we engage with each other in order to sustain our 'glocal' spaces, even though it can be painful and frustrating.

Develop feminist leadership The feminist leadership model conceptualizes leadership as a service. It allows for individual feminist leaders to guide and lead their movements responsibly, but it also decentralizes power and decision-making so that everyone in the movement becomes a leader in her own right. Within organizations, feminist leadership should, it is hoped, provide vital political content, ideological clarity and commitment to the ethos and principles of feminism. It should promote the learning and teaching of feminist principles, including, among many others, the centrality of the fight for women's personhood, the necessity of providing a voice for women, the validation of women's knowledge, a respect for women's bodily integrity, norms for working across diversities, and values for working in solidarity with strategically chosen allies.

Developing feminist leadership is fundamental to the survival of our organizations. For feminist spaces to survive, we need a reconceptualization of power and leadership within organizations. Furthermore, as organizations grow more complex and try to cope with the demands of juggling various projects, acquiring funding and servicing a variety of stakeholders, they need effective feminist leaders to manage them. Non-governmental women's organizations have the ability to provide the necessary conceptual, analytical and practical tools for emerging leaders. Producing well-grounded feminist leaders through awareness-raising, self-esteem promotion, intergenerational capacity-building programmes and other types of strategic training should become the *raison d'être* of feminist organizations.

Replenish our ranks Simply stated, we need more young women in the global women's movement. Furthermore, we need to develop institutional cultures of intergenerational organizing. While many have recognized this need, actually addressing it remains a sticky area in the women's movement. On the one hand, younger women note the conservatism and the matronizing, often selfish, behaviour of older women. Older women, on the other hand, point to the lack of commitment of younger women, who are perceived to be less willing to challenge power relations because of where they are in their life cycle.[16] It has also been noted that, in the North, the feminist movement has become a victim of its own successes. Young, middle-class women, armed with their college degrees, the right to control their bodies, their credit cards and a marked improvement in the quality of their lives compared with those of their mothers, say that we are now in a 'post-feminist era'. But, as has been stated so many times before, there is no such thing as 'post-feminism' until there is a 'post-patriarchy'.

Overthrowing patriarchy is quite a revolution. If ever we are to achieve our revolution, we must prioritize replenishing our ranks and take the actions necessary to bridge generational gaps.

Take care of ourselves and each other Addressing the physical, spiritual and emotional needs of women has been a major shortcoming of our work as feminists. The compounded effects of the growing backlash against the women's movement, media harassment, cultural and religious fundamentalisms, the pressures of running organizations, and the challenges of balancing family and professional obligations, make the task of sustaining individual women's energies very difficult. Many of us are tired, burned out, depressed and angry, and many of us have gone through intense periods of crises characterized by a breakdown in relationships, problems with our children, betrayals of trust, bitterness and deep hurt. Increasingly, we are cynical and are just 'going through the motions'. And while many of us are aware of this, we seldom talk about it. For a movement which has thrived on the slogan 'the personal is political', we have not reflected on how much of what we do to and with one another is both personal and political.

It seems that we have taught ourselves to put everything and everyone first before ourselves. There is of course a good reason for this – we simply do not have time for everything! In order to address this problem, we need to go back to the old feminist strategies of consciousness-raising and developing women's self-esteem, whatever our age. We need to teach ourselves how to feel pain and how to talk about what we are going through, rather than denying it or seeking comfort in all the wrong places. For those of us who are mothers, let us take great joy and pride in motherhood even while we reject the identities of enforced heterosexist institutions. For those of us who have partners, male or female, let us feel free to love them without feeling that we are losing anything. We have to learn how to like each other, to respect each other and to love each other, and, most importantly, how to take great joy in doing that. Let us put the soul back into our movement.

Conclusion

We need more opportunities like this for reflection and dialogue on the new challenges facing the global women's movement. We will have to be cautious, brave and vigilant to ensure that the gains we have made are not lost at the same time as we push towards new targets and goals. We need to preserve our feminist spaces in any way that we can, at the same time as we build new spaces and put forward new visions. To do this, we need commitment, solidarity, critical dialogues, effective leadership, power and finances. We need a diverse, interconnected and interdisciplinary feminism, which is radical, local, global and collective, linking theory with practice. Let us stop diluting our language and agenda; let us stop being apologetic about our choices, our dreams and our visions of justice. Together, let us create a new world with new visions.

Notes

1 The term 'glocalization' is said to have been coined by sociologist Roland Robertson. See R. Robertson (1992) *Globalization: Social Theory and Global Culture* (London: Sage), pp. 173–4.

2 United Nations Economic Commission for Africa (1999) *Report of the Sixth African Regional Conference on Women*, E/ECA/ACW/RC.V1/99/12 (November).

3 African Regional NGO Report on the NGO Consultations (1999) Sixth African Regional Conference on Women, Addis-Ababa, 22–26 November 1999.

4 <http://www.urgentactionfund.org/af-desk2.html>

5 <http://www.uneca.org/eca_resources/Publications/ACW/new/acgd_publications/Political%20empowerment.htm>

6 United Nations Economic Commission for Africa, *The Political Empowerment of Women. Summary of Progress Made by African Governments*, Sixth African Regional Conference on Women, Addis-Ababa, 22–26 November 1999.

7 Ibid. Getting women into decision-making positions is one thing, but

ensuring that they make an impact is another. There are four key issues involved here: (i) access for women to political spaces (e.g. through quotas, voter education, public support and awareness, affirmative action, party support, etcetera); (ii) participation (e.g. representation of women in decision-making structures and their level of political engagement); (iii) transformation of the institutions themselves (e.g. meeting times at parliament, childcare arrangements, women-friendly language, etcetera); and (iv) external transformation (e.g. how gender considerations are integrated into legislation). See *Women in Politics and Decision-Making in SADC: Beyond 30% in 2005*, Report of the proceedings of the Southern African Development Community (SADC) Gender Unit Conference, Gaborone, Botswana, 28 March–1 April 1999.

8 'Health Care Still a Dream for Some', see <http://www.sardc.net/widsaa/sgm/1999/sgm_ch8.html>

9 For more information on these cases, visit <http://www.now.org/issues/global/091202couple.html> or <http://www.amnesty.org.au/women/report-nigeria.html>

10 This new partnership for African development is described as follows: '[it] is a pledge by African leaders, based on a common vision and a firm and shared conviction, that they have a pressing duty to eradicate poverty and to place their countries, both individually and collectively, on a path of sustainable growth and development, and at the same time participate actively in the world economy and body politic. The Programme is anchored on the determination of Africans to extricate themselves and the continent from the malaise of underdevelopment and exclusion in a globalizing world.' From <http://www.dfa.gov.za/events/nepad.htm> For more information: <http://www.nepad.org/>

11 I talk about feminist space and faith in *The Dame Barrow Distinguished Visitor Lecture* (1999) (Toronto: Ontario Institute for Studies in Education/University of Toronto).

12 For more information on Women's Budget Initiatives, see <http://www.case.org.za/gender.html> or <http://magnet.undp.org/events/gender/india/Soutaf.htm>

13 B. Abzug (1996) 'Women Will Change the Nature of Power', in B. Abzug and D. Jain, *Women's Leadership and the Ethics of Development*, UNDP Gender in Development Monograph Series, 4 (August).

14 For more information on this point, see: C. T. Mohanty, A. Russo and L. Torres (eds) (1991) *Third World Women and the Politics of Feminism* (Bloomington: Indiana University Press).

15 An international network of women's funds was started three years ago. There are now up to fifteen autonomous women's funds in various parts of the world, most of which have been supported by pioneer women's funds such as Global Fund for Women, Match International and Mama Cash. There is a vibrant network of women's funds in the United States called the Women's Funding Network, which also shares its resources and lessons with other women's funds around the world.

16 This is a complex relationship. It is usually older women, free from the challenges of looking after young children, who have the time and space to

concentrate on public advocacy. Younger activists, especially those who are in the early stages of relationships ranging from dating to marriage and caring for young children, do not have the same time to devote to rounds of meetings and outreach, even while they are still deeply committed. On the other hand, we have seen many young activists challenge the conservative, accommodating politics of older women, calling for newer, more radical approaches. Through the work AMwA has done at the African Women's Leadership Institute, for example, we have provided platforms for these discussions to take place and develop strategies which take on board the positive contributions and insights of all generations.

4 | Rights of passage: women shaping the twenty-first century

MAHNAZ AFKHAMI

The concept of women's rights is rooted in history rather than culture. Historically, the role and status assigned to women have been remarkably similar across the world. Until relatively recently, nowhere in the world could women choose a field of education, train for a job, get a job, or get paid equally if they were given a job, nor could they marry, have children, space their children, get a divorce, own property, nor travel by their own free choice. Until the last decade of the nineteenth century when the women of New Zealand gained the franchise, no woman in the world had the right to vote or to hold elected political office. Everywhere, patriarchy was the foundation of the social order based on the concept that there is a 'natural' place for women in accord with their assumed physical and mental characteristics, and in line with the dictates of culture, religion and tradition. Across the globe, otherwise diverse and varied societies uniformly believed in the complementarity of the roles assigned to women and men and developed a complex system of economic, political, legal and cultural substructures that reinforced each other and the overarching patriarchal framework. Given the premise of complementarity of roles, the system was and is rational, comprehensive and efficient.

Women in all cultures have struggled throughout history to improve their position in society and within the family. Until recently, the struggle took more or less the same form everywhere. Women tried to get what they wanted by using the means available to them: their sexuality and their position as mothers in the household. To express the human urge for freedom and equality they had to break the accepted rules of conduct and employ means that were often not considered honourable. To behave honourably, they would have to behave according to the norms that imprisoned them in their allotted place.

Measured by historical time, the discourse for women's freedom and equality was developed only recently. Mary Wollstonecraft's *A Vindication of Rights of Women* (1792), perhaps the first treatise of its kind, was considered an oddity. Even John Stuart Mill's *The Subjection of Women* (1869), was ahead of its time and Mill himself was subjected to ridicule by opinion-makers in such influential journals as *Punch*. About the same time as Mill's essay,

Tahereh Qurrat al-` Ain, a woman priest in Iran, made a public appearance unveiled to claim rights on behalf of women. Tahereh lost her life for her courage but she left a legacy that influenced thinking about women's position in society, religion and culture among Iranian women and men for years to come. The 'woman question', as it was called in mid-nineteenth-century England, touched on issues of sexual inequality in education, economic life, social relations and politics. Women began to play a more important role in society, but few practical changes to their position happened legally until the beginning of the last century. The struggle that brought about the changes sprang from ideas and concepts of justice, fairness and human dignity, which were, as were the concepts underlying patriarchy, embedded in cultures, literatures, histories and religions across the world. Women began to take a new look at these building blocks of social structure and began to develop and articulate alternative feminist interpretations in each area.

The discourse of women's rights is intricately tied to the discourse of freedom and equality. At its centre is the course that individual consciousness takes. Individual consciousness, as distinguished from communal consciousness, is a discovery that comes with time as science and technology provide the foundations for doubt about communal law, that is, law that springs directly or indirectly from God or nature. In this sense, history moves from law to right as the individual begins to perceive that she has a right to participate in the making of the law rather than submit to the existing law as unchanging and eternal. In this, all societies that develop and change move in the same direction. To the extent that feminism means anything, it must include the right of women to freedom of choice and equality in law. Otherwise, the term loses meaning since, without that basic belief, we would have to consider all men and women who have ever tried to improve the condition of women within existing patriarchal structures.

The world and women

The world has become a difficult place to fathom. This is partly because we are not sure whether we should take it as it is and try to adapt to it the best we can or to refuse to accept it as a given and try to change it to our liking. In fact, we can do neither: instead, we must opt for both. The values we have developed as feminists cannot be achieved within a patriarchal setting, whether local, national or global. To ignore the systemic forces that shape our interactive lives, however, is to become Quixotic. Let us examine some of the systemic forces that are particularly relevant to the rights of women.

Globalization Globalization as a process has been going on for at least two centuries. Its beginning coincides with the rise of modern imperialism and its corollary, colonialism. It is a condition of economic and technological change. Its centre was and is the West: first Europe, then increasingly in recent years, the United States. Because it is a condition rather than a policy, it must be taken as a systemic characteristic and therefore qualitatively different from situations that can be reversed by political decision or wished away by appeals to ideology or gender.

The distinction between condition and policy is important for the choice of strategy. Most Third World countries that fought colonialism assumed that it was a consequence of policies adopted by Western politicians. Anti-colonial struggle often took the form of xenophobic nationalism. A few countries took the foundation of colonialism to be a fundamental imbalance between the economic and technological capabilities of the colonizer and the colonized. These countries, including the Asia-Pacific rim for example, opted for a different approach than that of the xenophobic nationalists. They chose interaction with the West to acquire and implement the know-how to build the infrastructure of development. They are now invariably in a better condition, not only economically but also politically.

Globalism subjects local and national conditions to forces beyond local and national control. The new configuration of power has both positive and negative consequences for the rights of women. To the extent that nations will have to adjust to the requirements of economic competition at the global level, a tension arises between the requirements of competition and exigencies of justice. This tension is often resolved in favour of competition rather than justice, thus negatively affecting the condition of women. This is particularly true in the global South where we see many examples of this negative impact in both villages and cities. Alternatively, by transcending national boundaries globalization opens the national and local spaces to international influence, making the flow of ideas and political pressure possible. A new venue has opened for women across the world that, used properly, may produce a synergy that can multiply power and energy many times beyond the simple addition of separate capabilities. But it takes understanding, planning and commitment to reach this synergy.

Technology Communication is the foundation of contemporary globalism. In theory, modern information technology (IT) has made it possible for women in the North and the South to interact to produce the synergy needed to make a difference in the world along feminist lines. This, however, is easier said than done. Practically, IT fuels the machinery of power worldwide; not only in the economic and military realms, but also socially and culturally. In this, as in every area of human endeavour, power has been structured by men, gendered in masculine terms. The tools of technology are overwhelmingly owned and operated by the North and women's access to these tools remains minuscule in the South. To change the balance we need to understand the relevance of the established structures of power to our own distinctive values and objectives.

Culture as competition The culture of masculinity is based on competition. Individual women may succeed in this culture, but unless the structure is changed they will reinforce the masculine culture rather than alter it. We have numerous examples of such women, including some of us who appear reasonably successful in the world of men. The Thatchers, the Gandhis, and the Meirs of this world are well known, and we take some pride in their ability to break certain traditional stereotypes. But they do not change the world for the better. We succeed only if we transcend culture as competition, not by doing away with competition, which is an impossible objective, but by subjecting it to a culture that is infused with the feminist ideals of fairness and justice. We must change the meaning of success by turning hierarchical relations into communicative relations, and by changing leadership by command into leadership by sharing and consensus.[1]

Privatization as economic salvation Culture as competition forces all nations to adjust to the most powerful impulses of the global economy. The global need for capital and talent atomizes societies by releasing individuals and groups from the bonds of economic justice and social security that connected them to the community and to the nation-state. Privatization becomes the end-all of economic planning, a process particularly hard on women because in many societies women are the lowest paid and least equipped to provide for themselves. The disconnection between the individual and the community makes everyone insecure and, in the absence of rational alternatives, more responsive to irrational and destructive ideas.

Religious zeal as politics of regression Culture as competition, merit as material possession, and privatization as economic salvation signify the void in the value system associated with globalism. The ideologies of the nineteenth and twentieth centuries, including socialism, Marxism, communalism, humanism, liberalism and utilitarianism, have yielded to an ideological system that has little to offer beyond greater material gain. The new global capitalism is a powerful regime, forcing every other system to convert or perish. In the absence of reasonable alternatives, religion has gained new vogue. Fundamentalisms of all kinds are growing across the world, in both developed and developing countries, turning religion into regressive ideology. Islamic fundamentalism is a particularly violent reaction to poverty, normlessness, dictatorship and despair. God is turned into an avenger in whose name all manners of atrocity are committed. Religious zeal makes democracy problematic because it turns every attempt at understanding and compromise, which are the hallmarks of democracy, into an evidentiary test of religious righteousness. In Muslim societies, women are particularly targeted because there is no better proof of return to a golden past than pushing women back into their 'natural' place. Thus women's position becomes the yardstick, the measure, for the success of the fundamentalist agenda.

Terrorism as protest/war as counter-policy The concept of war as 'politics by other means' was the beginning of the development of the concept of total war, a consequence of Napoleon's taking the ideas of liberty, equality and fraternity to Europe by the sword. The concept was tested in the American Civil War, developed during the First and Second World Wars, and perfected during the US–Soviet bipolarity in the threat of thermonuclear warfare. The fall of the Soviet Union has left the United States as the only superpower, separated from other countries by a seemingly unbridgeable economic and military gap. In the global world, the USA, representing the West, is everywhere, and everywhere a growing number of people live under insufferable conditions. But it is not poverty, disease, illiteracy or despotism that leads them to support politics by other means; rather, it is hopelessness about the future that drives them to desperation.

Terrorism as war and politics has had a long history, mostly as a personal act of political vengeance. As structured politics, it is a new phenomenon. We have the beginnings of it in the wars of liberation, whether of the Zionist type in the genesis of the state of Israel, the anti-colonial wars of the Third World countries, the political abductions and assassinations by leftist extremists from a variety of countries in the 1960s and 1970s, or the Palestinian intifada during the last twenty years. All these cases are aspects of war as politics waged against manifestly superior military power. They are horrifying because they target innocent people, particularly helpless women and children. But they are no more terrible than wars carried on by established military powers that target, with enormous destructive force, helpless civilians in cities and villages.

Terror as policy has engendered war as counter-policy. We are now faced with a new phase in the development of terror as a chain of action and reaction. The United States is waging war on terrorism but neither the definition nor the perimeter of this war is clearly stated. It is a war without end against an enemy unseen. Innocent men and women have been killed in the United States; innocent men and women will be killed in revenge. If the aim of terror is to level the field of warfare by instilling fear in a far more powerful country, causing it to give up the most cherished principles of individual liberty and right, then terror has already triumphed. Fear leads many people, including many women, to accept violence that can only lead to more violence as a rational policy prescription.

Strategic choices for women's movements

In the last quarter of the twentieth century we witnessed a blossoming of women's movements. Across the world women are now active in unprecedented numbers, conscious of the need to be involved in the decisions that affect their future. More importantly, they have succeeded in including the concept that all issues are women's issues in setting the context for sociopolitical and economic debates. It is now accepted that women have a stake in everything that affects individual and communal life. This is a great leap forward, a revolution in thinking and a new perception of women's roles in shaping the world. The emerging consciousness, though activist and intellectually expansive, is neither homogeneous nor inwardly tranquil. Nothing is more natural for women than to differ on points of analysis, issues of priority, or choices of strategy. The world imposes itself on us no less than we seek to impose ourselves on the world.

Though men still run it, intellectually the world is no longer seen only through masculine eyes. Men, as well as women, are increasingly conscious of the relevance to women of the decisions made in the name of society. Even governments and movements that are philosophically against equality find it necessary to deal with this development by defending their position and offering an alternative theory on the role of women that they hope will counteract the growing feminist consciousness across the globe. It may be that in many parts of the world men's awareness of the relevance of gender has led to reactionary politics leading to a contraction of rights and an expansion of violence. Important and regrettable though this is, it points to an irreversible historical moment that is a harbinger of what is to come: women playing their part in defining the world in ways that will transform exclusionary behaviour into communities of equals working together harmoniously in the quest for a shared vision.

Interactivity Modern information technology has allowed women to communicate across the world. So far, the communication has been North to

South, mainly because Northern women have greater access to the means of communication than the women of the South. Moreover, feminist debate has a longer history in the North and is often better organized. Northern non-governmental organizations (NGOs) were the first to make a dent in the essentially male-dominated governmental policy-making at national and international levels. Partly as a result of the United Nations world conferences of the last quarter of the twentieth century and the networking and solidarity that developed through them, women's NGOs have expanded in the South, demanding a place in the political process. They need international support because they operate in social systems that are, for the most part, hostile to their demands. The support and solidarity from international NGOs and the donor community in the North are vital to their progress. There are, however, some caveats that need to be addressed.

Northern women's advantage reflects Northern advantage in general: that is, with the same processes that have led to globalism as a condition rather than a policy. They belong to the culture of the powerful, the rich and the politically and culturally dominant. Alert to the pitfalls of such hegemonic conditioning, some Northern women, or, alternatively, some Southern women residing in the North, have tried to level the field by taking intellectual stances that at first glance appear reasonable, but upon deeper reflection are not. One such intellectual stance is cultural relativism, possibly a defining concept for making strategic choices about the future of women's movements in an increasingly globalized setting.

Culture as concept determines how we look at feminism as theory and how we approach the politics of achieving the essentials of the theory in different cultural and political milieux. The problem with cultural relativism may be easily discerned by its political effects: it brings together women activists who wish freedom, equality and choice for women as allies with regressive governments and movements that want exactly the opposite, namely, to keep women in bondage. The idea of cultural relativism nurtured in Western universities begins with the principle, though not necessarily the fact, that women are free to choose, and because they are, no one has the right to impose her cultural preferences (parochialisms) on them. Ironically, in Iran, Sudan, Saudi Arabia and many other countries where the rights of women are severely curtailed, governments and regressive movements base their claims on the same principle, accusing those who object to their treatment of women as cultural imperialists. They justify their usurping of individual rights by pointing to the fact that many women support them, seemingly of their own volition. The anomaly between the two positions is clear: one begins with the foundation of individual right, the other with the primacy of community and traditional culture. Clearly, a decision about the core of feminism, namely individual space and choice, is indispensable to any theory of women's rights. Conversely, practical policies for achieving space and choice will depend on the characteristics of each society.

Western thinking about cultural relativism is closely related to the resurgence of religious fundamentalism more in the South but also in the North. Women's movements across the world are strongly affected by religious doctrines. In some cases, such as in the discourse of Islam, epistemology has been mistaken for sociology. The history of Islam as religion has been substituted for the history of the people who happen to be Muslims. The result has been to favour the clergy as arbiters of social norms and moral values with devastating consequences for democracy, development and especially women's human rights. In the Muslim world, wherever traditional interpretation of religion has prevented modernity and spirituality from becoming reconciled, the contradiction has paralysed life. Perhaps the best example of the conflict between doctrine and reality is Iran, where an Islamic theocracy is imposed on a modern people, including almost all Muslims, resulting in constant contradiction and paralysis. We Muslim women especially must make sure that we do not confuse right with law, or the right to choose with choices that have been imposed on the basis of preordained law.

Gendered development 'A room of one's own' as a precondition of space and choice or empowerment is now well established in women's movements. This idea has transmigrated to the theories of development and aid, where women's participation in development decisions is seen as a requirement of both sustainable development and equitable distribution. The concept must be refined in women's rights theories and made a focus of practical politics for promoting women's rights in the South as well as in the North.

Gendered development points to human development, a more comprehensive concept than economic development. It springs from gendered thinking, bringing to development a complexity of values that supersedes the materialism of global capitalism, while it shuns both the morass of religiosity as well as the void of the socialist Utopias that in the past opened the way to totalitarian politics. Gendered development takes off from the feminist idea of a participatory world, a system of sharing that has its roots in interaction among equals, not just before the law but each in the eyes of the other. Such a world may not be easily attainable but it is perhaps the only possible way in which humanity may reach peace in prosperity, liberty, equality and justice. The other way is that of hierarchy, senseless growth, militarism, normlessness and terror.

Strategic communication for the expansion of women's movements How do we make our interactions purposeful without either dictating our point of view, losing sight of our point of view, or in the bargain, forfeiting our principles? Strategic communication is efficient communication: that is, it conveys the message and gets the job done without producing unwanted consequences. The goal of strategic communication for women is to achieve shared vision. The only way to do so is to develop respect for the other, not as a ruse to achieve one's goal but as genuine respect. This genuine respect springs from within; it is a property of the 'self' rather than that of the 'other'.

Leadership as dialogical communication We need leaders in order to get important things done. Important things, however, are not achieved by fiat, at least not in the world we seek. In leadership, as in dialogical communication, everyone is assumed to have something of worth to contribute, not only towards doing what each of us considers essential, but also, more importantly, to help each of us determine what it is that we truly want. In this context no one is a leader all the time; everyone is a leader at some time.

Individual freedom versus coercive community We are all social by nature, creatures of community. The point, therefore, is not to disparage community; it is rather to distinguish between community as a set of coercive rules, such as habit, custom or law, and community as an interactive system in which each of us is a free contributing agent. The cohesiveness of community, made up of family, clan, village or city, should not be maintained at the expense of individuality. I, as a woman, understand that I can be a happy human being only as a member of a community. We, the community and I, must therefore come to an understanding. Historically, this understanding has been achieved by force at my expense, even when I accepted the communal norms because I had internalized them, believing that they were eternal rules based on the will of God and exigencies of nature. It was then not possible for me to object because I did not know that I could. Now I do. This does not mean that I no longer accept the norms. I only know that I must have a choice to accept or not, that every other woman ought to have the choice, and that each of us is obligated to help the other discover that she has, or ought to have, the choice.

Feminist worldview versus empowered women patriarchs Feminism distinguishes between women-cum-men, such as the Thatchers, Gandhis and Meirs who achieve high political or managerial positions, and women leaders who promote feminist ideals. There is, however, a dialectic that must be considered. The more women there are in decision-making positions, the higher the probability that women's points of view will have a hearing. When the number of women in decision-making positions reaches a critical mass, we have, or we come close to having, a qualitative change. We have reached such a critical mass in certain Scandinavian countries with palpable political effects. It seems that although, individually, women may rise in the world of men by becoming like men, collectively they exhibit many of the qualities we have associated with the feminist point of view. It is important, therefore, for women's organizations across the world to help an increasing number of women to gain positions of leadership under existing circumstances while also advocating the values and methods that are an integral part of strategies of the future.

Strategies for the future

We must insist that the rights of women are rooted in history rather than culture At the moment this is the most crucial strategic option women can adopt if they are to maintain a theoretically sustainable position while they deal with the plight of women across cultures. This is also at the heart of the controversy about relativism and universalism in the discussions of women's human rights. Feminist theory, regardless of preferences its various branches may have, must make a sharp distinction between universal rights of women to individual freedom, space and equal access to the protection of the laws universally acclaimed, and the practical ways and means of reaching these rights in different cultures and political systems.

- We must insist that no one, man or woman, may claim a right to a monopoly of interpretation of God to human beings or a right to force others to accept a particular ruling about any religion. The upshot of this position is that women ought not to be forced to choose between freedom and God. The same applies to claims on behalf of tradition.
- We must insist that international governmental and non-governmental organizations, national-states, civil society organizations, as well as national and multinational corporations, decide their policies about international, national and local issues in cognizance of the universal rights of women.
- We must educate the decision-makers at all levels about the plight of women and the reasons why they should try to shape their decisions to help women achieve their internationally recognized rights.
- We must hold governments and organizations responsible for the effect on women of the political, social, economic and cultural choices they

make nationally or internationally. Such choices must have a political cost and the nature of the cost ought to be defined based on the characteristics of the deciding organization or state.

Women's vision of the future must become holistic and comprehensive The patriarchal system in operation across the world is cohesive, internally rational and structurally comprehensive. It is, however, anti-historical because it is based on a uniform definition of the role of women as naturally subordinate and complementary to the role of men. We need to conceive the future in which women play a decidedly different role, as equal to men and complete in themselves, in terms that are also cohesive, rational and comprehensive. This means we must take a new look at the structure of human relations broadly defined. We need to achieve a balance between the sexes not only in the public arena but also at the level of family. Women must remain aware of the multidimensionality of the required change, and they must also show the areas in which men and women should work together to construct the social, economic and cultural structures needed for the successful operation of the desired society.

- We must move beyond the theory of women's human rights as a theory of equality before the law, of women's individual space, or 'a room of one's own', to a theory of the architecture of the future society where the universality of rights and relativity of means merge to operationalize an optimally successful coexistence of community and individuality. This architectural theory will point to a dynamic design where broadly conceived human relations evolve with the requirements of the times as they also satisfy the needs both of individuality and community. We already have the beginnings of this kind of thinking in the idea that all issues are women's issues.
- We must take the statement 'all issues are women's issues' as a preliminary proposition opening the door to reformulate the issues emerging from the contradictions in the patriarchal society to create solutions that lead us to non-patriarchal relations. Only then will women's empowerment make a real difference.
- Men must be regarded as actual or potential partners. Women must educate men to a future that is significantly different from the past and present. Women's movements must 'infiltrate' the institutions that influence the mind-sets, inclusive of men and women. Education at all levels must clearly be a primary target. Women's studies at the universities must be reconceived to become an integrated component of the courses that affect gender relations as well as individual–commu-

nity relations. Courses in culture and religion are obvious choices. Just as important are such fields as social, economic and political studies, public and business administration, architecture, city planning, development studies, and everything having to do with war and peace, including military–industrial relations.

We must accommodate the strategic demands of globalism Globalization has brought about new opportunities as well as seemingly insoluble problems. It is changing the architecture of human relations across the world. We must adjust our understanding of the ways and means of achieving our ends to the evolving global conditions.

- We must acquire the intellectual wherewithal to foresee future trends and their effect on women's lives and values. It may be that we must now begin to define our interest in wider perspectives. We must bring into our organizations talents beyond those traditionally concerned with women's issues. We now need a variety of informed input to our planning and operation, from economics to statistics, from concepts of human security including the problem of terror and counter-terror to a more precise definition of cultures of war and cultures of peace. Women's organizations across the world, but particularly in the West, should be infused increasingly with the so-called 'hard' sciences.
- Because globalism is a condition and not a policy, it follows that we must address the factors that have created it and that will affect its future make-up, such as the multinationals and the military–industrial complexes. Women have tended to shun organizations such as the World Bank, IMF and OECD because they are government-oriented and masculine in character. But these traits are precisely the reason we must infiltrate and reorient them. Otherwise, women's movements will tend to remain at the periphery of the developments that shape the world.
- Women must be increasingly integrated in global information technology at both scientific and operational levels. To bring information technology to women in the less developed world ought to be an overarching strategy of women's organizations everywhere, particularly in the West. Women must use whatever clout they can muster to force the organizations of the type mentioned above to make the extension of information technology to women an integral part of their relationship with governments and the private sector everywhere.

Women must work to empower women across the world We must learn how to appropriate and use political power. Women everywhere must help women to become leaders. To achieve equitable participation of women leaders requires us to reconsider the essence and form of leadership. We need to reconceptualize leadership so that the chances for women to become leaders are optimized, the probability that women leaders become surrogate men is minimized, and a critical mass of women leaders in positions of political authority is achieved.

- We must work to encourage women to communicate with women everywhere – in their community, city, country and across the world. An important part of the encouragement process is to help women in the developing parts of the world gain access to the means of communication, including the telephone, the internet and mass media. The technology exists; it must be liberated for constructive, humane use.
- We must use modern information technology to encourage women everywhere to become participants in the political process broadly defined: that is, participating in the making of the decisions that affect their lives and the lives of others in the family, community, state or, where possible, the world.
- We must bring to women everywhere an idea of leadership that is dialogical, non-hierarchical, communicative and communal. We have developed the appropriate methodologies and begun to experiment with such leadership formats. We must develop them further to make them operational in complex political environments.

Conclusion: subjecting the inevitable to feminist choice

I began with defining globalization as a condition rather than a policy. Because it is a systemic tendency, it appears impervious to political decision-making. This may only be so because the system has been constructed on masculine foundations of competition and aggression. We can change the system by infusing it with feminist ideals. We must change the rules of the game, using modern techniques to subvert the system that has produced the techniques. As we negotiate our passage into the new century, we know that if we insist upon our rights, our movements will be the force that shapes the future.

Note

1 An example of participatory, horizontal leadership based on collaborative partnerships for implementation is described in M. Afkhami, A. Eisenberg and H. Vaziri (2001) *Leading to Choices: A Leadership Training Handbook for Women* (Bethesda, MD: Women's Learning Partnership).

5 | Challenging power: alternatives to the current global order

AN INTERVIEW WITH JOSEFA (GIGI) FRANCISCO

When we think of cutting-edge work on women's rights and gender equality, Development Alternatives with Women for a New Era (DAWN) inevitably comes to mind. Since 1984, DAWN has been putting the gendered impacts of macroeconomic policies on the gender and development agenda. DAWN has very close links with another innovative and essential network – the International Gender and Trade Network (IGTN), a group of gender advocates based in different regions of the world, working to advance gender-equitable and sustainable trade. IGTN is at the forefront of gender advocacy on trade issues and, like DAWN, draws on regional experiences to inform global advocacy.

Josefa (Gigi) Francisco is a member of both these networks. She is an articulate, strategic activist with an intimate understanding of women's rights and gender equality issues within Asia, and of how women's rights are advanced or hindered by the interplay of structures of power and institutional arrangements, as well as by global trends. In addition to being the South-East Asian Regional Coordinator of DAWN, and the Coordinator of the IGTN Asia regional node, she is also the executive director of the Women and Gender Institute of Miriam College Foundation in Quezon City, Philippines, and a long time faculty member in the International Studies department. Gigi's work is grounded in political sensitivity to and respect for local realities and she is connected to the key regional players and movements, bringing to both her research and her advocacy the depth of understanding that is needed to build up truly effective inter-connectivities, cross-cutting analyses and broad-based activism. Indeed, Gigi's is an invaluable voice in regional and international women's movements that come together in strategic dialogue and collaboration with partners and other social activists from around the world to devise grounded and strategic approaches to women's rights and gender equality in the new global reality. What is perhaps most striking about Gigi is her ability to identify connections between the current political climate and the longer-term struggle for women's rights, and her ability to project into the future on how these politic realities will impact on the abilities of all peoples to live freely and without fear of oppression.

In the following interview, conducted in August 2003, Josefa (Gigi) Francisco shares some of her impressions about power and the political realities that define the challenges to women's rights and the opportunities available to advance justice and equality throughout the world.

AWID/Mama Cash: *What do you think are the most critical issues that will challenge our efforts for women's rights in the next five to ten years globally?*

Josefa (Gigi) Francisco: US unilateralism at the global level. I think the full extent of US unilateralism and its very serious implications remain to be seen. Here I'm speaking of US unilateralism on two fronts: the economic front, particularly around trade liberalization pushed through different arenas such as the World Trade Organization (WTO), the Free Trade Area of the Americas (FTAA) agreement, and the Asia–Pacific Economic Cooperation (APEC); and the security front, specifically in the so-called US-led war against terror. We are also witnessing the convergence of these two fronts, where they are colluding with each other and reinforcing one another in more open and apparent ways. For example, the USA recently issued a policy statement claiming that they would only engage economically with countries who are 'friends' and who are supportive of the war against terror, especially in terms of aid and economic concessions. This is now a declared policy of the United States. We can trace the roots of the convergence of the two fronts of unilateralism to 'the hawks' and 'the conservatives', that is, the right-wing forces that are now in the White House. Given these forces, the coming election in the United States, in November 2004, will have important implications for the democratic and economic justice struggles in the USA and worldwide. It presents a vital opportunity to try to move the ultra-conservatives out of the White House, raising the chance that there would be an opening up of a space in the USA for more respect for citizens' rights, democracy and multilateralism.

As I mentioned earlier, we have not yet seen the full impact of this unilateralism. The most recent manifestation of global resistance to it took place in Iraq. We lost the UN Special Representative of the Secretary-General in Iraq, Sergio Vieira de Mello,[1] and others in the bombing of the UN headquarters there. This was a result of US security-based unilateralism and their insistence on staying in Iraq. What we are witnessing now is a blurring of lines between those who would like to dominate in Iraq, like the USA, and those who would like to help build a shattered society that I believe de Mello and others were trying to do, as opposed to US aggression cloaked in democratic garb. I could understand retaliation against UN security forces, the US military, or British occupation forces, but I cannot understand targeting people and organizations that are trying to make a positive difference in Iraq. I suppose that the line has been blurred around the question of who is responsible for global misery and insecurity, and in this case Iraq: it is now the USA plus the UN. The line between those who dominate and those who are trying to re-establish multilateralism and democracy amid difficult times is now very unclear.

I believe that one of the major factors in whether US unilateralism will consolidate or weaken in the next five years is the American people themselves and how they will elect their next president, that is, whether democratic forces will prevail and remove Bush or the American people will continue to be deceived by the pseudo-nationalist rhetoric of the right.

AWID/Mama Cash: *In terms of strategies for advancing and ensuring women's rights now and in the future, would you say that getting Bush out is a key strategy?*

JF: Yes, definitely. Ousting Bush from the White House is not going to solve all of our problems but it will definitely give us some breathing space.

However, it isn't as if I am naïve about and totally supportive of the existing possible alternatives to Bush. His opposition doesn't seem to be very dynamic, but hopefully it's better than him in terms of being less interested in taking the unilateral route.

AWID/Mama Cash: *Is the war on terror affecting countries outside Afghanistan or Iraq?*

JF: Yes, definitely. Part of the impact on the South is the emergence and/or strengthening of internal security acts, just like the US Homeland Security Act. These include the security laws or regulations that now allow unconstitutional searches and detention of people suspected of being involved in or supporting terrorist activities. These laws violate human and political rights, and similar regulations are being created in countries of the South. What we are now seeing is an erosion of democratic political space and an undermining of people's civil liberties. The imposition of these new laws is a result of powerful political elites in both the South and North who are using US unilateralism in a very opportunistic way to advance their interests, and to suppress popular opposition.

It is nothing new to suggest that US unilateralism is only part of the problem, and linked to this is the opportunism of the political elites of the different regions of the world, including the South. There is not only a formal, but also a substantive mimicry of the war against terror that has been unleashed by the rhetoric of the Bush administration. This mimicry is resulting in the erosion of civil rights by new anti-terrorism laws that are serving the interests of political elites. Here again we see a convergence between US security-based and economic unilateralism. It is the same political elites that are implementing the new anti-terrorism acts that are also driving the economies of their nations towards the trade liberalization agenda. A contradiction within states is being initiated through this process, where a state asserts its sovereignty on the war front but on the economic front is giving up that sovereignty in the name of trade liberalization. Why is that so? Because the elites are simply being opportunistic on both fronts. This contradiction will be maintained as long as it is benefiting those in power – they are able to make political gains by restricting those that oppose them through new laws, even while they reap economic gains from trade liberalization.

This crisis of state and governance is very fundamental and links to the relationship between US unilateralism and the opportunism of the elites wherever they are found. This crisis of governance exists at all levels and puts civil society organizations or social movements very much on the offensive, on the one hand, but, on the other hand, they are left with difficulty about alternatives. So while we are now critical of how global governance is manifesting and transforming itself, and how state governance is being captured by the elite and is not responsive to people's needs, we actually used to be very comfortable with elite-led state governance because, on some level, the system was working. We were very much kidding ourselves in believing that – and it had created a comfort zone – we did not need to fundamentally challenge state or global governance. However, now the system is breaking down, and that presents an opportunity for us to be on the offensive.

When I say 'breaking down', I am referring to an increasing right-wing agenda that has intensified the oppression and alienation of people. This creates an opportunity for advancing a critique of governance. But, the fact that there is fragmentation and weakening of the state as an institution also leaves civil society organizations with no 'ready' alternative to the emerging US unilateralism that is transmogrifying global governance. Based on the existing paradigm, a rejection of US unilateralism implies a strengthening of states, but this is being eroded by that same unilateralism on both economic and security fronts. This has meant that civil society does not have an alternative proposition to the global governance crisis that is located/positioned in sovereign state-led institutions and understanding. If this is the case, is the alternative to totally re-create the world?

That is the crisis of governance, and the dilemma of civil society organizations. Out of this crisis and dilemma rises another critical issue: how religion will fit into this. Will it come to fill the void created by this crisis?

In the next five years, what may happen is that as non-secular institutions and non-secular actors, including civil society, fail to provide any alternatives, political opportunists will promote religion as the only established institution that can provide direction. It will be the only haven, location or space where people can still gain some comfort and reassurance. And this is where our biggest problem now lies as advocates of women's rights. I mean, there are liberating aspects in institutional religion, but there are also its very conservative or oppressive aspects. Unfortunately, in a period of disenchantment and confusion, political opportunists may easily converge with conservative religious leaders. In a context of ever-present chaos and frustration, religion becomes not only a refuge, but is manipulated by political interests as the image and embodiment of an alternative.

If religion has the potential to be manipulated, we need to have a considered position as a social movement *vis-à-vis* this phenomenon. What is the ideological position or location from which we could be a countervailing force to conservative religious groups? Most progressive women and men believe that human rights can be advanced as an alternative means of reforming institutions and neutralizing the emergence of the Right, as a way of democratizing power and opportunities, as well as wealth in countries. But, the human rights framework is itself a contested terrain that came out largely from the bosom of the United Nations, a non-secular institution whose legitimacy is currently in question. In this sense, it will be difficult to carve out human rights as an alternative that challenges people's reliance on politically motivated religious zealots. An interlinked concern might be: if people are turning away from institutions such as the UN, then how do we reshape human rights in such a way that it becomes a more autonomous concept that people do not reject along with the UN?

AWID/Mama Cash: *In your perspective, how can human rights be an alternative in the current global context?*

JF: I believe that human rights are a domain from which we can create alternatives. The problem is that human rights are a contested concept. Rights themselves are contradictory. For example, if you talk about cultural rights and then you bring in women's rights, there is an immediate cognitive clash of frameworks. To speak of women's rights is to aim for cultivating universal, individual-based rights, which are contradictory to the notion of cultural or group-based rights and to the women's movement's understanding of difference among women. I believe this is one thing that we should try to be more open about in our feminist dialogues.

Human rights are a set of universal principles, and we need to recognize their historical context and what had been cultivated early on, but equally important how these concepts are dynamically changing as new ideas are debated. Yet until now, the search for universal ideals has been mainly carried out within the rubric of the United Nations. Academia has lost its edge and has been de-legitimized because of its complicity with commercial and political interests. Formal religious institutions are also suspect, particularly with the rise of exclusivism and intolerance within their ranks. Without the United Nations, where are we going to pursue discussions about human rights?

The alternative space that some women's/feminist groups are looking at is the World Social Forum. The World Social Forum itself, as a process, is an alternative space but it needs to be nurtured in a way that it will bring about more radical and diverse options. It needs to advance strategies that are not limited by existing institutions or rely on them in a strait-jacketed way as a reference point for creating alternatives. It needs to break away entirely from existing structures, mechanisms and institutions to challenge the crisis of governance and avert a capture by conservative political and religious forces that present themselves as alternatives to corporate-led globalization and US unilateralism.

AWID/Mama Cash: *How would you begin to create alternatives that aren't based within existing institutions? Do you have a vision for the future?*

JF: No, I am not a seer of the future! What I do believe in is the process of change. I have enough faith in people that I believe that once the process of change is begun and enough well-meaning people around the world are willing to take a stand (and I do not think we have a shortage of that in the women's movement!), then good things will emerge. But we will have to go through a very painful process, a process that includes our own collective and individual self-critiques, in more consistent and penetrating ways. In both the North and the South we have to address identities, locations, positions, standpoints, viewpoints, assertions, and see again how a new ethics will emerge, away from the gilded documents of the United Nations or the words of official declarations. We were able to achieve a universal understanding of women's human rights in terms of citizenship rights and how violations of these should be addressed by the state. States received orders at Beijing, Cairo and other UN conferences, but all of these venues were making demands only on the state. We failed to make demands on ourselves.

AWID/Mama Cash: *If current forms of feminist activism are primarily directed at the state, how do you see that being different in the future?*

JF: Maybe it is time that we demand something of ourselves, of our own movement. Part of the alternatives-creating process is stepping away from state-centred demands that are made in the context of the institutional space of the UN. The state and UN ground is shaky now, so we have to demand things of ourselves and of the movement. We have to do that through political construction. What I am talking about is a whole political reconstruction of the women's movement and of social movements in general.

AWID/Mama Cash: *How would the women's movement reconstruct itself?*

JF: Again, it is a process. It is a combined intellectual and political exercise that will be built upon. For instance, what we are doing now in this dialogue where you are trying to bring in different perspectives is political constructivism. But we have to be clear about what exactly we are trying to reconstruct and what in fact is the direction of that construction. In this reconstruction, then, we cannot keep relying on global institutions like the Commission on the Status of Women (CSW), UNIFEM and the UN to give us the space for women's conferences. I would rather support a different type of reconstruction: of ourselves, of the women's movements, and of our linkages with other social movements.

AWID/Mama Cash: *Where do you see this reconstruction taking place?*

JF: It has to take place in different spaces and through diverse efforts, building on but not bound to existing solidarities and networking. I know I am being very vague, but I don't have the answer for the reconstruction of the world. Or of the women's movements. I just have faith in feminist processes and our capacities to re-create.

AWID/Mama Cash: *How is your region being affected by today's climate of unrest?*

JF: There is some gossip going around that, after Bali,[2] Manila will be bombed. I also just came back from Indonesia and there are bomb threats all over the place. It is a different kind of existence. People are just trying to be happy but there is a lot of anxiety and insecurity. Even if people claim to be accustomed to this sort of threat, the threats are very persistent right now and it does affect the society's mental health and functioning.

It is ironic that one of the directions of the women's movements, before the war on terrorism was unleashed, was to come up with a set of innovative indicators on women's mental health, happiness and sense of security, as a part of national indicators of prosperity or development. Now, how could one talk of mental health in the context of the global war against terror, and in the context of the erosion of jobs and of livelihoods under rapid trade liberalization? There are many things that the women's movements tried to imagine, in a context that was what I would call more of a 'comfort zone'. That comfort zone is no longer here, and its absence is affecting every one of us. When you ride on a plane, you don't know what is going to happen to that plane. When you go out to the mall, you don't know if there is going to be a blackout as in Toronto and New York.[3] There is more crime on the streets. So we try. We try to live on a day-to-day basis.

AWID/Mama Cash: *What are the strategies that you see as most effective for challenging the current climate?*

JF: The women's movements need to link up with other social movements. We cannot change the world by ourselves, especially during this time when everybody's sense of comfort, including the progressive movements', has crumbled away. It is not only us. It is not only on the women's human rights front, or the women's equality front, so we have to look for friends and allies. We also have to rebuild our constituencies. We are losing the younger people and there are so many young people out there. In the Philippines, for example, 60 per cent of the population is fifteen years and below. It is a very young population. There are also many women's movements that have very weak relations with women in the poor and marginalized communities. We should re-establish these connections and make them stronger.

AWID/Mama Cash: *How do you see bringing younger women into the women's movement, or younger people if you are wanting to include men?*

JF: Yes, it will have to include men. We will have to bring both young women and men into the interconnected movements in a planned way. We have to plan it more systematically. We have to bet on it. We have to retire people like me and bet on the young. Those of us already in the movements could just teach; that is what many of us do anyway. We can write, we can teach, and we can listen more. We can be the outer circle and young people can be the inner circle. We can be a human shield.

AWID/Mama Cash: *I like the image of a human shield of activists.*

JF: You know how this early feminist picture goes, you know how collectives are: you have the inner circle of senior feminists and then the outer circle of younger feminists. Another similar picture is with mothers inside and daughters outside. It's always the young people who are outside. Instead, this time it should be the older women who are on the outside in the bigger circle, and at the centre would be the younger women.

AWID/Mama Cash: *I like that. It's a great representation. You spoke of the women's movement connecting with broader social movements. Do you think that women's movements are well connected to each other?*

JF: Coming from the Philippines and the Asian context, you will find that women's organizing is primarily on an issue-basis. This means that some women work on reproductive and sexual rights alone, other women work solely on violence against women, and still others only work on women's economic rights, etcetera. I think we now have to move out of this issue- and sector-focused way of working and organizing. We need to come together multisectorally around major advocacy efforts.

Globally, that is already happening with the help of the internet and email. I think email is great; it helps broaden our perspectives and helps us to interlink. We need to interlink. That is what DAWN has been saying over and over again, we need to interlink and move out of myopic single-issue focus. We can still have our respective 'turf', in the sense that we can still have a major focus area, but that major focus need not be the centre of the universe. It need not always be at the forefront of our advocacy. It has to come together with other issues.

AWID/Mama Cash: *Do you have an example of an area where working multi-sectorally could be beneficial?*

JF: The issue of peace. The issue of women and peace is something we can work together on, that is, peace and sustainability, or peace and economic justice. This 'sustainable development' concept has been abused, but peace and sustainable futures maybe, or a just, equitable and peaceful future. These things where women could just come together and, from our different advocacy efforts and viewpoints, try to talk, to exchange, and to imagine a peaceful world. Imagine what we can do together for that world, for that imagined future.

We need that kind of a reimagining again. Intellectual work is dominating that creative, imaginative space but in an uncreative and unimaginative way. I don't want to read the next new women's studies book. The intellectual field of gender and women's studies has been captured by the demand of mainstream education. Similarly, in development literature, there is a lack of creativity and challenge, and some of the 'best' work falls short of critiquing the neoliberal growth framework. Much of it falls short of that. The moral of this story, then, is not to leave the project of strategizing and imagining for the future to those with money to publish. Instead, let's talk together.

There are many attempts by larger civil society organizations, and partly in academia, to try to imagine a future beyond what we have now because people everywhere recognize that there is something terribly wrong with the way things are. However, some of these attempts seem to lack a real understanding of grassroots work and genuine alternatives-searching, and instead limit themselves to corporative and unimaginative mainstream understandings. I think women and women's networks should come together away from these larger institutions and try to envision the future. I don't know how we should do it. Bringing people together requires money, meaning that women from larger institutions tend to be more involved in international conferences. Not that I have anything against them, but the debate doesn't really come out as a debate in these venues. The World Social Forum seems to offer a better format for people to come and say 'this is my perspective'. The women's movements should create spaces within the WSF for more feminist debates.

AWID/Mama Cash: *You had talked about the finances to be able to come together in different forums. Does the World Social Forum overcome this obstacle?*

JF: The World Social Forum may not be the place to overcome financial barriers either but there is now a multiplicity of social fora – at the regional, national and continental levels – which are more accessible to people. As well, the debate does not have to be a massively orchestrated nor heavily funded thing. Whoever is there, you go with that, and fashion an open process. This does not resolve anything, but it does begin the process of critical and creative imagining on the part of women and men, minus the baggage of institutional and organizational locations. For some women, it has become difficult to shed their institutional and organizational identities. Their membership in an organization has become much more important than their personal identity as a citizen of a country, or as a member of a nation, or a member of an organization. Even in my case, there are times when it is more important for me to be DAWN than for me to be simply Gigi, the individual.

AWID/Mama Cash: *Do you see a way of working within organizational identities, given that that is a reality for so many women?*

JF: Yes, I see debate and discussion emerging from a space that is not heavily funded. It is possible that among a group of networks that have an international reach, maybe five, six, seven networks, we could all commit to doing such a thing. We could develop the questions to ask and commit to generating that process without stamping it with a network, organization or other identity. I would love to be part of a political project that is committed to something like this – putting together groups of four or five women all over the place, and then asking them all the questions we created. We would create a space to envision a future. That would be nice, back to basics. That is how we started, through consciousness-raising and education work.

AWID/Mama Cash: *In closing, would you share your personal dreams or goals for the future?*

JF: My biggest dream is to be able to retire, put up my computer shop, and from where I am release a virus that will change all rightist politicians into leftist activists! No, really, I don't have any big dreams. Except, I suppose I remain positive about life in the sense that I am still hoping that there are enough womenfolk who can facilitate a process of regeneration. And that is what we need, to regenerate ourselves personally as individuals but also as members of women's movements for social transformation.

Notes

1 On 19 August 2003, the UN headquarters in Iraq were hit by a truck bomb killing seventeen people, including Sergio Vieira de Mello. De Mello was acting as UN Special Representative of the Secretary-General in Iraq. This position was taken as a four-month leave from his post as United Nations High Commissioner for Human Rights.

2 On 12 October 2002, two Bali nightclubs catering largely to foreign tourists were hit by a suicide bomber and a car bomb attack, killing 202 people.

3 On 14 August 2003, a power blackout shut down the electricity grid in large parts of north-eastern United States and central Canada, affecting 50 million people.

6 | An action framework for South Asia

DEEPA DHANRAJ, GEETANJALI MISRA AND SRILATHA BATLIWALA

Old problems with new faces

The worldwide impact of the women's movement, and its quest for gender equality and justice, was undoubtedly one of the hallmarks of the twentieth century. Beginning with the struggles for women's suffrage in its early decades, and the participation and leadership of women in freedom movements to end colonial rule, women's struggles for social, economic and political equality generated sufficient impact that by the end of the century the concept of gender equality had been accepted by the majority of the world's nations in principle, if not in practice. By the Fourth World Conference on Women held in Beijing in 1995, activists, advocates and scholars who had brought to light the persistent and systemic nature of women's subordination and subjugation had much to celebrate. Since then, however, a good deal of ground seems to have been lost; in many contexts, it is hard to even state with conviction that a women's movement exists at the global level, though a number of national and local movements, with significant capacity to mobilize and intervene, still persist.

From our perspective, several forces seem to have eroded the gains made by women's movements over the past three decades. In the South Asian context, the most significant of them are: the increase in poverty as a result of accelerated global economic integration ('globalization'), the expansion of war and militarism, and the rise of various fundamentalist movements which, in combination with the other factors, are re-creating and reasserting traditional feudal and patriarchal social relations. This is very evident in the South Asian context in the manner in which fundamentalists are reasserting notions of masculinity and femininity, as well as chastity and modesty. Most of all, it is evident in how ethnic and religious identities are centrally constructed around the roles of women in order to protect the power and privilege of men, particularly of the dominant classes and castes.

Thus, the critical future challenges for the global women's movement are poverty, conflict and militarization, and the rise of fundamentalisms of various kinds. These are not parallel, but are interconnected forces that have served to erode women's position and condition, particularly in the Third World, reinforcing or mutating traditional patriarchal controls and weakening women's security and survival. None of these is a new challenge, but they have taken on new dimensions and complexities, and greater urgency in the current geopolitical scenario.

While these forces affect all women, for Southern feminist activists and scholars, women have never been a single, universal category, class or social group. In our societies, gender discrimination has always operated through other forms of exclusion and oppression: colonialism, caste, class, race, region, religion, ethnicity, sexual orientation, age, marital status, points in the life cycle and so forth. For women in the South, gender relations operate through these other social and institutional structures, determining their status not only *vis-à-vis* men and women of their own social group, but also men and women of other groups. Thus, you will rarely hear us speak of 'women', per se, but of 'poor rural women' or 'Dalit women labourers' or 'lower-middle-class Tamil women'. This fundamental understanding shapes both our concept of gender and our struggles for liberation.

In this chapter, therefore, we are addressing ourselves to the challenges faced by poor and labouring women, and we build our analysis from the experience of poor women in South Asia. Our rationale for this is simple: it is these women who must negotiate in their lives the enormous burdens and impacts of globalization, fundamentalism and conflict. In South Asia's villages and urban slums, it is poor Dalit, tribal or women of religious minorities who bear the major brunt of structural adjustment reforms, of the lifting of trade barriers and new intellectual property regulations, of religious fundamentalism, of caste discrimination, of both domestic and structural violence including sexual violence, of the militarization of their neighbourhoods, of state repression such as by army, police or even forest department functionaries, and of repression by private interests such as landlords' militias and slumlords. Despite these disproportionate burdens borne by poor women, their political agency has been circumscribed because of the perceived threat they pose to the status quo, or it has been appropriated or subsumed by religious extremists and movements for political autonomy or nationhood.

This is a task of great urgency given the current political context, and certainly in the Indian subcontinent. Right-wing religious fundamentalist organizations, such as the Hindu Durga Vahini RSS women's wing, the Jamaat Islami, and the Kashmiri Dukhtarein-e-Milat, are aggressively recruiting poor women who were previously outside their traditional political base. Other political and civil society formations have provided women little space or power. Organized trade unions, for example, have been greatly weakened, and even when they were stronger, women were neither in decision-making positions nor were their issues part of union agendas. In the unorganized sector, workers' federations are again male-dominated, their demands gender-blind, and women's roles in them are insignificant or non-existent. Political parties are struggling with shrinking membership and they are waning as sites of participation. In India's local councils, where women's participation is legally ensured through a quota system, women are not encouraged to develop their own political constituencies or agendas; on the contrary, they are encouraged, and often coerced to depend on a range of patrons, be they landlords, upper-caste leaders, or even NGOs. While women's movements have provided alternative spaces in many locations, they have not had the human or material resources to cover the map and could not stem the mobilization of poor women by reactionary forces.

Given these political conditions and extreme impoverishment, poor women will have to mobilize politically in large and visible numbers, and enter the political domain through every forum and association possible. It is only the collective energy of this kind of mobilization that will release their transformative potential, and force even the most cynical of both local and global political structures to take cognizance of them and respond.

Global processes and growing poverty

While global economic integration has provided new opportunities for some poor women, overall it is further impoverishing millions of already poor people, and is creating new pockets of poverty. The majority of the world's women still live in either dire poverty or constant economic insecurity. In a region like South Asia, the dominant concerns of most poor women and poor men, are: year-round employment and adequate income to ensure at least two square meals a day, affordable healthcare and education for their children, decent housing and basic amenities, and secure land tenure. Among the poorest households, women's labour and income are vital to the survival of their families and the well-being of their children. Poverty, ecological degradation, traditional gender division of labour within households and the skewed access to, or loss of, common property resources, have all exacerbated the burdens on women for gathering fuel, fodder and water. Poverty also affects women's health and educational opportunities in both direct and indirect ways: long treks for basic needs deplete women's already low nutrition reserves and increase the opportunity costs of education, healthcare and participation in community life. Inadequate food and water, and cultures that enforce silent suffering, mean women develop a range of chronic diseases such as TB, anaemia and reproductive tract infections that go untreated.

In regions like ours, the majority of poor people live in rural areas and the majority of poor rural women are engaged in agriculture, foraging and artisanal activity. In spite of their crucial contribution in the field of agriculture, women's access to land either as tenants or sharecroppers is limited. Land rights for women is still a contentious issue in countries like India. For example, though Hindu women now have equal legal rights to inherit the self-acquired land of their parents, in practice, the male family members appropriate this right. In the case of land owned by a Hindu joint family, there is no legal recognition of women's rights to inherit a share of the land. Women-headed households, which are on the rise due to desertion, bigamy and widowhood, may own land but in most cases male relatives will control the land. Water rights are tied to land rights, and thus women's access to water is both inadequate and fragile.

Rural poverty is further aggravated as common property resources get 'grabbed' by rural and urban elites, often by government agencies acting for them. For example, open grazing land in peri-urban areas get 'acquired' to develop housing projects for the middle class. Thus, women from landless or marginal farmer households are losing the few benefits that free access to fuel, fodder and grazing areas conferred in the traditional subsistence farming economy. Add to this the displacement caused by civil and political conflicts, by dams, by mining, by the enclosing of forests and by large-scale migration to cities, and the problems of urban poverty swell. Displacement and migration have devastatingly worse effects on poor women in terms of economic, social and personal security and survival. The destruction of traditional livelihoods and the 'opening up' of whole sectors of production to multinational corporations, as a result of globalization-led 'modernization' programmes, is particularly devastating for women.

Here are some damning examples of how economic reforms have affected poor women in India:

- In the small town of Sircilla in India's southern Andhra Pradesh state, there have been hundreds of suicides of handloom weavers. These artisans were caught in a debt trap after they 'upgraded' their traditional handlooms to powerloom technology and increased production as part of a state-supported modernization programme. They were unable to market their increased production and, at the same time, the state government increased power rates at the insistence of the World Bank. The weavers could no longer pay their electricity bills or meet their loan payments. The cruel irony is that they could never keep up with the changes. Driven to desperation, hundreds of weavers committed suicide. Of course, their wives were then forced to hold the family together while being hounded by creditors. In some cases entire families took their lives together.

- The country is also witnessing the large-scale migration of young women and girls from drought-prone and otherwise devastated rural economies to big cities for sex-work. This migration is now occurring outside the parameters of what has been thus far understood as trafficking in women; there is no money offered to their families, no procurement chains in the usual sense. These young women are using their own relatives or contacts in the city to migrate for sex-work. Even within cities, daughters of retrenched factory workers in dying industries like textiles are forming the new base of recruits into sex-work. The notion of 'procuring' girls into the trade is already changing as economic forces push girls and young women into the trade under their own agency. While there are a growing number of sex-workers' organizations in the country to protect and advance their interests as workers and as women, they cannot stem the tide.
- Again in the southern Indian state of Andhra Pradesh, the dairy industry was highly developed as part of the planned 'white revolution' – an almost exclusively female activity. Powerful women-led milk producers' cooperatives and cooperative federations had come into being, with strong trickle-down effects on the status of women in these households. Now, the federal and state government is allowing, or has been forced to allow, multinationals like Unilever into the branded milk market. Given that there is surplus milk production, there is commercial interest in processed milk products such as milk powder and cheese. Multinational entry into this sector means the imposition of international sanitary standards (phyto standards) that do not allow hand-milking, and require milk to be frozen immediately after milking. This will drive dairying out of the hands of thousands of rural women, and into those of bigger players who can command the resources for investing in such technology and supply-chain infrastructure. How can poor people participate in a global market where the standards are set, and changed, by others?[1]

These examples demonstrate that the people most affected by economic policy changes and reforms, especially poor women, have no power to play a role in such decision-making, but are more often its victims than its beneficiaries. In the case of the weavers, we see how standards of what is 'efficient' production are not determined by the producers, but by global market standards and institutions with far greater political clout, and they can keep raising the bar or shifting the goalposts with impunity.[2] They are victims of a global economic paradigm in which poverty is not viewed as the result of structural inequalities, but because the poor are not trained, not capable and lack capital.

Increased conflict and militarization

Poverty eradication is going to be much more difficult in the future given the unprecedented and dramatic militarization of the world since September 2001. The United States spends over $25 trillion on defence, which is more than the combined military budgets of all other nations in the world.[3] The post-September 11 foreign policies of the US government, such as the 'war on terror', have not only expanded the militarization of several regions of the world, but have given sanction and legitimacy to other nations to enhance their defence spending, curb the civil and political rights of their citizens, and conduct genocidal campaigns against selected minorities charged with breeding and harbouring terrorists. The challenge is not only of the militarization of areas by their own governments, but by foreign powers that move with impunity into these regions and dictate or override domestic compulsions.

This is clearly evident in South Asia, one of the most conflict-ridden and militarized regions in the world. Countries like India and Pakistan allot huge proportions – 14 to 15 per cent – of their national budgets for defence,[4] even as the majority of their populations struggle to eke out a bare and brutish existence. So while their armies acquire more and more modern weapons and equipment, the majority of their women are illiterate, undernourished and in poor health. And after developing nuclear weapons, both countries have lost a significant degree of their sovereignty, with foreign powers mediating and monitoring their every step. Consequently, outside regimes will have the power to influence national policies and budgets that have enormous impacts, particularly on the poor of these countries, as we are already witnessing in the subcontinent.

The links between conflict and poverty, or, rather, between peace and prosperity, are well known but strangely absent beyond the level of lip-service from both the discourses on poverty and on international 'strategic' issues and peace. It is time for the women's movement, regionally and globally, to expose and build widespread awareness of these links at the grassroots level, and to help build a groundswell against war, civil conflicts and militarization. It is also important to build an awareness of the gendered impact of conflict on women both as participants and victims, as well as their potential in peace processes.

When doing so, women's movements will be up against another countervailing force: declining support in our societies for pluralism, given the long history of political, ethnic and religious conflict, and the spread of fundamentalist movements of all kinds. In this respect, the women's movement both globally and locally has long been a progressive force, advocating policies and cultures of tolerance, inclusion, secularism and pluralism. In many of our countries, it has stood for the adoption and protection of the full range of human rights, for equality under law and for equal protection from both the power of the state and reactionary religious forces. But women's voices have now been drowned in this arena. Women are being instrumentalized by governments, like that of the United States in its 'war on terror', but that very war is contributing to their exclusion or re-seclusion in societies where some degree of voice and public participation had been achieved, such as the Middle East, Pakistan and even Afghanistan.

A case study of the decades-old ethnic conflict – some would say civil war – in Sri Lanka brings out the full range of complex dynamics and impacts on women that result from conflict and militarization, even when women act as agents of peace.

We know that women, especially poor women, suffer most of the 'collateral damage' caused by wars and conflicts. In Sri Lanka, the long and violent struggle for a separate Tamil state, and the widespread state repression and human rights violations by the forces of both sides, have widowed thousands of women. Even if husbands are alive, they may be in combat, missing, detained or disabled. In all cases, women have had to become primary earners in an uncertain economy, and provide for children and the extended family, all in situations of extreme physical insecurity. Data show an increasing number of female-headed households in Sri Lankan free trade zones, plantations, or among migrant workers.[5] Taking on this role also implies dealing with immense mental stress: constant fear of adolescent children or other family members being detained or 'disappearing', which is code for being abducted or killed by security personnel and militant groups, and making decisions about where to relocate after being displaced from ever-expanding 'security zones'. Despite their ability to adapt to such unfamiliar roles, they neither gain new status within the family nor receive acknowledgement from society at large. Needless to say, there is no attempt to support them either through policy or with infrastructural resources. It must also be stressed that, in South Asian cultures, a widow is not just a woman whose husband has died but someone who carries a social stigma that creates loss of status, exclusion from community life and greater vulnerability to sexual harassment and assault. The point is that while conflicts may kill larger numbers of men, it is women who bear the consequence of those deaths in a particular, gendered way.[6] This demonstrates how 'gender, class, race, nation, ethnicity, fundamentalism and globalization [sic] intersect and connect up with militarism and each other to form a grid of oppressions that are mutually supportive'.[7]

Women are also coopted to support militant movements in multiple ways, from recasting and giving new political significance to their traditional roles such as 'motherhood', to offering them the promise of new, apparently 'liberated' identities outside the family. In the early days of Tamil resistance to Sinhala domination and discrimination, women's participation as propagandists was central. They were used as speakers at public meetings, where they constructed women as victims of the Sinhala state and exhorted their sisters to raise brave sons who would fight to restore the pride of the Tamil community. (Hindu fundamentalists use the same rhetoric, exhorting Hindu mothers to rear their sons like warriors.) Tamil women were pressed to use all possible tactics to fuel their men's commitment to the cause, from encouragement to humiliating the unwilling. Thus, their role in the struggle was to nurture and sustain sons and husbands in peak physical and psychological fighting condition, to construct the militant version of masculinity.[8]

Later, when the resistance changed into a militant armed struggle, women joined Tamil nationalist organizations in large numbers. In the early 1980s, all the major Tamil nationalist groups were addressing women's subordination in society as part of their political agenda, with a promise held out to women that in the liberated society that would emerge after their victory, women would enjoy equal status with men. Autonomous women's groups joined women members of militant groups to debate and challenge traditional patriarchal constructions of women in Tamil cultural ideology and notions of emancipation. The concept of 'Pudumai Pen' (the 'New Woman') was constructed.

The single exception to this was the Liberation Tigers of Tamil Eelam (LTTE), the group that later obliterated all other Tamil movements and took over the nationalist struggle. It never addressed the woman's question, but was the first to recruit and train women in armed combat, building on the base of militancy and women's liberation that had been created. And here we see the other dimension of women in conflicts: their cooption into struggles as combatants. It is a little-known fact that 50 per cent of the LTTE's fighters, and most of their suicide bombers, are women, such as the young women who assassinated India's former Prime Minister, Rajiv Gandhi, and attempted to assassinate Sri Lanka's own President, Chandrika Kumaratunge.

While urging them to renounce their femininity, and to prepare to die for a Tamil homeland, the LTTE does not permit any discussion of women's subordinate status, provide an equal role within the movement, or promise future equality in the Tamil homeland it intends to create.[9] Women cadres are subordinate to male control, and no woman has been allowed into the higher echelons of LTTE leadership. Clearly, even entry into struggles as active combatants, and shunning traditional concepts of femininity, does not necessarily assure a fundamental transformation of gender relations. Nor is this unique to Sri Lanka; we see evidence of this particular form of exploitation of women's potential for militancy and armed struggle around the world.

What about women's roles in peace and conflict resolution processes? In the subcontinent, examples of women participating in protests against human rights violations, and in conflict resolution and peace movements abound. Again in Sri Lanka, 'Women for Peace', which was a coalition of women's groups and women professionals from all religious and ethnic groups, were the first to demand an end to the war and to start moves for a politically negotiated settlement. For over ten years, women activists worked to free political detainees, repeal 'anti-terrorist' legislation, protest about illegal detention and 'disappearances', and ensure compensation for civilians affected by the conflict. This they did at tremendous personal risk, exposed as they were to death threats from the state, police, army and the contesting ethnic armed groups. Many women lost their lives in extrajudicial executions; this has happened in many other countries of South Asia as well.

On the other hand, there are women's movements for peace and for the rights of the affected that have been suborned and exploited. The Tamil Mothers' Front, formed as a non-violent autonomous organization in 1984, challenged the state to return their children, end human rights violations, and begin a process of investigation to establish accountability for the abduction and killing of their children. They invoked the notion of motherhood as a universal value that obligated them to protect life in all situations. The consensual moral authority accorded to mothers in society permitted them to step into the public domain in a legitimate gendered role. The LTTE cynically supported their demands from the Sri Lankan state until they had physically eliminated all other Tamil groups and established total control over the Jaffna Peninsula. Thereafter, the political role of the Tamil Mothers' Front declined, and it deteriorated into a welfare organization under the dictatorial and patriarchal LTTE regime.

The Sinhala Mothers' Front in the south, inspired by the Tamil Mothers' Front, experienced political exploitation and marginalization in another form. They were not an autonomous group, but were organized under the main opposition party, the Sri Lanka Freedom Party (SLFP), the main challenger to the pro-Sinhala party that held power at the time. Many of its members included mothers and wives of police and military personnel who had been killed in the war. Their political demands were for an end to armed conflict, a return to democracy, and an ending to human rights abuses and extrajudicial executions. The Sinhala Mothers' Front intended to act in an unbiased way as 'watchdogs' on whichever party was in power, and to become independent of party protection and develop their own organization. But they were unable to resist their campaigns and agendas being used to overthrow the existing government. Even when that was achieved, by being dependent on the SLFP for political protection and leadership, the Front was unable to transform itself into a genuinely independent political force.

Both of the above examples are cautionary tales in how women's roles in and organizing for peace can be subverted and exploited. In contrast, in north-eastern India, a region that has seen self-determination movements and intense militarization for many decades, women have mobilized a broad range of people into their movement by successfully initiating dialogues with both armed militants and the Indian Army. The Naga Women's Front has been better able to resist being silenced by raising human rights violation issues within an integrated set of demands that addressed the living conditions of all civilians under army occupation, such as subsidized food, schools, hospitals and holding of elections. Since they were asking for full and efficient governance and administration, they could not be labelled 'anti-national secessionists'. Militant national armed groups have also found it difficult to attack them as being pro-state because of the widespread popular support they enjoy among the people. Here, women have been able to expand the role of women beyond 'mothers' to the role of engaged, active and democratic citizens.

Clearly, the impact of conflict on women is highly complex and varies widely in terms of cultural and political context. What is clear, however, is that it requires a complex level of analysis, constant monitoring and examination, and sustained intervention strategies by feminist groups. But with the spread of conflict throughout the world, it is clear that women's movements will have to develop a greater degree of sophistication in their analytical frameworks and greater political acumen in developing strategic and empowering responses.

Rise in fundamentalisms and identity politics

In the absence of peace and the continuing pervasiveness of poverty, fundamentalism, both religious and ethnic, gains new momentum, and today we are witnessing what amounts to a virtual division of the world into fundamentalist regions. This, of course, means that all forms of patriarchy gain new and clever footholds. Old practices mutate into new forms of disempowerment: the Hindu woman becomes an icon for both the 'modern' woman, unlike her backward, oppressed Muslim sister, and for traditional values of chastity, modesty, self-sacrifice and devotion to family. She will help make petrol bombs for her husband, sons and brothers to throw on the Muslim slums next door while cooking their dinner like a good Hindu wife and mother, and going to work as a schoolteacher the next morning, in her 'modern working woman' avatar.

While women's movements have focused strongly on domestic violence – a valid focus given the essential and ubiquitous nature of the family as an institution – the nature of identity politics, because of its inherent complexity, poses far greater challenges to feminist thinking and organizing. In Pakistan, conflicts between different sects of Muslims, separatist movements in areas like Baluchistan, and attacks on the oppressed post-Partition migrants (called 'Mohajirs') have had terrible effects on women in these groups and areas. In Bangladesh, silent and almost unnoticed pogroms against the Hindu minority have displaced and widowed hundreds of thousands of poor women. In Sri Lanka, the civil war has left thousands of women widowed, or deprived them of sons and daughters either killed in the conflict or forcibly abducted to serve the Tamil separatists.

In India, low-intensity wars on the Indo-Pakistan border, in Kashmir, the repression of struggles for self-determination in the north-east, intertribal warfare such as between Kukis and Nagas, of course periodic conflagrations between Hindus and Muslims, and, increasingly, massacres of Muslims and attacks on Christians, have had an immense impact on the lives of thousands of civilian women. Most recently, the selected targeting of Muslim women in the Hindu fundamentalist-led pogroms in India's Gujarat state, and the horrific sexual violence they have endured, creates a sense of deep despair. Most disturbing of all, this form of attack on women has achieved a frightening degree of 'normalcy' as a form of legitimate reprisal in wars and sectarian conflicts. The comment by India's Defence Minister during the Gujarat pogroms that the sexual violence against Muslim women was nothing either surprising or new reflects this trend. In other words, it is normal for women to be raped or have their foetuses torn from their bodies when there is a massacre, riot or war.

While these issues have been well analysed by feminist scholars, it has been difficult to translate their insights into strategies on the ground. The notion of a national, homogeneous women's movement against fundamentalism was challenged given the particular class, caste and religious status of feminist leaders and their organizations. The politics of difference could not be successfully negotiated and many groups retreated as the fundamentalists appropriated and distorted the very issues they had been raising. In India, for example, feminists had long embraced the adoption of a common set of civil laws, earlier called a Uniform Civil Code, to govern marriage, inheritance, divorce, maintenance and adoption.[10] In the early

1990s, Hindu fundamentalist groups repositioned this issue as one between the state and the religious and cultural exclusivity, and disloyalty of specific groups posing a threat to the integrity of the nation. They reconstructed the Uniform Civil Code around a Hindu norm, built around the practices of a few upper-caste and upper-class Hindus, ignoring the great diversity of customary laws among Hindus themselves. They ignored the fact that the Hindu code itself had been reformed in a very reactionary fashion, in some instances restricting the advantages that women actually enjoyed under customary law.

Many progressive feminist organizations withdrew from the debate, which became a minefield given how the fundamentalists were defining the notions of nationalism and minority rights. Feminist groups did not know how to reconcile the notion of individual rights and equality of women with the notion of the rights of specific communities: whose rights should be privileged? An important lesson learned from this experience, however, was that in highly diverse societies like India, with growing levels of polarization along religious and ethnic lines, the concept of 'uniformity' was deeply problematic, especially if one did not want to contribute to the fundamentalists' agenda of creating a Hindu state. This realization led to the emergence of far more complex frameworks and a spectrum of positions among women's groups. These range from a common gender-just code, to reforms from within communities even if this does not ensure absolute gender justice, to rejection of formal court procedures in favour of community-based arbitration fora.

Perhaps the most difficult challenge posed by the spread of fundamentalism is the mass cooption of poor and working-class women by fundamentalist groups and their ideologies. Progressive women's groups have been among the first to condemn sectarian violence and militarization, and all forms of fundamentalism and its projects. In Pakistan, women's groups offered the only opposition to the Hudood Ordinance, which placed a range of restrictions on women's movements, imposing medieval penalties for crimes such as adultery; Bangladeshi and Sri Lankan women's groups have mobilized against the growing powers of the Islamic and Buddhist clergy; and Indian women's groups have long struggled against the forces of Hindu fundamentalism. Yet, impressive numbers of women have been mobilized by those very agendas; by the Islamic fundamentalist parties such as the Jamaat Islami and other groups in Pakistan and Bangladesh, by Sinhala and Tamil fundamentalists in Sri Lanka, and by the Hindu fundamentalist organizations like the VHP[11] and RSS.[12] When the Babri Mosque in India was demolished by raging mobs in December 1992, 50,000 of the 'kar sevaks', or religious volunteers, at the site were women.

This phenomenon is a testimony to the way in which fundamentalists have offered women new notions of 'emancipation' and power in the public realm. These become attractive in the absence of other kinds of progressive mobilizing spaces that offer women a different agenda. Women's movements will have not only to reclaim women in general from these formations, but ensure they do not successfully mobilize the poorest and most marginalized women.

Strategies for the future

We believe that three critical strategies must guide women's movements to face these enormous challenges and threats: revising the conceptual frameworks from which to develop our strategies, the building of a large and powerful mass base, and recasting our own structures to deal with these overwhelming tasks.

Revisiting our frameworks An important first step for charting any future course for women's movements is to interrogate and analyse the conceptual frameworks, whether implicit or explicit, that have informed our thinking and our action thus far. Given current political realities, we may have to revise our frameworks to provide clearer directions for our future work, and use older frameworks more strategically, with an awareness of their strengths and limitations.

Let us examine why this is important with a concrete example: in South Asia, women's movements have used legal reform extensively to fight gender discrimination, and have operated between two basic frameworks, namely the rights framework and the substantive equality framework. The rights framework focuses on formal equality, such as on equal rights under the law, assuming that every individual/citizen is essentially the same. Its proponents argue that gender difference has been used to deny women equal rights. But this is problematic in societies with wide social and economic differences, and where access to legally enshrined rights may be difficult for most people. Thus, the demand for sameness in rights to property, which is a formal right, can be meaningless if the majority of people in a country are landless labourers. The equal right to property for men and women becomes useful when combined with struggles for land reform.

The substantive equality framework recognizes this distinction that individuals may be different. It is not simply based on equal treatment under the law, but on the actual impact of the law.[13] It takes into account inequalities of social, economic and educational background of people, and seeks elimination of existing inequalities by positive measures, including legislation that favours women. The focus of the analysis is not with sameness or difference, but rather with disadvantage. 'When equality before the law is interpreted as men and women being the same as each other, courts do not uphold any legislation intended to compensate for past discrimination or to take into account gender-specific differences (like childbearing). The sameness approach cannot distinguish between differential treatment that advantages and differential treatment that disadvantages.'[14]

The dilemma that feminists confront with both of these approaches is that they empower the state as the prime agent of social transformation and protection. This assumes a neutrality on the part of the state which is false: the state is constructed, most of the time, to protect and advance the very class and gender interests that such changes will jeopardize, and thus often finds ways of accommodating the changes in principle – for example, passing highly diluted versions of a pro-women law – while vitiating them in practice, as has been the case throughout South Asia with land reforms. They also reduce the focus on building transformative change processes within communities on the ground. Thus, each legal or policy victory of the women's movement could often evaporate on the ground as the struggle for implementation and enforcement begins. This experience is not unique to South Asia, which is perhaps why there is a growing critique worldwide that the rights approach has not worked.

We therefore have to explore and create frameworks and strategies that, first, are not situated within the paradigm of the state as the primary agent or enabler of change, and not premised primarily on formal legal intervention, but are instead based on the agency of poor women and their constituencies to bring about larger substantive transformation. While the state will continue to have a role, it will be a partner rather than the patron. Second, given our understanding that the experience of gender and disempowerment is specific to culture and location, we can no longer assume the existence of certain 'universal' moral principles that guide our framework; we must instead create a process actually to locate them. This requires a widespread, bottom-up process of debate and discussion. This is a vital role for women's movements in the coming phase.

Strengthening the base It is imperative that women's movements rebuild themselves as social and political forces. In order to do this, they will have to revitalize their organizing strategies. A key priority is to facilitate and support the emergence of strong, grassroots-based organizations of poor women, and facilitate their access to multiple political spaces. We need a churning up from below at the village, town and city levels. This also means creating alternative spaces for women who bear the brunt of neoliberal policies, displacement and loss of habitat and livelihoods due to wars and civil conflicts, ethnic violence, domestic violence and state repression. If they can be mobilized, we will see an incredible revolution, as has already occurred in some locations.

This task places a special responsibility on middle-class feminists, who may have to surrender forms of leadership and control over articulation of priorities and concerns that they may have had in the past. They must learn to facilitate the emergence of grassroots leaders and autonomous organizations, and help them form links and alliances both with other progressive movements, such as labour and economic justice, and human rights, as well as with campaigns and organizations working at national, transnational and global levels. Several excellent examples of this can be found, such as the role played by NGOs working on urban poverty in India, South Africa and Thailand in creating and supporting mass-based federations of the urban poor who are now directly negotiating with local and national authorities and international financial institutions to secure their rights to safe and sustainable settlements.

This example also brings out the importance of a more intersectional approach, which is the way of the future and the only way to address the huge challenges of poverty, conflict and fundamentalism. It is to be hoped that this will counter the rather sectoral and narrow project-based approaches that funding agencies have fostered, compartmentalizing work on violence, income and employment, health, education, law reform, and sexual and reproductive rights.

We believe that a strong focus on building the base will also create the conditions for grassroots women and their formations to launch and take leadership of mass movements against poverty, conflict and fundamentalism. By articulating dynamic new approaches and creating innovations on the ground, they will create a magnet for other movements and struggles to join them. This will help expand movements, transform their character and leadership, and engender their approaches, thus overcoming one of the limitations of the past, where women were participants in, but not leaders of, larger social justice movements. It will also change the character of alliances and coalitions. The choice of collaboration partner will therefore not be based on affiliation, but on how it creates value and adds to social impact.

Recasting structures The process of taking the leader and building vibrant organizations to take the movement forwards necessitates an examination of what we have learned from our experience of creating and sustaining alternative structures. We know that women's organizations have faced multiple challenges and problems with power, as manifested in democratic functioning, delegation of authority, hidden hierarchies, questionable leadership styles, conflict resolution and lack of support to younger leaders, within their own structures. In postcolonial societies, the asymmetry of power is based not only on class or education, but also on access to world languages such as English. This is carried over into women's organizations, where the lack of access to English results in exclusion from critical theoretical debates and developments. These gaps must be closed: gaps between 'thinkers' and 'doers', between vernacular speakers and English speakers, and between web-surfers and others. These gaps become even more critical when the main challenge is to build mass-based women's organizations and grassroots leaders both nationally and internationally.

We therefore need to build learning movements based on principles of critical introspection, questioning assumptions, inclusion and consciousness of our own differences and hierarchies, and being genuinely open to change. This is difficult to sustain without periodic, systematic processes of reflection that are consciously created and protected. When this is assured, women in turn will ensure that their movements change, evolve and remain vibrant. Finally, we need to build fluid and open movements, whose constituency has expanded in real and visible ways to include all those affected by hunger, deprivation, conflicts and hate.

Notes

1 Personal communication with K. S. Gopal, development analyst and planner, Hyderabad, India.

2 Ibid.

3 The United States Defense Department requested $379,347 million for the 2003 fiscal year. See <www/defenselink.mil>

4 C. R. Reddy (2002) 'The Road to Ruin', *The Hindu* (opinion leader page), 25 May 2002.

5 C. A. Chandraperuma (1991) *Sri Lanka, the Years of Terror: The JVP Insurrection, 1987–89* (Colombo: Lake House).

6 K. Samuel (1999) *Women and Armed Conflict in Sri Lanka*, unpublished monograph.

7 A. M. Chenoy (2002) *Militarism and Women in South Asia* (New Delhi: Kali for Women).

8 S. Maunaguru (1995) 'Gendering Tamil Nationalism: The Construction of Woman in Projects of Protest and Control', in P. Jegannathan and Q. Ismail (eds), *Unmaking the Nation: The Politics of Identity and History in Modern Sri Lanka* (Colombo: Social Scientists Association), pp. 158–75.

9 K. Samuel (2001) 'Gender Difference in Conflict Resolution: The Case of Sri Lanka', in I. Skjelsbæk and D. Smith (eds), *Gender, Peace and Conflict* (London: Sage).

10 These are currently determined by the customary laws of different religious groups that create wide differences between the rights of Hindu, Muslim, Christian and Parsee women.

11 Vishwa Hindu Parishad (World Hindu Forum).

12 Rashtriya Seva Sangh (National Service League).

13 R. Kapur and B. Cossman (1999), 'On Women, Equality and the Constitution: Through the Looking Glass of Feminism', in N. Menon (ed.), *Gender and Politics in India* (Delhi: Oxford University Press).

14 N. Menon (1999) 'Rights, Bodies and the Law: Rethinking Feminist Politics of Justice', in N. Menon (ed.), *Gender and Politics in India*.

7 | Different worlds possible: feminist yearnings for shared futures

SARAH BRACKE

> We fight our bid for collectivity, its difficulties and its limits. We stretch ourselves, mobilising and pushing ourselves, daring ourselves to share our concerns and express our desires. We are many, different, each one with her story; the alliance is neither neutral nor a priori but rather a continuous process of recognition and communication into which we launch ourselves again and again, committed to a strategy of uniting ourselves.[1]

Struggles in times of late global capitalism: contradictions and possibilities

Feminisms in transit Discussions about women's conditions and rights in our societies are often marked by a tension between two seemingly opposite positions. Many women, it is affirmed, have gained a great number of rights during the course of last century, such as economic and political rights, and rights concerning bodily integrity and sexuality. The twentieth century has indeed been characterized as one of women's emancipation, with the emergence of new horizons of possibilities for every new generation. In a number of societies, including many Western European ones, it sometimes seems as if formal and juridical equality is (almost) a fact and very few juridical changes can be made in order further to improve the status of women on that level. The discrepancy between this formal juridical equality and the obvious and all-too-familiar realities of inequality is usually bridged by focusing on the need to *apply* the existing legal instruments in order to reshape realities of continuing gender inequalities. Moreover, in the light of the acknowledgement that social differentiations, such as geopolitical location, class, ethnicity, citizenship, sexual preference and age, structure access to women's rights, the emancipatory agenda is further considered in terms of the need to *enlarge* access to existing rights.

At the same time, many feminists and activists are concerned with the deterioration of scores of women's lives in the last decades, and wonder whether strategies focused on 'applying' legal instruments and 'enlarging' access to them are sufficient. Of course, we all find ourselves struck by examples of sheer backlash against women's struggles and their achievements, not least in the context of various economic crises and the coming to power of right-wing governments. But the concerns of many activists reach further, as we question the terms in which we organize our struggles and wage our battles. Much of the reformist politics and policies of emancipation, often framed in the language of 'equal opportunities' that tends to sit so comfortably within a neoliberal framework,[2] leaves us with so much less than we bargained for. Are not some of these political strategies part of the problem, many of us are asking, to the extent that they might effectively emancipate some women's lives but are complicit with the deterioration of other women's lives? 'The master's tools will never dismantle the master's house', Audre Lorde wrote in a previous moment of intensity of the women's liberation movement,[3] and the prophecy of her vision clearly manifests itself in the current conditions of late global capitalism.

Perhaps the point is not to decide which of these perspective really reflects conditions for women in this world, whether the instances of progress or those of deterioration are more real. While these perspectives are no doubt related to different visions on social transformation, it is perhaps more urgent to understand how they constitute different layers of the complex and contradictory realities of late capitalism at the beginning of the twenty-first century. We need to understand, for instance, how a greater amount of women painstakingly slowly breaking through (a limited number of) glass ceilings in the economic sphere, politics or higher education coincides with a feminization of poverty and a general increase in the precariousness of many women's lives. Or how policies concerned with the 'reconciliation of work and care' in Western Europe coincide with women from the South legally or illegally migrating to the West to perform domestic services, often in what has been called 'chains of care' as they leave the care of their dependants in the hands of other women. As Laura Agustín puts it:

> Nowadays, when more and more European women are going out to work, we are seeing one kind of gender equality. But since more and more European men are not staying at home, and most men have not taken on more than minimal domestic responsibilities, this apparent equality has to be qualified. [...] 'Equal' gender relations therefore may crucially rely on the employment of a third person. And while this in itself might not give cause for alarm, the nature of the typical domestic employment offer should.[4]

Furthermore, we need to understand how the increasingly rigid closed border regimes of Fortress Europe coincide with a rise in 'trafficking in women'.[5] Merely denouncing conditions of sexual exploitation is an insufficient response if it is not based on the recognition that networks of traffickers constitute for many women the only accessible 'immigration office' in the current geopolitical situation. And we need to question, as new forms of governance turn to feminism as a possible source for legitimacy,[6] how familiar feminist demands for women's safety in the streets relate to the new security ideologies so popular in the West. These ideologies are blatantly racist in the ways they set up questions of safety and violence in relation to issues of migration, integration and citizenship. At the same time, they are also sexist in the ways they promote an ideology of particular women in need of 'protection'.

These are different types of 'coincidences', each provoking different sets of questions. But they do have something in common: they complicate the inherited and familiar feminist struggles and discussions on women's rights and they create a sense of urgency for the making of new alliances. Our feminist perspectives and struggles need to be informed by the contradictions within and between the lives of women living in late global capitalism. Simply adding new concerns to the existing feminist agendas, without letting those new questions and concerns upset and reorganize the agendas, is insufficient. Many of us find ourselves torn between the fact that emancipatory politics and policies are too comfortably nestled within existing structures to destabilize the system, on the one hand, and the fact that the brutality of the conditions of global patriarchal hetero/sexist racist late capitalism makes it hard to give up on those emancipatory politics, on the other. Throughout the 1980s, as Cristina Vega analyses with reference to the Spanish context, the aims of the women's movement became codified in terms of planned equality, hence turning the law and the state into the ultimate horizon of feminist politics.[7] In a discussion of black feminism in the UK, Hannana Saddiqui relates the professionalization of the movement to its depoliticization.[8] Within the current horizon of 'equal opportunities' and professionalization of the women's movement in the West, we often find ourselves confronted with impossible choices. In what Saddiqui refers to as a moment of 'coming of age' of the movement, Vega proposes that we see 'feminism in transit'; we find that the need to reinvent and re-create shared horizons of liberation is urgent.[9]

On maps and tools In order to work through this moment of transit, and to envision and practise effective resistance in the current system of patriarchal hetero/sexist racist capitalism, we need to be able to 'read' the new and rapidly changing geographies of power. Donna Haraway, for example, elaborates on these power relations in terms of an integrated circuit,[10] while Avtar Brah writes about contemporary capitalist globalization.[11] In other words, we need good maps. The debate on whether or not we need another United Nations conference on women's rights, the discussion in this volume on the possible futures of our struggles, and our various meetings at the social fora[12] are just some examples of how we are trying to understand, in a collective way, how to move in these new geographies of power. Together we are trying to figure out in which directions to take our struggles.

I want to pause briefly to consider how to make these maps, in a desire to affirm some tools emerging out of our feminist genealogies. The maps we need are inevitably collective projects, informed by the experiences, practices and knowledge generated by various struggles in a multitude of locations. Theories and practices of situatedness and of positioning are at the heart of the women's movement. They are crucial impulses that brought and continue to bring women together politically *as women*, thus undermining both an assumed universal political subject and the established boundaries between the personal and the political. Politics of location or the practices of positioning, however, equally function as powerful tools within women's struggles and movements, through the often conflictual mobilization of differences of ethnicity, class, geopolitical situation, sexual preference, and so on, that undermine the attempts to construct a universal 'woman' and/or feminist subject.

Hence, the politics of location function against a background of universalism that continues to have a strong hold on the political field in general and also on women's struggles. For instance, as a result of questioning the universalism of the new political subjects of the alterglobalization movements[13] at the European Social Forum (ESF) in Florence in 2002, a project of a feminist 'gathering of forces' preceded the ESF in Paris in 2003. In its turn, however, the preparation of what eventually became the 'European Assembly of Women's Rights' remained marked by an underlying universalist idea of 'women', in which very quickly racism, heterosexism and homophobia are considered 'specific' issues, and subsequently general 'women's issues' are set up according to dominant white, heterosexual and middle-class norms. Nowadays such practices are often legitimized by a call for a 'back to basics' feminism that, in the light of the backlash against women's struggles, could speak with one strong voice, at the expense of suspending differences between women. Differences, however, are our strength, not our weakness, and while a practice that suspends those differences in the name of unity might seem effective for prompt action, do we honestly think that we can afford its costs in terms of the building of our movements and alliances?

Some have understood the politics of location and situatedness in a relativist or paralysing way. In a happy 'everybody his/her own truth' mode, this amounts to the 'united colours of diversity', as yet another version of neoliberalism in its favourite game of ignoring relations of power and inequality. However, to paraphrase a key sentence in George Orwell's *Animal Farm*, a striking parable of the workings of power in modern societies, we might all be different, but let's not forget that *some of us are 'more different' than others.* In an anxious 'who owns the authentic voice' mode, on the other hand, a relativist understanding of the politics of location leads to an impasse where difference gets translated as an absence of communality, undermining any possibilities for conversation, let alone alliance. 'We are different,' Saraswati Raju critically responds to such an impasse. 'But can we talk?'[14] Moreover, 'authenticity' in this case is often linked to 'the most powerless'; it is always the 'other' woman who is deemed 'most authentic'. The notion of 'grassroots', for instance, continues to be marked by a certain romanticization of the 'authentic' site of struggle, hence inscribing existing hierarchical relations.[15]

Against such (mis)understandings and neutralizations of situatedness as relativistic 'diversity' or incommensurability, we need to keep in mind that universalism and relativism are simply two sides of the same coin.[16] They both refer to speaking from nowhere and/or everywhere and hence miss the point that we always speak from somewhere in particular, however complex, multiple and multilayered those locations might be.

Grounding our maps in the politics of location thus implies not only that we need to start from multiple situated positions, namely the different material conditions of our lives, but at the same time map out how these conditions stand in relation to each other in terms of power and inequality. Another way of saying this is to insist that gender or sexual difference, as a regime of differentiation and inequality, is always already ethnicized and racialized, structured according to class relations and articulated within a particular regime of sexuality. Such a starting point can provide us with grounds for radical democratic practice.

Politics of representation and its crises A radical democratic perspective is an alternative to the crises of representation and representational politics that we are currently facing. Historically, feminism has emerged in the interstices or cracks between a hegemonic representation of 'Woman' – those images of what a woman should be that are presented and sold to us – and the material realities lived by actual embodied women.[17] And similar to the politics of location, such a crisis of representation not only founds feminism, but equally continues to nurture it, in a continuous mobilization of that question which Sojourner Truth raised more than 150 years ago: 'Ain't I a woman?'[18] Women's struggles and feminism indeed generate and come to rely upon certain representations of women that in their turn are questioned. In her crucial intervention, *Under Western Eyes*, Chandra Mohanty exposes the discursive colonialism marking representations of 'Third World Woman' circulating in Western feminism.[19] Written in the 1980s, Mohanty's essay urges us to look at neocolonial, neo-oriental and racist representations of women today. The colonial continuities in the representations of 'Muslim women' are striking in this respect,[20] as 'the plight of Muslim women' is used to mobilize for imperialist and right-wing agendas that search to establish a new global geopolitical hegemony or to restore the deadly discourses of 'cultural homogeneity' in the West European 'multicultural debates'. Another problematic representation, which plays an important role in the reconfiguration of Europe after 1989, is that of 'women as victims of trafficking'. Reducing the whole issue to sexual violence against women, and disavowing the dimension of women's migration, are useful to the agenda of Fortress Europe and its deadly border regimes. In both examples the crucial question is: what are the feminist complicities with, and counter-strategies against, representations of women that figure centrally in xenophobic right-wing agendas? The point of refusing such problematic representations, as Mohanty and many others make clear, is that they hinder fruitful alliances. We must come up with adequate responses to such cynical uses of 'women as victims', responses that take into account the complexity of women's lives and women's agency.

Representational politics have not only shown signs of exhaustion within women's movements, but many feminists have also denounced the problematic logic of policy-making based on an idea of the 'representative' woman. In this logic, differences are redistributed in the framework of 'target-groups', such as 'the (representative) migrants' and 'the (representative) poor', hence excluding any vision on how power inequalities work through their articulation or intersection.[21] For example, EU policy has, generally speaking, constructed women as a unified and homogeneous category, viewing this category mainly as 'white women in paid employment'.[22] In response to policy-making that attempts to resolve the social needs of women through endowments for the family, women from la Eskalera Karakola write:

> The problems of family management are just some of the many that we face. The generalised flight of women from the traditional family and from reproduction makes ever more absurd this attempt to speak of the necessities of women as if they were identical to those of reproduction in the bosom of the family. This practice constitutes an effort to deny and invisibilise the tremendous diversity among women, we who are young and old, who are

singles, lesbians, transsexuals, migrants, students, precarious workers and so much more.[23]

Also in the context of social movements we are confronted with inadequate and underlying notions of representation linked to the imaginary and imagined constituencies upon which movements are built. This is the question of who can speak for humanity as a whole and who for 'its small bits', as Nirmal Puwar puts it.[24] 'Are you representative?' often becomes an awkward question sanctioning the transgressions from established representations of what 'the women' should say, what 'the black women' should stand for, what 'the lesbian' should embody and what 'the poor women's' interests are.[25] These representations make metaphors out of concrete material lives, measure people by their otherness, and, against a politically subversive understanding of the politics of location, tie their speaking up to social location.

In the context of the intensification of anti-capitalist resistance, the politics of representation are problematized from yet another perspective. Looking back at her student activism around claims for better representation of women and ethnic and sexual minorities in the early 1990s, Naomi Klein asks, 'why were our ideas about political rebellion so deeply non-threatening to the smooth flow of business as usual?'[26] And while questions of representation re-emerge within these anti-capitalist struggles, in their old and familiar guises of universalism and the marginalization of 'particular' struggles, perhaps the strategy of denouncing those movements as 'not paying enough attention to our claims' is not the most interesting one. As Cristina Vega argues:

> This is the old trick of who is central and to what we concede centrality, a double move that makes us complicit with subalternizing strategies. And tell me, my sweet friends, who if not feminists and queers of various kinds have put desire and pleasure at the centre of politics? Who has transformed the way of taking the street and brought the black block outfits back to their performative potential, who has been responsible for breaking the discontinuities, public–private, work–non work, etc. of traditional politics, who has reflected around the question of autonomy, horizontality, [...] more than the feminist movement? Who has brought the question of hybridity – sexual, ethnic [...] – into the scene if not the queer and anti-racist movements? Who has put their bodies against social death and invisibility more than those migrant activists that are locking themselves up in churches all over Europe?[27]

In the light of the increasingly visible dead-ends of the politics of representation, we need to look for, name and nurture alternatives that *we already practise*. Let us consider politics in terms of *affinity*, as for instance the ecofeminist and peace activist Starhawk does.[28] Or let us look at the politics of the *alliances* in which we are involved, such as the process of creating the social fora.[29] And what about the politics of *weaving webs* between different local groups, as the World Women's March does?[30] Or the *politics of contamination* that grounds the activities of networks such as Women in Black[31] and Act Up,[32] both of which started as local actions that subsequently developed into a concept spreading to many locations, intervening in and transforming local realities? Let us remind ourselves of our politics of *reappropriation* as we occupy language, images and spaces for our struggles, like the Eskalera Karakola and other autonomous feminist spaces in which we try to reconstruct social relations in a different way. In the same vein, consider black and migrant movements that radically reappropriate notions of 'security' in a context of security-focused state ideologies, such as BRAIN, the Black Racial Attack Independent Network, or the Arab European League. And what about the politics of *becoming* that we are engaged in and affected by? As Cristina Vega envisions: 'If we are going to discuss alternatives in, let's say, regulations on the sexual identity of transsexuals, let's let transsexuals lead the way, let's involve ourselves in a *becoming transsexual* that is not the same as being transsexual, giving voice to transsexuals, or expressing punctual solidarity with transsexuals and then getting back to business.'[33]

Political subjects – a point of departure common to these examples – cannot be assumed; time and time again they are made.[34] When we assume that the subjects of the feminist or women's movements are simply 'out there' waiting to be mobilized, we forget that political subjects and agendas need to be continually reinvented. Let us not be mistaken that we 'have' a feminist movement and feminist political subjects to which, at best, new issues or subjects can be added. No, as feminists and activists we are involved in the creation of such movements and agendas, in the light of new and changing conditions.

Situated observations

Locating Europe After arguing for the importance of speaking from embedded and embodied positions, I want to pause for a moment on the geopolitical context from which the thoughts in this text are articulated, namely Western Europe. This is a geopolitical space that is characterized by great difficulties of considering itself in specific terms. For example, the heavy legacy of eurocentrism envisions Europe not as a concrete place on the map and in history, but rather in universal terms, as an idea of civilization.

Europe has always viewed itself as 'autochthonous', as Stuart Hall argues, as producing itself from within itself, thus disavowing interconnections with other histories and its foundational hybridities.[35] Locating Europe, in other words, is connected to the decentring of Europe, a process that found a great impulse in the political independence struggles of decolonization, but does not end there. The material and symbolic expulsions of ethnic and religious 'others' – the legacy that enabled Europe to construct its identity as white and Christian – still continues today. However, those 'in but not of Europe', the postcolonial subjects, the migrants, the 'East' Europeans, and those slipping through the various border regimes, are increasingly involved in the construction of a different Europe because of their growing numbers and their strong political claims.

The difficulty in 'localizing' or decentring Europe continues to mark social movements, including (white) women's and anti-racist struggles. This point was brought home once more at the first World Social Forum in Porto Alegre, Brazil. Following the decision to divide into regional caucuses in order to develop more regionally embedded visions on the effects of neoliberal globalization, European participants only hesitatingly got together, I was told, as if they were not sure what they could talk about. Their hesitance seemed related to the absence of various 'others', notably the victims of neoliberal globalization in the global South; many Europeans find it easier to think about the struggle in the South than within Europe. But also, I suspect, the absence of 'the other' as hegemonic actor of neoliberal globalization, namely the USA, played a role. Many Europeans find it much easier to take up a critical stance against the hegemony of the USA, than to interrogate European complicities within the 'integrated system', which implies holding to account structures and networks of power that have anchors in Europe, such as national governments, the EU, and also the G-8, WTO, NATO and IMO. More generally, decentring Europe implies the development of embedded perspectives on how global late capitalism works and what it looks like in various concrete locations in Europe. This is what I meant in a previous section by 'maps'. Considering that we need to construct our maps in collective ways, I offer the following elements that I see as important to our maps, only as a preliminary list.

- The new transnational division of labour and mobility of capital results in a profound restructuring of the labour market. In Western Europe this has meant deindustrialization, with multinational companies moving their production activities to the South and East, and new forms of unemployment. In general, employers are increasingly fleeing any kind of employer's responsibility or accountability. In addressing these conditions, the challenge for our struggles in the West is to avoid protectionist fantasies and calls to close the borders to 'foreign' products. Instead, we need to realize the necessity of transnational struggle in response to transnational movements of capital and production.

- The global reorganization of care and domestic services constitutes another important reality of global late capitalism that is usually obscured by masculinist perspectives on work and economic activities. Domestic labour, care and sex-work can be grouped together, as Laura Agustín for instance does, not because they constitute the same kind of activity, but because these occupations are solicited by Western Europeans willing to pay for them; hence, in classical migration theory they are 'pull factors'. However, various 'progressive' European discourses, notably parts of the white women's movements, are failing to address these predominantly female migrations.
- The dismantling of the welfare system and undermining of social security have disproportional impacts on the poor, migrants and women and children. Common goods and public services, such as health services, education, public transport, water and electricity, are increasingly privatized and commercialized. In this regard, resistance against the General Agreements on Trade in Services (GATS), developed in the context of the WTO but partly in the hands of national governments and the EU, should be a top priority on the agendas of our women's movements.
- Exclusionary notions of citizenship and restrictive border regimes increasingly shape the national and European landscapes, resulting in social exclusion that too often amounts to social and actual death. Women's movements in the West need to oppose the criminalizing of social movements, including migrant movements, and expose the facts behind the state's fascination with 'security'. The normalization of rampant xenophobia and racism must be a preoccupation of all progressive Europeans.

The consensual hallucinations[36] *of neoliberalism* I would like to pause on a crucial ideological formation that accompanies the operation of late capitalism, namely neoliberalism, as an important obstacle in our feminist struggles in the West. Let us briefly return to the observation that women breaking through 'glass ceilings' coincides with the feminization of poverty. From a feminist perspective, this strikes me as a contradiction. To paraphrase Emma Goldman, *If it's not about all of us, it's not my revolution.* In the ideological landscape of neoliberalism, however, this contradiction is neutralized. Women who do break through 'glass ceilings' are regularly regarded as evidence that the conditions for emancipation for all have been achieved. Subsequently, the feminization of poverty is considered largely to be the result of the personal failures of individual women. In other words, both of these phenomena in women's lives are framed through the Western value of free choice.

Thus we are constantly confronted with the argument that the individual, if she really wants, can get anywhere she likes, in a kind of Nike-feminism: 'Just do it'. In the same breath, women in old and new forms of poverty are also evaluated through the lens of free choice and judged as lacking the real will to change their condition. A poor woman might not manage to 'just do it', for a variety of reasons. Her inability to deal properly with the challenge of her situation can none the less be addressed through neoliberal 'corrections to the system' developed especially for people like her. This ideological framework has produced the notion of 'workfare', for example. Moreover, the 'success story' of the poor, single mother who manages to 'make it' gets a paradigmatic function in the neoliberal fairy-tale: it proves that if you want, if you *really, really want*, you can still 'do it' no matter what your starting position.

Post-feminist discourse is a popular and crucial part of this neoliberal ideological formation. Feminists are indeed constantly asked about, in the words of Ingrid Robeyns, the post-feminist ghost that haunts discussions on gender inequalities in Western Europe.[37] When a young activist housemate returned from working in a refugee camp in Bosnia, she commented that after witnessing the conditions of women in rural Bosnia she finally understood why feminism was still needed. And in the process of setting up a monthly feminist gathering in an autonomous political centre in the Netherlands, a young white male activist carefully asked whether we could discuss 'women in Afghanistan' since there was not really so much to discuss any more in relation to the Netherlands.

Post-feminism thrives on the idea that women in the West are 'beyond emancipation' and that remaining differences between women, in consequence, are a matter of free choice. It operates through a systemic evacuation of the question of women's emancipation and feminism from the here and now. In many public discussions on women's emancipation and feminism in Western Europe,[38] the need for women's political struggles are often cast in terms of 'back then', when women did not have the right to vote, and 'over there', outside the West. In their bourgeois individualism, neoliberal post-feminist tendencies find themselves in an unholy alliance with neocolonial, racist and sexist ideas by which a West European emancipated self-image has been marked for the longest time.

Neoliberalism depoliticizes; it disavows questions of power inequalities. We need to recognize the many forms this process takes, including, for example, the apolitical celebration of cultural differences, sociobiology and evolutionary psychology as modes of explanation,[39] the naturalization of differences during religious and nationalist revivals in the name of a natural or divine order, and the repression of differences in the name of a shallow notion of equality and integration. In sum, the material conditions in which we find ourselves are marked by an intensification and sharpening of power inequalities while, at the same time, these inequalities are naturalized or neutralized in a dominant neoliberal ideology in an attempt to take away grounds for political mobilization against existing power inequalities. This is a crucial contradiction from where to start our struggles.

Yearnings for our futures

> The antagonistic force demonstrated by the movement, with its claims to horizontality, creativity, scope, diversity and capacity for interruption are appealing for a stale left that has suffered from the neoliberal touch and the incapacity to generate a new discourse that would cede protagonism to the social movements. Those that say we do not have proposals when we say 'no one is illegal', 'social income now', 'share the global burden', 'papers for all' or 'no to the privatization of education and public health' want, in fact, to arrive at a intermediary state between the way the world is now and some decreased version of our high pointed goals. To those that have sold again and again our desires we say one more time: we want it all and now.[40]

Throughout this chapter I have tried to articulate some visions on how to continue our struggles. The sections have spilled over into one another as I failed to neatly disentangle analyses of the problems we are confronted with in our feminist struggles, affirmations of tools and practices with which we are already familiar, contradictions that we live with in the integrated circuit of global late capitalism, and the ways in which these reflections are embedded in a West European context. In this concluding section, therefore, I can only pull together some of the red threads that spiral throughout the text.

First of all, our women's movements need to politicize. Politicization is the (im)pulse running through our feminisms. For the longest time, our agendas have been shaped by the intense moment of politicization of the 1970s; indeed, the professionalization and institutionalization of the 1980s and 1990s were very much rooted in feminist agendas emerging out of this earlier decade. However, the 'horizon of liberation' intimately connected to that early agenda was gradually left behind, as many feminists started to operate within a horizon of the law and the state and of 'equal opportunities'.

But only at the expense of losing its destabilizing power, and our women's movements losing their beating heart, can 'the personal is political' be considered as an achievement once and for all. Rather, 'the personal is the political' is a continuous process,[41] a process of transformation that demands personal engagement time and again. It cannot be 'delegated' to other women or eras. It is literally the process of getting together, telling each other the stories of our lives, and crafting collective visions and practices of resistance out of these stories. This process bears divisions of labour such as 'authentic voices' and 'experts', 'grassroots' and 'representatives', 'activists' and 'theorists' quite badly.[42] Instead, the sustainability and radical democracy of this process rely precisely on creating new ways of relating to each other, which undermine existing hierarchies. In the light of the current neoliberal climate that depoliticizes power inequalities, we are in great need of the intense politicization of the increased precariousness of our living conditions wherever we are situated,[43] discourses on security, production and consumption, and of notions of citizenship and border regimes. In sum, we need to unmask global late capitalism's 'realisms', which are blatantly hetero/sexist and racist, and their very material and differentiated effects on our bodies and lives.

Second, such a process of politicization situates us within the current alterglobalization and anti-capitalist struggles.[44] This affirmation anchors us in our feminist genealogies of transnational organization grounded in the multidimensional character of oppression and power inequalities. The Chipko movement, for instance, articulated their struggles around issues of poverty, neoimperialism, environmental destruction and sexism. Their activism and ways of organizing were transmitted by Vandana Shiva to a great number of women's activists from all over the world at the UN Women's Conference in Mexico in 1974. This is just one well-known example of mobilization that has paved the way for the current alterglobalization.[45] Affirming this radical history and future of our feminist struggles decentres certain mainstream feminist approaches, which became focused on 'equal opportunities', conceived within an existing capitalist framework that remains unquestioned. Moreover, it also disrupts and works as a creative force within the alterglobalization movement, confronting the whiteness of the movement as we know it in a European context, as well as the sexist, heterosexist, racist, eurocentrist and nationalist tendencies that run through it.

It is against this background that the NextGENDERation network found it important to create a feminist space at the first European Social Forum (ESF) in 2002, however small the space of one workshop might seem in the context of a massive forum with tens of thousands of participants.[46] As many of the reflections throughout this chapter come out of my engagement in this collective creation, I will briefly pause on this experience. NextGENDERation is a network of students, researchers and activists with an interest in women's studies and feminist theory, and the desire to participate in the ESF was in itself a result of a gradual process of politicization. An engagement in women's studies led to a concern with the institutional context of education and knowledge production, which is increasingly shaped by neoliberal agendas that promote financial cutbacks and push towards privatization. Moreover, protest actions in singular educational institutes are confronted with reactions from the institutional authorities claiming 'their hands are tied' by increasing competition and regulations from supranational organizations such as the EU. Such developments undermine the democratization of education and the available spaces for the generation and transmission of critical and liberatory knowledge.

Starting from a feminist perspective based on a multiplication of the axes of power, and therefore the axes of political action, we found it appropriate to name the workshop at the ESF 'Missing Links: Feminism and Globalized Resistance', hence putting our yearnings for links and alliances at the centre. As we articulated a small 'Missing Links' project in a large and diverse movement, some of the contours we meant to question were rendered immediately visible, as a discussion with one of the leading white male figures of the French branch of Attac illustrates. After we informally addressed the marginal presence of women's movements, black, migrant and refugee movements, and gay and lesbian movements in the ESF organization team, we learned what he thought of this unfortunate situation. 'Listen,' he said, quite irritated after a while, '*we* are trying to organize this globalized resistance. If *they* don't come, than that's their problem.' In a fatal state of blindness, he, and many others, failed to see that it is precisely not 'their' (our!) problem, but the problem of the alterglobalization movement. And while his response reflected an attempt to construct a centre ('we') of the movement, this centre does not hold because different formations of 'we' – like the 'we' that I have risked using in this chapter, realizing very well that this is only the beginning of actually constructing our collective subjects and alliances – are already in the movement, continuously transforming and decentring it.

'Missing Links' opened a small space to gather feminist forces and look for common ground, and hence create, rather than presume, a basis for collectivity and alliances. At the time of writing, the NextGENDERation network, together with other groups and individuals whom we have encountered in those few feminist spaces at the ESF, are preparing a range of activities for the next forum. These activities include moments of exploring and repositioning certain questions in seminars, notably on 'embodied leadership' and representation, on feminist counter-strategies against security-focused discourses and on the ways in which women's migrant labour crucially figures in current global economic restructuring. They also include the occupation and construction of a feminist space allowing us to meet and build collectives, as well as the preparation of feminist interventions in the form of direct actions during the forum and demonstrations.

In a sense, this is about creating feminist 'centres' within the movement, by which I mean 'spaces of one's own' where we can ground our actions, visions and desires in our various feminist genealogies. This point of departure differs from justifying, yet again, the need for feminism – a need that is reflected in the difficulties of placing gender on the agendas, as it is either deemed to be irrelevant or referred to 'after the revolution'. These are old and all-too-familiar scenarios and the alterglobalization movement is in fact generating new feminisms, as many women activists, confronted by left-wing machoism, have decided not to put up with it. Out of Attac, for instance, FeministAttac has emerged. In both points of departure, where reality often overlaps, feminist organizing takes on an autonomous dynamic. What we need to refuse, however, is performing 'the woman question' within a larger movement, that can be raised in certain moments of good-will ('now-explain-to-us-what-exactly-the-problem-is'), only to be dropped later on when it's time to get 'back to business'. The European Assembly of Women's Rights that opens the ESF in 2003 is for instance to a great extent set up along those lines, hence asking to be subverted by feminist desires. Feminism is hardly a question of 'explaining', but rather it is about a shared engagement, in anger but more importantly in joy, in laughter, in desire, in solidarity. When Adrienne Rich proposed that women try 'to see from the centre', she did so precisely in the context of refusing to be 'the woman question'. 'We are not the "woman's question" asked by someone else,' she comments, 'we are the women who ask the questions.'[47] Questions that disrupt, contaminate and create.

Third, in these collective constructions of feminist grounds, the need to practise and nurture politics of alliance between our different struggles – or the linking of 'scattered resistances'[48] – should not be underestimated. Much lip-service has been paid to alliances, often skirting the hard work they demand in practice. Alliances are about engaging with others and therefore also about dealing with positions invested with power. In particular, whiteness, the great blind spot that too often manages not to recognize itself as a position profoundly invested with power, but also geopolitical location and neoimperialist and neocolonial attitudes, along with class position and the patronizing attitudes of classism and normative heterosexuality all need to be addressed in the way we set up our alliances. Alliances are inevitably based on the involvement of our subjectivities; they are about working with differences and working through conflicts. Perhaps they are about love. In any case, we cannot render them into abstract models and can only try to share our pedagogies and methodologies. But we can find words of inspiration for the yearnings that push us to engage in them. Writing about that previou s moment of intensity of the women's movement, Adrienne Rich recalls that we 'never meant anything less by women's liberation than the creation of a society without domination; we never meant less than the making new of all relationships'.[49] Our struggles are about nothing less.

Notes

This text is collective in that the reflections and yearnings of many dear feminist friends are profoundly writen into it. I particularly want to thank Cristina Vega, Elena Casado Aparicio, Ingrid Robeyns, Maayke Botman, Maggie Schmitt, María Puig de la Bellacasa, Nadia Fadil, Rutvica Andrijasevic and Selma Bellal for ongoing conversations, friendships and daring.

1 La Eskalera Karakola is an autonomous feminist occupied space in Madrid. Quote from 'Spaces for daily life. Feminist foundation of the project'. See <http://www.eskalerakarakola.org>

2 S. Bellal (2002) 'L'Europe et l'égalité des "chances' entres les sexes: une égalité concrète devant les inégalités?', *Politique-Revue européenne de débats*, 3: 125–8.

3 A. Lorde (1981) 'The Master's Tools Will Never Dismantle the Master's House' (1979), in C. Moraga and G. Anzaldúa (eds), *This Bridge Called My Back: Writings by Radical Women of Color* (New York: Kitchen Table, Women of Color Press).

4 L. Agustín (2003) 'Sex, Gender and Migrations. Facing Up to Ambiguous Realities', *Soundings: A Journal of Politics and Culture*, 23 (Spring): 95.

5 R. Andrijasevic (2003) 'The Difference Borders Make: (Il)legality, Migration and Trafficking in Italy among Eastern European Women in Prostitution', in S. Ahmed, C. Castañeda, A. M. Fortier and M. Sheller (eds), *Uprootings/Regroundings: Questions of Home and Migration* (London: Berg). My reflections on the issue of 'trafficking in women' in this chapter are greatly indebted to many discussions with Rutvica and the generous sharing of her work and activism.

6 C. Vega (2003) 'Interroger le féminisme: action, violence, gouvernementalité', *Multitudes (féminismes, queer, multitudes)*, 12: 49–60.

7 Ibid.

8 H. Saddiqui (2000) 'Black Women's Activism: Coming of Age?', *Feminist Review*, 64: 83–96.

9 C. Vega (2002) 'Transitos feministas', *Peublos. Revista de Informacion y debate*, 3 (II). See <http://www.e-leusis.net>

10 D. Haraway (1991) 'A Cyborg Manifesto: Science, Technology and

Socialist-Feminism in the Late Twentieth Century', in *Simians, Cyborgs, and Women: The Reinvention of Nature* (London: Free Association Books).

11 A. Brah (2002) 'Global Mobilities, Local Predicaments: Globalization and the Critical Imagination', *Feminist Review*, 70: 30–45.

12 Here I am referring to fora organized at global, continental, national and regional levels all over the world, with the motto 'Another World is Possible', as spaces to meet, discuss and build alliances of globalized resistance against neoliberal globalization and capitalism.

13 'Alterglobalization' envisions possible different worlds, a resistance that is transnational and therefore shakes off the misleading 'anti-globalization' label.

14 S. Raju (2002) 'We are Different, but Can We Talk?', *Gender, Place and Culture*, 9 (2): 173–4.

15 N. A. Naples (2002) 'Changing the Terms. Community Activism, Globalization, and the Dilemmas of Transnational Feminist Praxis', in N. A. Naples and M. Desai (eds), *Women's Activism and Globalization. Linking Local Struggles and Transnational Politics* (New York: Routledge). Naples quotes D. Mindry (2001) 'NGOs, "Grassroots," and the Politics of Virtue', *Signs*, 26 (4): 1187–211, on p. 7: 'It is important that we begin to examine the ways in which moralizing discourses such as those concerning the "grassroots" and "poor, black, rural women" as targets of intervention structure relationships among women working in NGO's in ways that are remarkably hierarchical.'

16 D. Haraway (1991) 'Situated Knowledges: The Science Question in Feminism and the Privilege of Partial Perspective,' in *Simians, Cyborgs and Women*.

17 T. de Lauretis (ed.) (1986) *Feminist Studies/Critical Studies: Issues, Terms and Contexts*, Theories in Contemporary Culture, 8 (Bloomington: Indiana University Press).

18 S. Truth (1851) *Ain't I a Woman*. Transcription: <http://www.feminist.com/sojour.htm>

19 C. Mohanty (1988) 'Under Western Eyes: Feminist Scholarship and Colonial Discourses', *Feminist Review*, 30: 61–87.

20 On this point, see L. Ahmed (1993) *Women and Gender in Islam: Historical Roots of a Modern Debate* (New Haven, CT: Yale University Press).

21 For crucial work on the intersecting nature of power relations, combining perspectives from theory, policy-making and activism, see M. Botman, N. Jouwe and G. Wekker (eds) (2001) *Caleidoscopische visies. De zwarte, migranten- en vluchtelingenvrouwenbeweging in Nederland* (Amsterdam: Koninklijk Instituut voor de Tropen).

22 R. A. Cichowski (2002) '"No Discrimination Whatsoever": Women's Transnational Activism and the Evolution of EU Sex Equality Policy', in N. A. Naples and M. Desai (eds), *Women's Activism and Globalization*.

23 La Eskalera Karakola, see note 1.

24 N. Puwar (2003) 'Speaking Positions in Global Politics', *Derive Approdi*, 11 (23).

25 Note that notions of representation in social movements often mimic the representational politics of parliamentary democracy, in the absence,

however, of elections which underpin such a system. For a discussion problematizing notions of representation and participation in social movements, see S. Bellal (2003) 'La célébration de la "société civile": vers la dilution de la responsabilité politique par la "participation"?', in S. Bellal et al. (eds), *Syndicats et société civile: des liens à (re)découvrir* (Brussels: Labor).

26 N. Klein (2000) *No Logo* (New York: Flamingo), p. 144.

27 C. Vega (2002) 'Firenze, Feminism, Global Resistance'. See <http://nextgenderation.let.uu.nl/esf2002/> Some (personal and shared) tips about going to Firenze.

28 See various texts on <http://www.starhawk.org>, on how to do politics through affinity groups from an anarchist perspective.

29 I am thinking, for instance, of the projects of feminist interventions at the European Social Forum. See, for example, <http://nextgenderation.let.uu.nl/esf2002> and <esf2003>

30 For more information, see <http://www.ffq.qc.ca/marche2000>

31 For more information on this network, see <http://womeninblack.net>

32 For more information on this network, see <http://www.actupparis.org>

33 Vega, 'Firenze'.

34 For a theoretical elaboration on this point, see J. Butler and J. Scott (eds) (1991) *Feminists Theorize the Political* (New York: Routledge).

35 S. Hall (2003) '"In but not of Europe": Europe and Its Myths', *Soundings. A Journal of Politics and Culture,* 22 (Winter): 57–69.

36 I borrow the term from the science-fiction author William Gibson, who used it to characterize cyberspace in his novel *Neuromancer*.

37 I. Robeyns (2001) 'Het postfeministische spook', *Lover*, 28 (1): 14–19.

38 The question of post-feminism presents itself in a very different way in Central and Eastern European countries, linked to the fact that women's emancipation to an important extent used to be associated with communist state policies.

39 Sociobiology and evolutionary psychology propose societal models of sexual difference based on imaginary models of hunter-gatherer, or of ethnic difference based on imaginary homogeneity of communities and 'natural xenophobia' as self-defence. These explanations are gaining popularity at this time as Western societies are dealing with rapidly changing gender relations and 'multicultural debates'. Sociobiology and evolutionary psychology represent ideas of 'natural' models of human sociability.

40 Vega, 'Firenze'. 'The movement' here refers to the alterglobalization movement.

41 M. P. de la Bellacasa (2003) 'Divergences solidaires: autour des politiques féministes des savoirs situés', *Multitudes (féminismes, queer, multitudes)*, 12: 39–47.

42 For a critical reflection on the 'theory versus activism' binary, see R. Andrijasevic and S. Bracke (2002) 'Venir à la connaissance, venir à la politique: réflexion sur des pratiques féministes du réseau NextGENDERation',

Multitudes (féminismes, queer, multitudes), 12: 81–8. An English version is also available on <http://nextgenderation.let.uu.nl>

43 See, for example, M. P. de la Bellacasa (2002) 'Flexible Girls: A Position Paper on Academic Genderational Politics', see <http://nextgenderation.let.uu.nl/texts/flexible_girls.pdf> on precariousness in an academic context.

44 C. Mohanty (2002) '"Under Western Eyes" Revisited: Feminist Solidarity through Anticapitalist Struggles', *Signs*, 28 (2): 499–535.

45 See, notably, N. A. Naples, 'Changing the Terms', on this point.

46 Traces from the workshop, from its preparation to its outcomes, can be found on the website: <http://nextgenderation.let.uu.nl> See also R. Andrijasevic, S. Bracke and C. Gamberi (2002) 'The NextGENDERation Network at the European Social Forum: A Feminist Intervention', see <http://nextgenderation.let.uu.nl>

47 A. Rich (1986) *Blood, Bread and Poetry* (London: Virago).

48 L. M. Desai (2002) 'Transnational Solidarity: Women's Agency, Structural Adjustment and Globalization', in N. A. Naples and M. Desai (eds), *Women's Activism and Globalization*, p. 17.

49 A. Rich (1986) *Blood, Bread and Poetry*, p. 217.

8 | Diversity as our strength: transforming power, public policy and popular culture

ANA CRIQUILLION

In attempting to identify the primary, current and future challenges for women's movements around the world, it is critical to look at some of the international issues and dynamics that are affecting women in order to understand the effects of 'globalization' and its implications for feminism. Generally speaking, there are key processes that bind us together as women, yet, at the same time, increase the differences among us. Identifying and analysing the complexity and the implications of these processes are vital for defining our strategies.

As I see it, among the principal global trends are the following: citizens' growing mistrust of traditional political processes and politicians; the increasing importance and impact of the media in this political context; macroeconomic and demographic changes and their contradictory effects on women's employment, migration and power relations within homes and families; and the sweeping surge in fundamentalist movements and their impact on politics and cultural norms that reinforce the subordination of women. While these dynamics affect women throughout the world, their specific effects on specific groups of women are diverse. Rather than bringing women together, they are in fact widening certain kinds of gaps between different groups.

By analysing lessons learned about the achievements and successes of feminist movements in recent history, I will take another look at the importance of direct representation and participation of women in the public sphere and in decision-making, as well as the relevance of popular culture and the media in shifting the balance of public opinion in favour of women's rights. I will demonstrate how feminist movements have succeeded and been effective when they have been able not only to give a name to women's most shared and heartfelt problems, but also to suggest solutions that are concrete, attractive and feasible for the average woman.

I will also demonstrate that, apart from the trends that sometimes dictate the workings of government and the comings and goings of public opinion, there are certain core experiences common to all women despite the infinite diversity of particular experiences and situations. These experiences include relative poverty, restrictions on the ability to exercise a full and satisfying sexual life and on women's control over their reproductive capacity, and the violence that women all over the world still experience.

In the face of these three core issues or common experiences, the struggle against different kinds of fundamentalisms, from economic and military to religious, becomes a global priority. In this struggle, it is important to understand not only the ties between their defenders and the political elites, but also their attraction for many women to the extent that fundamentalist groups offer a type of 'answer' to uncertainty and feelings of meaninglessness.

Diversity is the challenge. On the one hand, the diversity of 'fundamentalist' activities gives the illusion of unrelated, separate acts, and hides the shared ideological offensive that motivates them. On the other hand, the diversity of reactions to these fundamentalist actions limits our capacity to stop their advance and makes us act in shortsighted and uncoordinated ways. In order to strengthen our own movement's capacity for mobilization and impact, it is essential that we go beyond our present discourse about 'diversity', which is limited to acknowledging the differences among women. We need to confront and overcome the multiple kinds of power relations and inequities among women, both within our movements and outside.

A broad view of emerging and diverging trends

When we think about how emerging trends are affecting or are going to affect women, it is difficult to imagine that their impacts would be the same, for example, for Nicaraguan women and for Canadian women, or for women within each country who live in very different situations and conditions based on age, race, sexual identity or preference, ethnic origin, migratory status, social class or caste or religion. We have to ask ourselves not only which trends we are talking about, but also which women. While many emphasize that the most relevant trend (globalization) tends to have a homogenizing effect throughout the world, might it not rather be that these global processes, more than homogenizing the oppression of women, in fact increase the differences and potential divisions among us?

In Nicaragua, for example, as well as in many other countries of the world, poverty is the determining factor in the daily life of the majority of women. It is a well-known fact here that seven out of every ten women live on less than two dollars a day, and five out of every ten live on a dollar or less. Women in Nicaragua experience poverty in different ways according to their specific circumstances; women in the Pacific region of the country and those on the Atlantic Coast, black and indigenous women and *mestizas*, professional women and illiterate women, adult women and girls and teens, and also single heads of households and married or partnered women, with small children or childless, for example, all experience poverty differently. Yet all women in Nicaragua share a common situation: the enormous weight of our foreign debt, the low price of coffee, our principal export, which is influenced by the World Trade Organization (WTO), and the conditions imposed by the International Monetary Fund (IMF) and the World Bank. That is to say, our situation depends more and more on decisions that are out of our control, made by agents outside our own country.

This scenario, which is repeated throughout Latin America and all over world, frequently translates into scepticism in relation to the capacity of governments to establish their own public policies based on the well-being of the people – assuming that this was ever their intention – as well as in the possibility of influencing these policies. We are living in an era in which political institutions have lost much of their credibility and have seen their influence seriously eroded. Representative democracy has come to be perceived as having serious limitations for any real participation in the decision-making that affects us. The right-wing voting trends in Europe and the United States, as well as in many developing countries, reflect the uneasiness of people who are in effect voting against, rather than in favour of particular candidates. Ultimately, they feel that neither the political parties nor their leaders serve their interests.

In this context, we see the growing influence of the media, including print, radio, television and, most recently, the internet, on the formation of public opinion and defining of spaces for debate on all kinds of issues. This influence has often been negative in relation to women's interests, but at times it has been favourable. For example, where women have seen conservative and fundamentalist moral forces take over governmental institutions, the media have often been the only progressive force that could be counted on to resist these influences and put forth alternative points of view.

One of the effects of globalization, in the way that it has developed until now, is the trend towards cultural homogenization, particularly the promotion of the 'American way of life', given the USA's enormous weight in the communication, entertainment and corporate marketing industries. At the heart of this trend towards homogenization, however, we are at the same time facing growing diversification. New cultural identities are being defined due to a growing recognition of the diversity of existing conditions among people and, most of all, due to the increasing migration of people from all parts of the world.

It is estimated that by the year 2050, developing countries will contain more than 85 per cent of the world's population. Migration will therefore play a crucial role in the future.[1] In the developing world there is a larger available workforce than there is demand for their labour, while in industrialized countries it is possible we will find the opposite trend, with more low-paying jobs available than there are people to take them, which has specific implications for working women. In recent decades, women in industrialized countries have had more access to education and to the means to control their reproductive lives. These factors, along with the lack of public services that alleviate domestic tasks and the care of children, the high costs of supporting large families, and women's growing integration into the labour force, have caused the fertility rate to fall to 1.6 children per woman. That is lower than replacement rate.[2]

This trend will probably intensify in the coming decades and will produce a rapid ageing of the populations in industrialized countries. Women, including older and married women, will in subsequent generations have even more opportunities to enter the labour force. We will face the growing demand of a market oriented to middle-aged people and senior citizens, in which issues such as medicine, gerontology, leisure and tourism will have increasing importance. Women are already working in these areas and have had opportunities to advance.

This new configuration of the labour force in industrialized countries, together with fewer or no small children in the majority of homes, should create a shift towards a considerable reduction in sex-segregated work, as well as changes in the gendered division of work inside and outside the home. It should also deepen the present trend in these countries towards a less sexual differentiation. These circumstances are favourable to achieving more equality and equity between the genders. But this can also increase the possibilities of unequal power relations between women, for example, to the extent that immigrant women work as domestics or nannies in the service of 'native-born' women. In this way, greater equality between women and men of the same social status and class may be achieved at the expense of other women's equality or of greater inequality between women. It is also possible that industrialized countries will once again resort to pro-natalist policies and other actions to reverse adverse impacts for men that these social and economic changes may entail. In so doing, they may well find perfect allies in the conservative religious and social groups.

Fundamentalist groups also have a growing effect on the lives of women all over the world: on their freedom of movement and expression; on their prospects for obtaining work or their access to resources; and on their sexuality and control over their reproductive lives. In the West, many people have a tendency to become alarmed by any type of restriction placed on women by certain fundamentalist religions, in particular, Islam. But Catholic fundamentalism is not very different. In the last decade in Latin America, for example, we have seen tremendous setbacks in women's sexual and reproductive rights due to the official position of the Catholic Church under the leadership of Pope John Paul II. Due to the fragile and unclear separation of church and state, many countries in the region have adopted population, health and education policies that impede women and adolescents' access to adequate sex education and information, as well as to contraceptives and abortion.

The Vatican's active opposition to the women's movements' positions at the United Nations' international conferences has, for all intents and purposes, thwarted the advances of the previous decade. Even the gender policies proposed by official governmental institutes and offices for women in the region are being questioned, at the same time as there is a clear shift towards a return to more traditional policies that take women into account only in their roles as mothers and housewives. From pulpits all over the continent, homilies are given urging women to return to these roles and to oppose those who preach 'licentiousness and the destruction of the family'.

This discourse finds receptivity among many women because it expresses their unhappiness and provides an answer to the sense of the meaninglessness and insecurity that they experience in their daily lives. In the face of so much war and street violence, the economic, political and military power of drug cartels, corruption, poverty, the dissolution of families, and the subordination and violence that many women live with in their own homes, religious fundamentalisms offer a community and spiritual refuge against isolation. In some senses they re-establish a measure of security by providing clear limits and moral norms, and promises of happiness in return for strict obedience and compliance.

The situation in Latin America is not unique. In fact, it is repeated in many countries, although since the contexts vary widely, we as women are placed in very different positions. Some of us live in rich countries, while the majority live in impoverished countries. Significant differences regarding the relationship between the state, market and civil society lead women to establish very different strategies at local, national and global levels. While the root causes of the phenomenon may be the same, the implications can vary widely for different groups of women, meaning that the actions taken will differ as well. Actions depend on the specific situation and on women's positions, both in relation to men and to other women.

Lessons learned from strategies adopted in the past

It has been said that the global feminist movement should be more proactive. Why isn't it? One of the underlying hypotheses is that we do not sufficiently anticipate the economic, political and social changes that affect us and our rights, and therefore our response is too slow. I, however, am not sure that a more 'timely' analysis of the emerging trends would be enough. In fact, I believe that it is even more important to thoroughly analyse the past, at least our recent history. What factors have positively or negatively affected women's advances towards gender equity and justice? Which factors have had the most impact, for better or for worse, and why? The answers to these questions would help us better understand where to focus our energies, which strategies to choose, and how to make the most of social dynamics.

It is clear that there is no universally applicable recipe that will miraculously eliminate worldwide gender inequalities. An interrelated multiplicity of factors exists that reinforce each other and influence their own increase and decline. Every economic, social and political phenomenon has a different effect on women than on men and is experienced in different ways by women according to their identities and conditions. It is beneficial to analyse the main globalization trends from this perspective. However, our agenda will once again become an interminable list of unattainable demands if we do not focus more on what really brings about change, not only in women's status and life circumstances, but especially in their position in relation to men in the same social stratum.

If we look back on the events of the last 150 years, the changes in women's status have been slow and highly unstable processes. We have observed how in diverse national and social contexts, rapid changes in women's status were reversed two or three decades later. We have also observed in distinct parts of the world a cyclical dynamic in the emergence of feminist movements or waves, as well as of anti-feminist groups and movements in reaction to these changes. In this sense, concentrating only on the present and recent past brings with it the risk of coming to premature conclusions and possibly mistaken predictions for the future.

Perhaps we should first focus our efforts on understanding which specific variables act, so that changes in them generate sustainable, large-scale transformations in existing sex/gender systems. Obviously, a determining factor in achieving changes in the status of women, particularly in relation to formal, legal and political equality, is the establishment of public policies that not only take into account women's specific circumstances, but also favour the promotion and defence of their rights. When changes driven by political elites coincide with favourable demographic factors and economic expansion, and are reinforced by the media and the educational system, the improvement in women's position and status can be quite significant and can contribute to the establishment of new definitions of gender and gender roles in society. The struggle for women's suffrage is a good example of this. While women's rights to vote alone do not constitute full equality, either formally or informally, voting rights have in fact contributed to changing gender norms.

Influence the political elite or change the rules of the game?

In recent years, an acute feeling of impotence and disempowerment has been growing within both women's movements and in general public opinion around the world, particularly in developing countries. This is a result of the limited economic and political power and manoeuvring room that local and national governments have *vis-à-vis* the growing power of the market, international agencies and transnational companies.

However, in the face of growing marginalization and exclusion of wide sectors of the world's population, we are also seeing a growing understanding both in general public opinion and among experts in international institutions like the United Nations and even the World Bank that the market alone is not capable of correcting the distortions it causes. This recognition has led to the belief that national and local governments should return to exercising a more regulatory role, and also to the belief that the international institutions in charge of resolving problems of coordination among countries need to be reformed and democratized.[3]

If this trend takes hold, and if we act together with other social movements to make that happen, there will be more political control over macrostructural factors and probably more opportunity for action and influence by the people, including women. Key elements are the strengthening and recovery of decision-making power by the states, particularly in the most impoverished countries; the citizenry's participation in political systems at the local, national and global level; and the direct representation and participation of women in decision-making at all levels, in parity with men.

This last element, women's direct political representation, continues to be a challenge for us. Despite notable advances in some of the developed countries, political, economic and religious elites are overwhelmingly male, and, like all elites, they normally act to conserve or reinforce their privileged positions, or at the very least avoid putting their positions at risk. Aware of this fact, and due to the lack of better representation and direct participation, feminist movements around the world have concentrated their efforts on attempting to affect the public sphere through their influence and/or pressure on the elites, primarily the political elite. The results have often been discouraging in spite of the organizational levels they have reached.

Reviewing the tactics utilized by feminist movements in recent history, we can see that, unlike other movements, violence, including the destruction of property, has not been much utilized, except in some fashion by British suffragists at the beginning of the last century. While strikes were common in the early 1900s among mostly immigrant women workers in the United States, the more recent use of strikes has not been very common except as one-day symbolic events, as in the case of the world strike initiative on International Women's Day on 8 March, which itself commemorates a strike. A mechanism more commonly used has been the active support of or opposition to specific electoral candidates. However, with the exception of the election of a few feminist candidates, there is little evidence that this type of activism has really had any particular influence on women's voting patterns or on political parties' platforms in any part of the world.

Other mechanisms, like the mass mobilization of women, marches in the street, and other demonstrations have had more impact. However, with the notable and inspiring exception of the widespread and massive demonstrations to protest against the US-sponsored attack on Iraq, these types of actions have been losing their attraction in recent years. There has been a growing resistance to using them, not to mention that the cost of international and national actions is high. Mass campaigns of political pressure by email, the creation of virtual global networks and discussions about collaborative action beyond national borders are taking their place. Other similar forms of pressure, such as the boycott of certain transnational companies such as Nestlé, have been effective but infrequent. Legal actions against discrimination and sexual harassment in the workplace have also had a certain amount of success, particularly in industrialized countries.

Direct lobbying of local and national authorities has definitely been the strategy most utilized in recent times. Through these actions, feminist movements have been able to initiate new legislation and press for legislative reform, and also to improve women's access to the justice system in some countries. At the executive level, feminists have campaigned for the creation of specific policies and programmes that take into account women's specific conditions and circumstances. The establishment of links between feminists and community and religious organizations, unions and associations, especially those that consist primarily or entirely of women, has facilitated the mobilization of new resources and increased support for their actions by taking advantage of ties and contacts previously established between these organizations and the political elites.

However, until we gain representation and the direct participation of women in significant numbers in the spheres of political power, the success of these efforts will continue to be greatly dependent on the political good-will of men in positions of power. The underrepresentation of women and in particular of feminists in the political elites throughout the history of humanity has been a result of the disadvantaged position of women in relation to men, which in turn perpetuates that position. Efforts towards parity require at least a partial recognition of this fact. It is interesting to observe how feminist movements, particularly those in the second half of the last century, have had ambivalent feelings and attitudes regarding the political elite. On the one hand, they have recognized the importance of having sufficient allies in key positions, and on the other, they have displayed hostility towards those who hold such positions.

The participation of women in political systems and at different decision-making levels cannot continue to be marginal. To the extent that it is, our actions remain short-term and isolated, obliging us to conform to the dominant political and institutional culture. We need to overcome our ambivalence and make a concerted 'assault' on institutions at all levels. We need to fight in a determined manner for the mass participation of feminist women of all stripes in representative positions in civil society, in all types of public positions and decision-making spaces, in the different branches of government and at the local, national, regional and global levels.

To do this, we will need a profound change in the political culture of feminist movements. This includes overcoming the authoritarian and personality-based styles of leadership that still persist within our movements, as well as overcoming our own difficulties with delegating authority and representation to other women and building real support among women for their representatives. It also means finding mechanisms that guarantee transparency and accountability of leaders to the women they represent.

To the extent that female representatives are in a position to do so, they could promote the creation of mechanisms and formal and institutionalized spaces for the participation of women's organizations in public policy discussions. These spaces could promote broad-based consultations with women's movements before approving new laws, establishing new policies, approving public budgets, designing strategies and national development plans such as Poverty Reduction Strategies, or approving international accords such as 'free trade' agreements, all of which have a tremendous impact on the lives of women.

However, participating in existing institutions and attempting to 'introduce a gender perspective' or working in women's organizations are not the only possible alternatives. Let us take advantage of our proven ability to establish new institutions and throw ourselves into the task of creating new mixed institutions, such as businesses, NGOs, community organizations, universities, institutes and schools, communication media, other civil society organizations and even political parties. These new institutions could work from a basis of ground rules that eliminate all internal gender segregation and follow an agenda that really takes women into account.

Popular culture and the media: key areas for change

It is true that these institutional-type changes are at the micro- and middle level. To achieve change at the macrolevel, we also have to alter public opinion and social norms. In fact, there is no doubt that gender norms play a determining role in the reproduction of inequality between men and women and legitimize the social structure on which inequality is based. In this sense, all efforts that contribute to influencing public opinion to replace traditional gender roles and norms with a new gender consciousness are vital to achieving greater equality and equity between the sexes.

In the face of the explosion of access to information, it is more difficult for the public to distinguish rapidly which information is useful. The competition for public attention increasingly forces the message-bearers, whether they are news broadcasters, advertisers or politicians, to focus more on how information is presented. Short, well-illustrated, attractive messages that include the option of interactivity will have advantages over more traditional media formats. While we should still look to increase our presence in traditional forms of media, we also need to take advantage of the window of opportunity offered by new information and communications technologies (ICTs) to directly influence the production of information that reflects women's realities and interests in all of their diversity. This would put us at the forefront of communication production and allow us to take advantage of innovative and attractive formats that will let us compete with the enormous quantity of information available to the public.

In addition to making these technologies serve us, it is high time that we recognize popular culture as a strategic medium and more purposefully enter into the creation and mass distribution of educational entertainment that can help tip public opinion on women's rights in our favour. The enormous influence of music and other forms of entertainment, including radio programmes, soap operas, television series, and videos that reflect people's daily lives, is increasingly evident in the popular imagination, formation and reproduction of ideas, attitudes and even behaviour, particularly among young people.

In the United States, for example, it is worth noting the growing influence of African-American, Hispanic, Jewish, and gay and lesbian perspectives in movies, television, documentaries and other kinds of materials made by and for these groups. Furthermore, there already exists a considerable amount of audiovisual material created by feminist women all over the world. It is likely that the process of transnationalization of communication products for specific social groups for entertainment and information purposes will increase.

Some experiences of feminist community radio like FIRE, musical videos like those made by Breakthrough in India, mass circulation feminist magazines like *La Boletina* in Nicaragua, and 'social soap' TV series like *Sexto Sentido* in Nicaragua and *Soul City* in South Africa, demonstrate that 'alternative media' do not have to be marginal. These media outlets can become as popular as commercial 'mass' media. In addition to reaching millions of people in some cases and getting such important issues as violence against women, women's right to choose and gay and lesbian rights into the public eye, these initiatives combine and reinforce the use of 'edutainment' with the activism of grassroots groups and coalitions, NGOs and feminist networks all over the world. So while it is a vital strategy to foment communication among feminists or among those that share certain common objectives, it is also vital to communicate with women who might not consider themselves part of these movements.

Battling fundamentalisms: a global priority

In reaction to the struggle for the equality of men and women, in which both women and men are involved, fundamentalist movements are erecting a barrier with beliefs that attempt to impose their own concepts of good and bad on the world. They are even using militarization, war and destruction. Included among these fundamentalist movements are religious fundamentalisms that do not recognize any truth or social norm other than what they themselves establish; military fundamentalism that claims the use of force and violence as the only way to resolve conflicts between nations and communities; and also economic fundamentalism that attempts to make us believe that the logic of profit is the only economy possible.

To confront these fundamentalisms and the growing backlash against feminism most effectively, we should publicly reveal the identity, the actual size (which is generally small in terms of member numbers), the personal interests and the operating style of these groups. They are trying to influence public policy to reverse the advances women have made towards obtaining their rights. We must respond.

At the same time, we should not underestimate the reasons why so many people receive these fundamentalisms favourably. How can we recognize the unhappiness of women, the feelings of impotency and isolation that overwhelm women in their day-to-day lives, without resorting to merely describing this desolation? How can we propose concrete alternatives for today that offer meaning to women's lives, a sense of community, and reachable goals for their own security and well-being, while acknowledging individual moral, religious or political convictions and promoting women's autonomy?

In addition to expressing adequately the desires and aspirations of women in all of their diversity, it is important that we find a style of language and discourse that allows us to get to the heart of public opinion. We can systematize and capitalize on our accumulated experience in this area. For example, public policies established in the last twenty years to prevent violence against women or to assist those who have been victims of violence are the fruit of feminist work to influence public opinion with very simple and universal slogans such as 'break the silence' and 'you are not alone'. In very little time, gender violence has changed from an invisible social phenomenon to being recognized as socially unacceptable, a public health problem and an obstacle to development. Through our campaigns we have simplified the legal and medical jargon related to the fight against violence against women and for sexual and reproductive health and rights. We have appropriated key concepts and translated them into language accessible to all. We should now use the same methodology to confront new subjects and threats.

One of the areas that has not received sufficient attention on our part, but which none the less determines the quality of life for a majority of women in the world, is neoliberal macroeconomic policy. We should appropriate macroeconomic concepts for ourselves and translate them to make sense in our everyday lives. It is urgent that we take the subject of the economy out of the closet! One method for achieving massive economic literacy could be through broad participatory studies from the point of view of women on the impact of public policies, and particularly of macroeconomic policies on their lives. These studies would provide evidence that would inform our analyses and proposals and strengthen our efforts to bring about change.

In order to mobilize women's movements around economic issues and not limit ourselves to the often narrow confines of social, health and education policy, we must share the design and results of these kinds of evaluations with women at the local, national, regional and global levels and think together about possible alternatives. We must learn to understand and manage public budgets. And we must defend our rights by pressing for the adequate assignment of resources and funds to meet our needs.

The same old challenge within feminist movements: monotonous similarity versus infinite diversity

Beginning with the feminist debates in the 1970s of equality versus difference, we have for years now been discussing diversity and intersectionality. We have made and continue to make numerous attempts to deal both theoretically and politically with the multiple oppressions that we live as women. The feminist reflections that were shared during the World Conference against Racism, Racial Discrimination, Xenophobia and Related Intolerance are just one recent example of such discussions. However, we continue to be entangled in internal debates at both local and global levels: How can we understand the diversity that exists among us? How can we understand the existing relationships – the intersectionality – among these different oppressions in each of our own individual identities? How can we avoid fragmentation without resorting to homogenization of the movement? We face a theoretical, methodological and organizational problem that remains unresolved.

It is interesting that many of us feel that we do not know how to incorporate this intersectional perspective into our work. When we talk with male leaders of other social movements and organizations, for example indigenous, environmental, farm-worker and union movements, we insist that they integrate a gender perspective into their work. We do not easily accept their arguments that they do not know how to do gender analysis or that they are unable to do it. As Mallika Dutt so elegantly stated at AWID's Ninth International Forum on Women's Rights and Development: 'Why is it that for us gender is the only issue of the struggle that we can understand and we accept that among us there are privileges for some and not for others, when we expect from everyone else that they incorporate a gender perspective in their struggles, whatever they may be?'[4]

Behind our profound desire to focus on what we as women have in common is the latent fantasy that we can erase the differences between us by acknowledging and recognizing them, as if naming them were sufficient to establish the desired sisterhood among us all. In this model of women as a homogenized group, identified on the basis of our status as victims of male oppression, we drift unconsciously towards this idea of a homogeneous feminism, a pure feminism that confronts gender oppression as such, even beyond other social conditions and forms of oppression. This model holds up only until other forms of oppression confront us, reclaim their right to visibility, and question this egocentric vision of feminism and of the rights of women. Then we are definitively faced with the power relations that exist among us. In order to avoid exacerbating the conflicts, to maintain this desired common identity and the possibility of fighting together for our rights, our response is to add up our multiple oppressions, never questioning the extent to which each one of us contributes every day to reproducing the oppression of others.

As Ms Dutt went on to say:

> Our power and our voice come from staging our oppressions and our discriminations. So at any given point what we use to assert that power [...] is to focus it around the ways in which we are experiencing discrimination, and that is the legitimacy that we claim in our fight for social justice and human rights. So, if I experience discrimination as a woman, but I do not experience discrimination on the basis of my class, or my religious status or my sexual preference, then what will I focus on? My discrimination on the basis of my gender as a woman. If you experience discrimination because you are a lesbian, then that is the identity which you will assert to claim power.
>
> What happens when discrimination and oppression become the cornerstones on which we assert power and identity? What happens when we come together only as victims and as oppressed people? What happens is that our ability to then connect our oppressions lessens because we all become focused on our little piece of the oppression puzzle. So I will do my work on lesbian rights and women of color in New York City and you will do work on HIV/AIDS with women in South Africa, and you will work on trade liberalization policies and their effects in Nicaragua [...] and the list will go on.
>
> We have to understand that [...] we have to come together around asserting power differently. We have to not just be against something, we have to be for something. And being for something means understanding human rights not just as a system of understanding violations but as a culture that we can build [...] a human rights culture that we can work towards that defines the economic structures we create, the political structures we create, the familial structures we create, [and] the religious and spiritual structures that we create.[5]

This necessary reconceptualization of our commitment to women's human rights has both organizational and political repercussions. The growth of feminist movements themselves and the process of diversification inside the movement causes us to confront, both at the national and global levels, one of the most common contradictions that is at the same time one of the most destructive for social movements. On the one hand, this contradiction involves the desire to respect the diversity of specific interests, objectives, strategies and leaderships, with the concurrent risk of fragmentation and of not achieving the kind of swift consensus necessary for an effective response to challenges. On the other hand, it is the temptation to homogenize organizations, by concentrating on one or just a few common objectives with the concurrent risk of not seeing the larger picture or having a perspective on more general problems. This often happens in thematic networks, or by reducing the number and diversity of group members in order to function in a more cohesive and effective fashion due to the greater ideological and political affinity among members, which happens in women's organizations with closed or specific criteria for membership.

The effects of these internal contradictions can be devastating. First, the time and energy invested in resolving these organizational and strategic differences detracts from the work of the movement to effect change. Then, a certain number of people, who generally identify with the feminist movements or consider themselves members of them, can lose patience and simply leave due to what they consider ridiculous confrontations or personal power plays. This has been particularly true in certain parts of the world among young women. Second, these kinds of tensions make it increasingly difficult to maintain a sense of a common cause, making alliances for the sake of shared objectives difficult, if not impossible to achieve. Finally, the image of internal division that feminist movements project robs them of credibility, permitting their opponents to question the legitimacy of their representatives and putting them in a situation of disadvantage *vis-à-vis* other social actors, the state and international institutions.

A first step in resolving this dilemma is to recognize and accept that the diversity of social conditions and ideological and political positions within the feminist movements, from the most moderate to the most radical, constitutes a challenge to organizational structure and internal management. At the same time, this diversity is functional for the kind of changes we want to bring about and therefore must be encouraged and nurtured rather than considered as contributing to division and separation. We will also have to recognize explicitly the power relations and discrimination that exist between women due to diverse social conditions, including age, skin colour, sexual preference or orientation, health, social class, nationality, ethnic origin, language and religion, among others. There is an urgent necessity to counteract such discrimination not only within feminist movements, but also throughout society.

Renouncing our privileges, overcoming our prejudices, unlearning discriminatory attitudes and behaviours, relearning empathy, building solidarity, developing our ability to listen, and establishing true alliances with other women as well as with men are the biggest and most urgent challenges of these times. Resolving the dilemma of monotonous similarity versus infinite diversity will define our success, or failure, in confronting the challenges we face in this globalized world.

Some conclusions ...

Beyond the diverse emerging trends associated with globalization, there are certain experiences common to all women despite the infinite diversity of their particular situations. Because of advances in the areas of gender violence and sexual and reproductive rights in some parts of the world, we might be tempted to focus on issues of globalization and relax our vigilance on these subjects. However, if we look closely, we will find that these subjects continue to be tremendously pertinent and completely interrelated.

In recent years, the subjects of relative poverty, where women are generally poorer and more vulnerable than men in the same social status and situation, and of neoliberal macroeconomic policies have been relegated in large part by feminist movements to the academic world, development assistance agencies, professional associations and unions and some specialized networks. Women in these groups have achieved significant advances towards a feminist analysis of the economy yet they have not been able to convince the rest of the feminist movement of the importance of economics or our ability to take it on as one of our central issues. The growing influence of neoliberal macroeconomic policies as public policy obliges all of us to reconsider our priorities and presents to us the challenge of tackling this traditionally masculine subject. It also obliges us to continue developing, perhaps with more dedication and urgency, better skills for negotiation and advocacy in civil society arenas that are focusing on working towards a more just and equitable world, including the fair trade movement, struggles for land access and ownership, the struggle of sweatshop and *maquila* workers, and others. In fact, the battle against poverty should not be conceived as a purely economic one, but as part of a wider ideological struggle. Eradicating poverty has to do with working for a life with dignity and well-being, and with the same rights for everyone.

... and proposals for strategies

In light of the discussion thus far in this chapter, the methods or strategies are all that remain to be clarified. To this end, I would like to make four very concrete proposals. The first is to demystify the subject of the economy and to appropriate it for ourselves, mobilizing women around the issue of economic rights. One way to move forward with this is to involve women in their own communities and municipalities in exercises evaluating the impact on their own lives of macroeconomic polities that are being implemented by their governments. Consider the example of the participatory social audit. Following Hurricane Mitch in Nicaragua, a social audit was carried out involving a number of Nicaraguan grassroots civil society organizations. They were involved in the design of a survey and the analysis of the results, reflecting on the relationship between the actions of their central and local governments and their own daily lives and personal aspirations.[6] On the basis of the perceptions of the so-called 'beneficiaries', the Civil Coordinator, a coalition of Nicaraguan NGO networks and social movements, has been able to develop concrete proposals to modify these policies and has exerted strong pressure on both national and local authorities as well as on international development aid agencies. A similar methodology could be applied focusing specifically on women. It could generate among grassroots women's groups a new sense of ownership and knowledge about economic policies, as well as a critical vision about how poverty is currently being conceptualized by institutions such as the World Bank and the governments of industrialized countries. It could also generate a new sense of economic rights among the surveyed women, and the possibility of subsequent mobilizing in order to demand economic rights.

My second proposal is related to the need to reinforce or influence public opinion, particularly among women and young people. We know how important it is to influence public opinion through the media, and we also know how difficult it has been to influence the large commercial media: television, radio and the press. While we should always look to increase our presence in these media, at the same time we should drastically increase the number of radio and television programmes as well as print media produced by feminists and under our own editorial control. We need to move up to the next stage of influence. I propose that we multiply the type of 'edutainment' initiatives that I have described above. They have been successfully implemented by several feminist organizations in different parts of the world in order to share their visions with a broad-based audience. Films, radio programmes, TV soap operas, music videos and magazines may be able to reach thousands or even millions of people. We can also use these products in order to deepen the work of consciousness-raising in the workshops and campaigns that thousands of grassroots feminist organizations conduct throughout the world.

A third proposal is to change the rules of the game in the public sphere through concrete actions. In recent decades, we as feminists have demonstrated our tremendous capacity to found organizations by creating thousands of institutions all over the world to struggle for our rights. However, many times we have done this in women-only spaces, in reaction to our frustration at the lack of receptivity and disposition of men really to take women's situations and opinions into account within mixed organizations. I propose that we put our creative capacities into top gear and we take it upon ourselves to create and lead new mixed organizations of all types, and even political parties with the firm position of changing the rules of the game.

What would this mean? It means creating institutions that are firmly rooted in the core principles and values of respect and appreciation for diversity and differences. It means establishing from the beginning policies, norms and procedures according to those values and systematically monitoring their application in the daily life of the institution. It implies that wholly accepting these values is a *sine qua non* criterion for selecting candidates for leadership positions in these institutions and a central reference point for membership. This is not an easy task. Inside each and every one of us exist prejudices and discriminatory attitudes towards people who are different from ourselves. We can be more or less sensitive to one or another situation, but we all have to be open to listening to how the people in our organization who belong to minority or marginalized social groups feel. We need mechanisms that facilitate the regular exercise of active listening. In various parts of the world, there are experiments of this type.[7] It could be useful to gather these experiences, find out the lessons learned along the way and disseminate them so that we can multiply these kinds of initiatives in each country and in each region.

My final proposal has to do with the sustainability and autonomy of feminist movements in each region and globally. I have not yet talked about this; however, it is clearly an issue that is affecting our movements in many regions of the world. Over the last two decades, for the sake of mobilizing new resources for the work of our movements, we have tended to institutionalize ourselves and to find our sources of funding in state or municipal subsidies or, in the case of developing countries, in international cooperation aid. This strategy has borne fruit and at first we were able to create solid institutions that have been fundamental to the development of our movements. Thanks to pressure from feminists in the South as well as the North, we have been able to put the subject of domination and power relations between men and women into public debate and make visible the importance of a gender perspective in public policies and international cooperation policies.

However, after a period of notable growth, we are seeing a tendency towards the shrinkage and even disappearance of organizations and programmes dedicated to strengthening women's movements as agents of change and social actors. Funds for these objectives have little by little been diverted to helping the victims of natural disasters and emergency situations, or have been dedicated to the delivery of direct services. The requirements of development funding are becoming more demanding and the agendas they support are getting further away from our own strategic needs. It is urgent that we return to generating analysis and debate about these trends and that we exert political pressure to reverse them, or at least stop them from intensifying.

At the same time, it is necessary to analyse the feminist institutions that we have created. We may need to intensify and accelerate the search for alternative sources of funding for our activities, and further explore solidarity among women and the possibility of better sharing of our resources. Among other initiatives, the women's funds that are being created in different parts of the world, even though the majority are still small and recently formed, are one answer to this search for more economic autonomy for feminist groups and organizations.

Building from these four strategies, using the lessons of the past and facing the challenges of the future, we can have a strong and diverse feminist movement. We can find unity in our diversity and bring together the local and the global.

Notes

1 United Nations (2001) *World Population Prospects, the 2000 Revision Highlights* (Population Division, Department of Economic and Social Affairs).

2 See State of World Population (2001) *United Nations Population Fund Report* (UNFPA).

3 See A. Singh (2000) *Global Economic Trends and Social Development* (UNRISD).

4 M. Dutt (2002) 'Human Rights for All: Understanding and Applying "Intersectionality" to Confront Globalization', Plenary presentation, AWID's IX International Forum, Guadalajara, Mexico, 3–6 October 2002. <http://www.awid.org/forum/plenaries/day3mallika.html>

5 Ibid.

6 See CIET-CCER (2001) *The Voice of Poor Households about Poverty Reduction: Social Audit Phase 3 – Monitoring and Evaluation of Community-based Indicators*, Civil Coordinator (CCER) (Managua, Nicaragua: Editronic, SA).

7 For a concrete example of an institution created with these intentions, see T. Hernández and V. Campanile (2000) 'Feminism at Work: A Case Study of Transforming Power Relations in Everyday Life, in Puntos de Encuentro', in *Institutionalizing Gender Equality: Commitment, Policy and Practice. A Global Source Book* (Netherlands and Oxfam-GB: Royal Tropical Institute).

9 | Confronting globalization: feminist political spirituality as a strategy of action

ALDA FACIO

I originally developed the ideas presented in this chapter in December 2002 at the time of the IX Encuentro Feminista latinoamericano y del Caribe – Resistencia activa frente a la globalización neoliberal.[1] At that time, neoliberal globalization was my worst nightmare. In the months that followed, however, the globalization nightmare appeared to me as a mere disagreeable dream in comparison with the aggression that the United States and its allies promised us.

I clung to the hope that the people of the allied countries would come to understand that the war they were being made to believe would protect them against terrorism would in fact give rise only to more insecurity and violence. I hoped that they would manage to convince their leaders of the futility and horror of 'pre-emptive wars' and that this military phase of globalization would quickly come to an end. For this reason, I have written this chapter as if my worst nightmare continued to be capitalistic globalization in its neoliberal incarnation.

In other words, I have decided to focus on the problem of neoliberal globalization and what I think the feminist movements could do to resist it. At the time I began, the immoral and illicit war against Iraq had not yet begun. More importantly, I decided to focus on neoliberal globalization because it is my understanding that the mind-set that created it is the same that makes people think that it is right or natural to kill millions of human beings in the name of 'national security'.

Globalization and its impact on women

Globalization is not a new phenomenon. More than five thousand years ago the process of patriarchy was begun, and has continued with such success that today there is no question that patriarchy is global. Economic globalization is not a new process either. In the last five centuries, the economically strongest countries have imposed their way of viewing the world through trade and 'production activities' in the 'discovered and/or colonized' territories. What is more, the strategy of globalizing policies, economies, systems and beliefs, which we see so prominently today, is not new and it has not only been used for imposition and domination;

the socialist, pacifist, anti-colonial, pro-human rights, feminist and other emancipatory movements of the past centuries have also aspired to the globalization of their visions, but they have not called these dreams 'globalization'.

The neoliberal strategy of giving the name 'globalization' to the process by which they have managed to demolish national economic barriers, empowering financial institutions and transnational companies as never before, is very effective. Neoliberal ideologists have made us believe that 'financial globalization' is about the free 'exchange' of people, goods and services and constitutes progress for the benefit of humanity. They have made us believe that globalization is the technology that has made it possible and that we cannot have the best of it if at the same time we have protections against the flow of capital into or out of a poor country. Furthermore, their strategy is even more successful because they have made globalization synonymous with more freedom, progress, leisure and goods. The globalization that we are experiencing, however, which was developed at the end of the twentieth century and the beginning of the twenty-first, needs an adjective: *neoliberal globalization*. What has really been globalized is the market. In fact, the only thing that circulates freely around the world is capital. That is to say, only imperialistic financial globalization is total, while the globalization of merchandise, products or services is partial and that of people almost non-existent.

For example, every month we hear of 'wetbacks' who are left to die or are otherwise abused by 'coyotes' trying to get them into the USA or Europe. The mere existence of these coyotes is proof that there is no freedom of migration for the majority of poor people. In our region, hundreds of Colombians and Nicaraguans are denied entrance into the United States or any other country that has become a haven for migration from war, poverty or violence. And yet the free trade treaties that the USA is forcing Latin American countries to sign do not deal with the problem of migration from poverty to the USA, while insisting on the free flow of capital. In fact, financial liberalization has been the hallmark of neoliberal globalization, due mainly to the 'advice' of the international financial institutions and to the idea put forward by neoliberal economists, that there would be great benefits derived from opening up to inflows of international capital for 'developing' nations. And even though the Asian crisis[2] demonstrated the perils of the free flow of capital, the trade negotiators are still insisting on it.[3]

This neoliberal financial globalization is what I am referring to when I speak of the nightmare of globalization for women today. And although women are the poorest, the most violated and the most alienated thanks to globalization, many feminists feel that we have to 'look on the bright side' of it because we have been sold the idea that to be against globalization is to be against progress. It is time that we clearly identify this process of globalization so we understand that it does not have a bright side and it has not produced any benefits for the majority of people in the world. We must be clear that the globalization that dominates today is capitalist globalization in a neoliberal incarnation, so that if we decide to oppose or resist it, we are clear about what we are up against.

While some people identify a myriad of factors and processes implicated in globalization, we should be clear that the internet, scientific advances, social movements, environmental struggles, pacifism and feminism are not international thanks to globalization. They are internationally opposed to globalization and they are international in spite of globalization and/or before it. If there is any doubt, consider HIV/AIDS. It is because of feminist research and internet communications that today we know that this pandemic is primarily affecting women. Furthermore, it is because of technological and scientific advances that today we could end the AIDS crisis. It is thanks to globalization, however, that a few transnational companies have the power to put their avarice and greed before the possibility of ending the AIDS pandemic with impunity. *Why?* Because thanks to the globalization of neoliberal ideology, it is not considered a crime against humanity to make a lot of money at the expense of the lives of the majority by denying needed medication to those who cannot afford to pay for it.

Moreover, globalization has permitted the country with the strongest market in intangible goods, and the military force to support its dominance, to be seen as a world leader in questions unrelated to its economic and military power. The political, legal and educational systems of the United States of America are viewed as models to be emulated in spite of the fact that the current president of the United States was not elected by a majority of voters,[4] that American prisons are full of ethnic minorities, that women lack pre- and postnatal leave, and that greater access to higher education is not resulting in more women in solidarity with those who are excluded from the supposed benefits of globalization. Rather, more education is resulting in more women who enjoy the privileges offered by this system at the expense of millions of women who cannot even aspire to basic education. And even though the world is increasingly critical of the power that emanates from this centre of arrogance, pride and despotism, which has set itself up as a global policeman, few people question America's technology, science, medicine and interventions such as the Plan Colombia.[5] Few seem to realize that these products of the United States only appear to give us more leisure, liberty, health and peace.

Neoliberal globalization has not resulted in progress,[6] interdependence, equality, peace or happiness for the majority of the world's population, and even less so for women who are worse off than ever,[7] as has been proven in too many studies by academic, development, human rights and women's institutions.[8] So why is it that the feminist movement does not have a plan and consolidated strategies to combat this process called globalization, whose greatest impact has been the imposition of a necrophilic and misogynist culture on the whole world?

I believe that one answer, among many other possible answers, is that the feminist movement, or at least the one that I know best, the Latin American movement, has gone off course. It has lost its path and has become complacent with its past successes *vis-à-vis* the state. I think that our objective has been obscured because in our desire to eliminate the discrimination that we suffer as women of different ages, races, classes and abilities, we have been thinking only of the 'possible' within the state. We have stopped dreaming of new worlds. In this effort to work within the parameters of the possible, we embrace all women, independent of whether they identify with feminist thinking or not. We are so accepting of women today that you can be considered a feminist and also be on the executive board of the International Monetary Fund, the president of a neoliberal party or commander of a platoon. This is a crucial problem. I am not saying that women in those positions cannot be feminists or that they shouldn't be feminists. I am only saying that if feminism is something so diffuse and abstract that it can include an ideology such as neoliberalism which is responsible for impoverishing millions of women, maiming and killing many and making life more difficult for most, then we have a problem. And if we have a problem, we must begin to face it instead of pretending it does not exist.

Furthermore, I say that we have become complacent because while I recognize that we have achieved quite a lot, many of us act as if our successes within the existing structure are what is needed to end patriarchy. It is undeniable that in the 1980s and 1990s, this movement made incredible achievements in the public sphere. Consider, for example, the formal recognition of gender-based violence as a social problem and a violation of human rights; the repeal of almost all openly sexist laws; more women at most levels of decision-making and the creation of ministries or offices of women's affairs; the promulgation of laws and policies with a gender perspective; and the international and regional conferences that adopted platforms for action, which if implemented would end the discrimination and exploitation of women on the basis of our gender. Moreover, in the private sphere we also made some gains for some women, including more freedom of expression, greater freedom of movement, and more paths open to more women.

Despite these achievements, I insist that the movement is resting on its laurels. Why? Because it is also undeniable that gender-based violence has not only increased, but has become more sophisticated; that justice continues to be androcentric in spite of the repeal of most sexist laws and in spite of hundreds of training sessions, innovations and conventions with a gender perspective; that power continues to be masculine although it now may paint its nails; and that poverty continues to be a chicana, mulatto, black or indigenous woman, even though our enemies now use the language of diversity. So while for some women there are more freedoms today, it is also true that almost all women are prisoners of fashion, publicity, fundamentalisms, legal or illegal drugs or even of that self-same 'sexual freedom', technological 'advances', and the innumerable messages telling us we are always ill, foul-smelling, too fat, and of the wrong age, colour, hair-type and personality.

I am not saying that the deterioration or lack of progress is only due to complacency with our past successes within the women's movement. In fact, it is probably mostly due to ineffective strategies, and even more so to external forces beyond our control. But I do think there is an element of complacency when we do not see the urgent need to unite against those external forces, or to question and analyse our strategies in order to implement new ones, or, even more urgent, when we have decided that the personal is not political. Instead of re-evaluating our goals, strategies and identities, we just keep relying on those strategies *vis-à-vis* the state that were successful in the past. In my opinion, this is complacency.

For these reasons, I think that we have to (re)construct a movement capable of confronting both the old and the new challenges of neoliberal globalization. In the following paragraphs, therefore, I will outline some ideas about what kind of movement I would like to see in order to achieve feminist ideals, or at least what I consider to be feminist ideals. It goes without saying that these ideas are based on my personal opinions and feelings, and not truths written in stone. It also goes without saying that I have developed these ideas thanks to the contribution of many women, and obviously what is presented here is not meant to be exclusionary or a complete list of possibilities. On the contrary, I hope that these ideas generate much friendly debate that will help all of us create more harmonious, efficient and effective strategies.

By 'friendly debate', I mean that I am hoping that even though many women will not be in agreement with me, they will be able to say so with love, instead of accusing me of being this or the other or instead of reading my opinions as impositions. I also hope that I will be open or flexible and secure enough in my opinions to hear these disagreements in such a way that I can reformulate my ideas without feeling diminished or wronged in some way. I have seen too many meetings where a listener angrily accuses the speaker of something and the speaker becomes so defensive that nothing is achieved except the re-enforcement of patriarchy as we women continue to be each other's enemy. Essentially, I am saying that this kind of debate requires us to ask questions and respond to them from a loving heart and from an emotional space that is free of judgement or blame. This is not easy because, as women, we have been indoctrinated in distrust of each other and in the idea that women are always 'guilty' of something.

The spiritual is political

I believe that our most urgent task in creating a movement capable of confronting the onslaughts of capitalist globalization in its neoliberal incarnation is to re-create, redefine and reaffirm ourselves as feeling, thinking beings, autonomously interdependent and eternally infinite. We need to reaffirm ourselves as beings capable of thinking lovingly, living in the present without denying the past or forgetting the future, and perceiving ourselves as both unique and at the same time as part of a larger whole. This, I believe, is spirituality.

Instead of our understanding of ourselves proceeding in this spiritual direction, however, advertising by huge transnational corporations has created a globalized culture in which we need to consume and accumulate in order to fill the emptiness of our lives. We have become so alienated, fragmented and isolated from our interior selves that we look to the accumulation of objects and power to fill the emptiness that we feel. Because of this overwhelming tendency, I believe that the spiritual is very political at this particular historical moment. The spiritual is a transgressor of the demands of the market because it is about interior wholeness and the dialogue that we establish within ourselves. The spiritual is about a state of ultra-consciousness that lets us see and understand who we really are. My suggestion for global women's movements, therefore, would be actively to pursue feminist spirituality and develop a 'feminist ultra-consciousness'.

This feminist ultra-consciousness goes beyond a feminist consciousness, which is understood as a mind-set that allows us to 'see' sexism. A feminist ultra-consciousness would allow us not only to see sexism in societal structures but also how sexism operates within us and how it is linked to all other forms of oppression. It would also allow us to see the energy flowing in and out of these oppressions so that we do not reproduce this energy in our solutions. For example, the energy that flows out of gender violence towards women is misogynist and the energy that flows out of misogyny is hatred of the opposite sex. If the solution we propose for gender violence is only or mainly punishment of perpetrators, without regard or compassion for their construction as males, would this not be equivalent to 'hating men'? Are these not similar energies? Should we not try to find a solution that flows with a different energy? How about love or compassion or forgiveness? Not easy, definitely, but it is probably necessary.

When I speak of needing a feminist spirituality, I am *not* speaking about a religion as such. I am definitely *not* proposing that the creation of female religious authorities or praying to the goddess in place of a god is a political act *per se*. Of course, if people wish to do either of these things, that is their prerogative. It is not, however, the spirituality of which I am speaking when I say that the spiritual is political. Political spirituality is what allows us to re-create ourselves as interdependent and infinite beings, capable of confronting impositions from outside with a creative bravery. We need to be brave and creative because in the quest to discriminate between our conditioning and our true feelings, we will need to step into lonely and unknown lands. As I said earlier, spirituality has to do with a state of feminist ultra-consciousness that allows us to see ourselves as the women we are; but to be in touch with the women we are, we need to strip ourselves of thousands of years of indoctrination in patriarchal values and ways of understanding reality. We need to be able to identify which are our genuine feelings and which are those we have been taught to feel.

As women, we need to find this state of 'ultra-consciousness' that allows us to love intelligently as we think with our hearts, so we can undo the false dichotomies into which we have been divided by patriarchal ideology. With this new consciousness, we will be able to feel and think about the world in new ways that will lead us to imagine, dream and create alternative attitudes towards everything around us. In time, it will allow us to build lifestyles that are less consumerist, more cooperative and especially more respectful of the other beings that inhabit this planet. It will permit us to find ways of 'being our bodies' instead of treating them as objects that we inhabit.

One thing that is abundantly clear in this era of neoliberal globalization is that we need different attitudes and different values in order to resist it. We cannot continue in the disjunction of assuming 'the masculine' as our own, or presuming 'the feminine' to be superior. We have to end the masculine/feminine dichotomy and replace it with values of real inclusiveness. We need lifestyles that are less violent and misogynist; we definitely need more love, more forgiveness, more tolerance in our lives.

I believe that the fight against globalization can help us find these values that we need so badly to recover, and these new attitudes and ways of life that we need to adopt if we want to continue to exist on this planet. But we also need to remember that we are not only people within the globalized world, but also women for whom globalization is impoverishing, violating and fragmenting. We therefore cannot simply join in the fight against neoliberal globalization. We need to create a strong feminist movement that has something unique to contribute to the anti-globalization movement. The power and strength of our movement will rest in this contribution.

In order to recover and re-create the feminine on which we can base our contribution to the fight against neoliberal globalization, we should turn our eyes to the beginnings of patriarchy. We know that in prehistory, that is, before patriarchy, god was understood to be female. Understanding how the first patriarchs displaced the goddess can give us a clue as to how to recover and re-create her for our contemporary purposes. Our goal is not to adore her like a god, but to recover our love for the feminine and everything associated with it, such as caring, nurturing and giving. We know that one strategy of the patriarchs was to rend from female bodies their transcendent and spiritual meaning. As a result, the body came to be understood as devoid of all sacredness, while the soul was viewed as the repository of everything divine, spiritual and superior. The pre-patriarchal religions, however, did not make this distinction. For them the body was sacred because it was one with the spirit or soul. Female bodies, capable of giving life to other human beings, were therefore considered not only sacred, but divine. And as the body was sacred, so too was pleasure. The patriarchal religions not only took away our capacity for transcendence but also our capacity to feel pleasure without guilt.

Once again we need the spiritual to create a feminist movement that offers pleasure to women: sexual pleasure, bodily pleasure, mental pleasure, pleasure of the soul, and also pleasure in work and in activism. We do not need a feminist movement that kills us with work but a movement that dances, laughs and delights in the creation of choreographies against globalization. This is where feminist spirituality comes in. In contrast to that created by patriarchs, feminist spirituality does not deny pleasure; rather it illuminates for us the thousands of ways of enjoying each moment of consciousness, of work, of activism, of our power and especially of our bodies.

Feminist spirituality also teaches us that pleasure cannot be accumulated, reproduced, sold or possessed. Perhaps it is because pleasure is not merchandise that neoliberal globalization is not interested in it. For this reason, then, feeling pleasure and being happy can be our biggest rebellion against the dominant economic order. Why? Because a culture based on a market economy such as the one globalization has imposed on us, needs people to buy and buy and buy. And, if one is happy and content with what one has and with what one is, one buys less. Thus, it is only logical to assume that a market economy needs people who are unhappy with who they are and with what they have. The strategy is to make us feel unhappy, unworthy, dirty, sick, foul-smelling and dependent so we can buy things that will make us clean, healthy, free and independent. You only need to see any television commercial to understand this.

Furthermore, the spiritual is political because how one sees oneself and understands reality is how one behaves. If we see ourselves as the victims of men, we will behave with vengeance. If we see ourselves as superior, we will behave towards men as they have towards us. If we believe that we are only flesh without spirit, or if we believe that there is a god only outside of us, surely we will not fully feel the happiness and pain of others. But if we see ourselves as distinct expressions of the same energy and the divine, we will behave with the love and respect that this consciousness gives us. And that is political!

Consider violence against women in the domestic sphere, for example. In Latin America, the emphasis has been on criminalizing domestic violence and for many years the women's movement has dedicated most of its energy towards this. To me, this is an ineffective strategy in the long-run because it stems from the desire to punish those who harm us, which in the end is a desire for vengeance. Punishment and vengeance for domestic abusers, as with punishment and vengeance for terrorists, will only bring about more violence. We need to find strategies that come from a spiritual space that flows with compassion and understanding, even for our abusers, in order to end this violence.

So what would be a better strategy? I know that criminalizing this problem will not end it. But I do not have the answer. I do think that we have to learn really to hear what women who are victims of domestic violence want. We have to feel respect for them and understand their needs, but first of all we have to see ourselves and what we want. Do we want vengeance? Do we want punishment for the aggressors at all costs because of our own needs as victims too? I think we should question our motives and ask ourselves: are we so committed to this strategy because we really think that it will end violence, or because we are not able or willing to give time and energy to ending violence with other, more difficult and time-consuming strategies?

Towards a spiritual feminist movement against globalization

It is true that in the face of patriarchy we need public policies with a gender perspective in order to alleviate poverty and violence against women, but the current incarnation of patriarchy that is bringing us militarized and neoliberal globalization requires something more than just different strategies. In reality, the majority of our states and their governments do not have much power, nor are they capable of solving problems on their own. Moreover, globalization is not a process that has been decided on by us as citizens but rather by a few rich men disguised as the free market. National policies, therefore, are of ever decreasing importance in the free market because it is outside the reach of politics. What should our strategies be, then? Is it really through traditional politics that we will end discrimination and the exploitation of the majority of women? Furthermore, what specific challenges does globalization pose to women and how should we address them?

Personally, I am convinced that the feminist movement should not seek the same power that men have exercised; we should rather value the power that is found in the love of life, in friendship and in sisterhood. In the 1960s and 1970s, we met in consciousness-raising groups to discuss our position as women in the patriarchy and to seek the feminine that the patriarchy had made invisible and trivialized. We still need this type of mutual support and consciousness-raising. Today, we need a movement made up of thousands of women's groups ready to dream and to build the possibility of a new world, because, as the most revolutionary movement of this new millennium says, 'another world is possible'. It is around this realization, I would suggest, that we need to formulate our anti-globalization strategies.

In (re)constructing a feminist movement in the face of neoliberal globalization, a fundamental step will be to stop speaking in the abstract and to use the new feminist consciousness that I have been speaking about to give 'love', 'sisterhood' and 'friendship' substance. This implies feeling them and giving them space, not only in our everyday interpersonal relationships, but also in our public actions.

For example, in our public actions we need to continue to denounce the discrimination and violence that we as women face on a daily basis, but we also need to celebrate our life, our friendships, our history, with art festivals, with posters, concerts, poems and theatre. We need to envision a life with no discrimination and no violence. We need to create feminist Utopias that describe in detail how a society without sexism would look. And we definitely need to laugh at our own mistakes and learn from them.

Contact with our spirituality, moreover, can help us to have friendly relationships with all people without losing ourselves, which is essential in building an effective movement against globalization. Developing friendly relationships between all feminists involves changing our attitudes and believing in our own discourse. I am speaking here of treating each other as friends rather than envying, slandering, betraying, tricking and treating each other badly. I am speaking of believing in each other. Once again, with a feminist spirituality, instead of being divided by distrust and jealousy, we could reach a true understanding of what we have always said: that what is truly good for you will also be good for me.

Together, we need to construct a feminist movement made up of understanding, compassionate, sororal, loyal and respectful women. We need to recognize the different capabilities of each woman and therefore be aware that there are many kinds of leadership. We need a feminist movement willing to be an equal partner in the movement against neoliberal globalization. As a result, we need to recognize that even though we are all incredibly capable survivors of globalized patriarchy, there are some women who are more suited than others to the specific type of leadership that we will need in order to be part of this movement. This is vital: just because a woman is a leader in one specific space, it does not make her superior, or more intelligent or better than the rest of us. Within the feminist movement we all have certain leadership roles to play. It is with this type of awareness that we will be able to confront the nightmare of neoliberal globalization.

Globalization poses several distinct challenges to women, human rights and our planet in general. First, globalization is imposing one single culture throughout the world: the American Way of Life, which is spoonfed to the world through cable television and through what we eat in the shopping malls, what we wear in the streets and what we study in our schools. In response, with our new consciousness we need to create a feminist counter-culture. This requires losing the fear that others will brand us as self-referential, ineffective or antiquated idealists, *mujeristas*, *hembristas* or lesbians. We have to permit ourselves to be transgressors, without becoming malcontents who are useful to the system. We can only do this if we become a feminist movement dedicated to building and creating outside the limits that are imposed on us when we decide to be effective, by mainstreaming gender into state laws and policies.

Creating a feminist counter-culture does not mean imitating the misogynist culture that has been imposed on us by globalized patriarchy. Conceiving of another culture does not mean turning up the other face of the old, imperialistic coin. It implies the creation of arts, technologies, sciences, languages, symbols and myths from our true internal selves in connection with all other beings. This requires raising the veils that obstruct our clear vision of ourselves: veils of romanticism, Greek tragedy, patriarchal myths and ancestral guilt; veils that prohibit pleasure and that do not allow us to feel, smell, touch, see, hear or even dream about another world without patriarchal biases. Again, in order to achieve this, we need a spirituality that permits us to see ourselves as we are, without fear, without excuses and, above all, without judgements.

Creating this counter-culture will not be easy and that is why we need to work in consciousness-raising groups so we can collectively see the patriarchy's underbelly. But we must also work individually, with strategies that permit us to know ourselves and grow as human beings, such as meditation and yoga. Creating a counter-culture is difficult because it implies not believing or accepting ideas that have been held by humanity as universal truths for centuries: the nuclear family as the basic unit of society, obedience and discipline as values that make people better, guilt as god-given, good and evil as always recognizable and the body as separate from the soul or mind. We would also need to see how we have internalized the notion that erotic pleasure and violent and degrading treatment go together, that beauty is thin and young or skin-deep, and that security is more important than freedom. And all these things we would not only have to understand as half-truths or outright falsehoods, we would have to *feel* them as such in our bodies.

Decoding our feelings or even feeling them to begin with requires a sense of entitlement and bravery. But the challenge is not only to get in touch with our bodies by becoming our bodies, but also to create a context that makes this awareness possible and that validates our response. Individual feelings of anger or outrage for what has been considered 'natural' or 'god-ordered' for centuries requires a cultural legitimacy and that can only happen if we create this culture which will validate our feelings.

Of course, a feminist counter-culture would not be linear or a mono-culture, but a diversity of different options. Just as there are many feminisms, so too are there many Utopias and many feminist cultures. These different Utopias, and maybe even conflicting Utopias, may be a source of discontent in the future. But if we work on ourselves, if we create a space in and out of ourselves for friendly debate, the discontent may be minimized. Maybe in learning to create from the heart and not only from the mind we will be able to stop competing for the truth.

A second key challenge of the neoliberal incarnation of globalization is that it is substituting an economy based on production of goods for one based on speculation. To achieve an alternative vision, we need a feminist movement that places human reproduction as the central theme of all struggles for justice. In other words, in the face of a globalization whose success is based on contempt for human reproduction, of a globalization that so easily moves from overvaluing tangible goods to super-valuing intangible goods, we need a feminist movement that truly values reproduction and bases its economy both on this reproduction and the production of material goods needed for our welfare without destroying the planet. Our movement must make the other groups resisting neoliberal globalization see that it is essential that every one of us incorporate the entire gamut of issues of human reproduction, including eroticism and pleasure, but also valuing maternal thinking and nurturing as part of their vision.

As feminists aware that structural adjustment policies have impoverished even more those women who were already poor, we can not pretend that the neoliberal state can really benefit us because it supports the criminalization of some forms of gender-based violence or institutes quotas for political representation. The type of economy which the neoliberal state is creating demands that the feminist movement itself be leftist, socialist and in favour of the elimination of all privileges in order for it to be effective. We need a movement that is based on the belief that patriarchy is hateful, not only because it is based on masculine domination, but also because it promotes domination and control as ends in and of themselves. We must be a movement that opposes all forms of domination and strives to create economies and political structures based on principles of substantive equality.

When I speak of a leftist and socialist movement, I am *not* speaking of the Left or of patriarchal socialism. I am speaking of a Left that is against domination of any kind. I am speaking of a socialism that has still not been realized anywhere on this planet. If feminists have had the patience to train those who govern on 'gender' and 'gender-mainstreaming', why would we not have the same patience to convince the leftists and socialists that domination based on gender is as shameful as that based on class, race or any other category? Oppression based on sex and gender is, after all, the oldest form of domination and perhaps the most difficult to eradicate. I believe it is worth the effort to undertake this challenge because I am convinced that we can achieve much more by incorporating a gender perspective in socialism than in neoliberal policies or traditional parties. We were so successful in reconceptualizing human rights, democracy and public policies to include our needs and interests, I do not see why we would not be able to reconceptualize socialism so that it includes our desires for a society without domination or discrimination against women. More importantly, it should include the construction of a society that values the caring and nurturing of human beings more than the production of goods and far more than the accumulation of power.

Speaking of desires, I am convinced that a very powerful strategy against neoliberal globalization would be to know how to fill this internal emptiness that so many of us feel. We should ask ourselves why evangelical churches, as well as conservative and religious parties, are attracting so many women. I am not proposing that we imitate them in order to sell women more lies, as they do, or in order to create another religion imposed from outside, but in order to understand what it is that they offer to women which we do not. It could be that their success is due to the fabrication of the illusion of filling the internal emptiness that the stock exchange has left us. For this reason we need a movement that proselytizes, a movement that is willing to promote feminist ideas and practices in multiple new ways. Furthermore, we need a feminist movement that is relevant to the large majority of women.

The third element of neoliberal globalization that I would like to highlight is its tendency to fragment us even more by promoting the divisions between us and by capitalizing on our diversity. To counteract this, we need a feminist movement that does not fall into the patriarchal trap of diversity as political identity. As women we are not a homogeneous group, and neither are we as black women, lesbians, indigenous women or young women. Within the category of black women, for example, there are rich and poor women, and there are lesbians, bisexuals and heterosexuals. Similarly, in the category of lesbians there are Chinese and indigenous lesbians, there are young and old lesbians, there are lesbians from the North and from the South, lesbians who are disenfranchised and lesbians who are overprivileged. Identities are infinite and if we give them primacy we cannot defeat the patriarchy that is the root of our particular oppressions. Rather than fight over our multiple identities, we have to fight against domination, privilege and control as values that dehumanize us all.

I am *not* saying that we should not celebrate our diversity or, even worse, that it is unnecessary for us to recognize that among us there exist racism, homophobia or ageism, among other issues. We should do so, however, within the connecting framework of feminist struggle, always keeping in mind that what unites us is the fight against patriarchy in its capitalistic incarnation. If the most constant values during patriarchy's different incarnations have been misogyny, domination and control of women, then we must fight against these values both inside and outside ourselves. It is important that we also recognize that racism, homophobia and intolerance do not have a gender, sex, race, ethnicity, class or age; they live in all of us no matter how discriminated against we are. For this reason, I believe that instead of accusing each other of being racist, homophobic, ageist or classist, we should make a daily effort to eliminate privileges, whatever and wherever they are.

How do we achieve this? I believe it is by not thinking that our experience is *the* experience of women, and by writing or speaking about our ideas as just that, as ideas, not god-given truths or something to be discarded. We can speak in a way that does not exclude other women, even if it does not include them specifically. We can analyse each strategy, each proposal, and each law from the perspectives of different women so as not to reconstruct racism, ageism or other discriminations. But we must also understand that it is not easy to expel racism or other 'isms' from our lives, and therefore instead of reacting to a panel, or strategy, or action plan that has excluded certain women by accusing the organizers or planners, we can propose ways of including more women. Also, by not laughing at racist or homophobic jokes and by not recommending books or movies or art that excludes certain women or portrays them as inferior, we can reduce discrimination. More importantly, we can receive ideas, art and proposals with love instead of with distrust or judgements. By recognizing that we are all part of the system that dehumanizes some more than others and that, therefore, we are all responsible, we can all be part of the solution.

The first step

In all of my suggestions I am not speaking of abstract concepts. I am speaking of our feminist movement being made up of women who are not only of distinct physical or social conditions, but distinct in the ways in which we have internalized patriarchy and also in the ways that we have survived in it. I am speaking of a feminist movement made up of women who must change attitudes and behaviours not only in the intimacy of our internal selves but also in the public and private spheres. We must remember that our movement is about the transformation of a system that does not exist only in the public sphere, but also, where perhaps it is strongest, in our relations with ourselves. In order to obtain our objective successfully, we need to feel love and respect for others, *but we need to begin with ourselves.* We need the ability to put ourselves in each other's shoes and understand each other, to agree or disagree healthily, without treating each other cruelly. And we can do this only if our relationship with ourselves and with our interior self is loving, respectful and honest. Again, for that we need the path of spirituality.

As I have emphasized throughout this chapter, we need a movement willing bravely to confront its errors, prejudices and foolishness. We do not need a movement made up of women who will judge, accuse and bring each other down. For that reason, we need to exile the misogyny that lives in each one of us, and we will not be able to do it without the ability to see it, understand it and remove it from our lives with love and understanding. The path of feminist spirituality can help us with this since it teaches us to love or at least understand ourselves, even our 'evil side', because it allows us to see that we can learn from it. What is more, when we understand how internalized misogyny works, we have the most important key to eradicating it.

The poorly named 'anti-globalization movement' is against the existing globalization, not against a globalization of the best that humanity has invented and imagined. For this reason, they repeat the slogan, 'another world is possible' over and over. I believe that this movement needs feminism and feminists so that this other world that really is possible also includes our dreams of a world without discrimination against women, a world that values the caring and nurturing of others. Moreover, it is only with the inclusion of our desires that this other world will really be possible. But for that, we need a feminist movement strong in the recognition of its weaknesses, united in respect for its diversity, happy with the consciousness of pain and loving because we know there is a reason for it. *Is this so impossible?*

Notes

1 Ninth Latin American and Caribbean Feminist Encounter – Active Resistance to Neoliberal Globalization, Costa Rica, 1–5 December 2002.

2 The round of financial crisis that hit emerging markets, starting with Thailand in mid-1977 and spreading rapidly to other East Asian countries before also affecting Russia and Brazil, dramatically exposed the negative effects caused by volatile short-term capital flows and the grave risks and dangers that accompany financial liberalization in developing countries.

3 For information on this aspect of globalization, see, for example, O. de Rivero (2002) *The Myth of Development, the Non-viable Economies of the 21st Century* (New York City: Global Issues Series, St Martin's Press).

4 If in any one of our countries a president were elected in the same way that Bush was, Bush himself would use that as an excuse to 'liberate' us from undemocratic elections.

5 'Plan Colombia' was officially presented as a strategy designed by Colombian officials to fight drug-trafficking, achieve a peace settlement to end the decades of civil conflict, foster economic growth and strengthen the rule of law. Critics state that it was designed in the USA; that the majority of the budget is being spent on counter-insurgency weapons; that the Plan is focused on targeting guerrilla forces, the peasantry and indigenous people; and that it is resulting in widespread environmental degradation.

6 See S. Stiglitz (1998) *Globalization and Its Discontents* (New York: New Press).

7 See, for example, L. Benería (1995) 'Scholarly Controversy: Global Flows of Labor and Capital: Globalization Threatens Labor's Rights', *International Labor and Working Class History* 47 (Spring).

8 For example, a Central American Conference was held in Nicaragua in

2003, with experts from the Inter-American Bank, the UN Economic Council for Latin America, and hundreds of researchers and academics who talked about the dire conditions of women after structural adjustment programmes, in the *maquiladoras*, in the informal sector and so on. These studies can be seen at <www.gtzgenero.org.ni.confergen/>

10 | Globalization and reinventing the politics of a women's movement

VANESSA GRIFFEN

Prologue

At about the same time as I was asked to write this chapter, I was clearing my office bookshelves where materials had piled up over the years. Coming to hand was an issue of UNDP's *Choices: The Human Development Magazine*. The cover photo was of a man standing on a rooftop, looking at a sunset on the horizon. The main issue heading was 'Development the Afghan Way'. That's convenient, I thought, now I can read about what's happening in Afghanistan. Then I glanced at the date of the publication; it was January 1997.

From a pile closer to my current work I picked up *Cross the Lines*, the newsletter of the International Fellowship of Reconciliation (IFOR), Women's Peacemakers' Program. The cover story was 'Women for Peace in Afghanistan'. It was issue no. 14, November 2001/January 2002.

Back at the bookshelves, I found a black box-file stuffed with fading yellow foolscap paper. It turned out to be my notes for a talk on women and globalization for a 1997 meeting organized by the Women's Development Collective in Malaysia. I cringed to think of what I said then; we now know so much more about globalization and have years of feminist analysis and women's resistance to benefit from. To my great surprise the notes were not very different from what we would say now, other than to add a few recent events, the latest developments in significant decision-making meetings and some moderately hopeful views of recent cracks in the monolith of the globalization agenda.

In another recent newsletter were articles such as 'Iranian Women vs. Fundamentalism', 'Child Soldiers Getting Younger' and 'Sex Education Book Stirs Debates', indicating that the issues have not changed, even five, ten, fifteen and twenty years after the women's conferences and their perceived advances in human rights. The newsletter also had news of gender training sessions, new laws (progressive and regressive), protests and campaigns, as women continue to resist domination and work for social change in many areas. (I was glancing through *We!*, Isis International Manila, February 2002.)

Finally, I turned up a pamphlet featuring an older woman's face portraying anguish, her hands raised, titled 'Why are we still waiting? The struggle for women's human rights'. The publication date is 1998, Amnesty International, London. (The photo credit shows the woman is from East Timor, where some advances have been made, especially with independence in 2002.)

Admittedly, written records are limited reflections of the diversity of women's work for women's rights, gender equality and sustainable development, but sifting through a random collection of papers, newsletters, books and reports on women's individual and organizational actions on these issues was both startling and instructive.

Why a politics for the women's movement?

This house-cleaning exercise led me to ask several questions:

- What will we find in the future, browsing through the collective record of struggles for women's rights and gender equality? Will the headlines remain the same and only the dates of publication change?
- What has and has not changed in terms of women's rights, gender equality, the protection of women from violence, and in the many cultural forms of women's oppression?
- The women's movement has voiced critiques of development for decades. How have these interventions, including those specifically by women, advanced development alternatives that will sustain human needs for the vast majority, particularly for poor and marginalized women? (By the women's movement I mean the collective of women, even if they cannot be represented in a singular way – more on this below.)
- Are women in a cycle of advocacy, analysis, action, reaction, and then more action, which needs to be assessed with a view to time? That is, the time it will take to achieve desired changes using our present methods and the length of time we have used methods that have not particularly advanced women's rights or the development agenda. Are we aware of the subliminal assumptions about how change will be advanced which are evident in feminist and activist research, shared analyses, proposed actions and organizational activities? And if these assumptions were scrutinized, would steps be taken to revise feminist actions and to determine the most strategic and vital next steps by the women's movement?

Clearly, reflection on whether women's collective actions and strategies are appropriate and sufficient to meet the demands articulated in feminist economic analyses of development and their conclusions on transformative change is long overdue. We also need to reflect on whether the present politics and actions of the women's movement are appropriate and sufficient to address the persistence of women's daily oppression across cultures. Core social institutions do not change despite advances internationally in women's rights language and so-called international commitments to change women's status. Finally, we need to consider whether our focus of attention on the continuing struggles for women's rights and secure, sustainable and equitable development will carry forward across generations. Women of all ages need to have a clear sense of what the international women's movement is about, that is, resistance to patriarchy and to unequal development which is impoverishing so many people in so many countries and depleting the earth's resources.

We also need to wonder where women's rights and the global social condition will be many years hence, even five years hence, if the women's movement continues to act without pausing for a critical review of the political intent, likely impact and direction of its actions, issues and strategies. This assessment is required not only for achieving advances in women's rights and status, and for achieving equitable and sustainable development, but also for making the best use of our energies and resources so that we act as a powerful social movement in these critical times of political insecurity, global economic inequalities and the continued subordination of women. This chapter takes the first step in this critical assessment.

I should add that I come from many places in answering these questions on emerging trends, future developments and how the women's movement can be more proactive. In reviewing past and present struggles for women's rights and the role and achievement of the women's movement, the issues that first emerge for me are based on place and time. I come from the South Pacific and have been working for seven years in an Asia Pacific gender and development programme. My reflections are based on my own ageing and more than twenty-five years advocating women's rights and Pacific people's rights. I am also influenced by a disciplinary bias, that is, I have a certain discontent with the predominantly economic analysis of development and globalization put forward by the women's movement and the lack of a concomitant body of work that is explicit in political theorizing for and about women's efforts to bring about transformative economic and social change. This background influences how I see the women's movement's work, priority issues, and how we need to improve the ways in which we move forward collectively.

In this chapter, I will explore emerging trends and future developments that affect, or will affect, the rights of women. In the next section I will highlight key areas where work will have to be done in order for us to have more impact. These areas are in fact lacunae in the international and national women's movements' feminist analyses and therefore require assessment and strategic action in order that we more effectively achieve gender equality and economic and social security in the broadest sense, at the global, regional and national levels. In addressing these issues, the chapter raises the following issues: gaps in feminist analyses or action, such as security and defence policy, and challenging the global media, the politics of 'gender' and women's rights struggles and a re-emphasis on patriarchal institutions. In the third section I will consider whether we can create an 'international women's movement' and how we can improve our mobilizing and organizing efforts. In conclusion, I offer my suggestions on critical issues for going forward as a movement.

Issues where we need to refocus

Challenging security and defence policies: the need for feminist analysis and attention The impact of globalization on inequality within and between states, and on increasing poverty among economically powerless groups, including women, has been a preoccupation of the women's movement for some time. At local, national, regional and international levels, feminists, women's organizations and networks have spent many years analysing, anticipating and reporting on the impact of globalization on women's lives. Their main concern is the economic and social implications of the free trade agenda on disadvantaged groups and countries. At the international level, women have participated in meetings and joined with other movements in protest against the gender, social, economic and political impacts of globalization. This focus on economic policies and structures, and their impact on women's lives and livelihoods, is a continuation of the feminist economic analyses of development that have been critiquing macroeconomic and structural adjustment policies since the 1980s. At the same time, women's groups at the local, national and occasionally the regional level are primarily focusing on economic structures and policies, which they see as central to the subordinate and worsening conditions of women and marginalized peoples. In many countries, women and non-governmental organizations are also focusing on and responding to local experiences of gender inequality and discrimination and human rights and development issues. These 'on-the-ground' responses by women at the local and national level reflect the hardest struggles for women's rights, gender equality and economic rights and encompass a range of activities, including involvement in local, broad-based men's and women's struggles for the rights and livelihoods of workers, migrants, farmers, peasants and minorities.

While the economics of globalization and its predicted negative social impact have been high on the feminist agenda in the last few years, feminist analysis of trends in international relations, security and defence policies is extremely limited. Issues of global governance and trends in international geopolitical development are incorporated in feminist analyses of globalization but mostly in very general terms. There have been regional and international feminist analyses of the state and globalization, political structures, changes in the power of states in the international arena, and governance issues and representation of women in formal politics. The women's movement, however, has not taken a strong stand on issues of security and defence internationally or nationally, except in specific areas where women seek human rights redress or are pressing to participate in decision-making in specific areas such as peace-building. What is lacking are feminist assertions on defence and security issues and on women's rights to equal participation in decision-making with respect to the state's use of force to settle disputes or to gain or protect economic or political interests. As citizens, women have been relatively silent and accepting of male power to control the state's use of force and determine national, regional and international security and defence arrangements.

Consider, for example, the 11 September incident and the United States' unilateral responses in the name of controlling terrorism. These actions rapidly exposed the declining power of the UN Security Council to exert international control over the United States as a superpower. The rapid international acceptance of the United States' military responses to terrorism on its territory quickly led to ill-defined statements in simple and prejudicial terms with respect to terrorism and threats to 'global security' that have been echoed and continue to be broadcast by the multinational media. The international support for US policy has had repercussions worldwide that are still being played out. In the Asia region, for example, in addition to the US bombardment of Afghanistan, US military support was offered to the Philippines in order to 'fight terrorism'. Global security scenarios have taken a new turn with the fears of nuclear weapons being used in the conflict between Pakistan and India and in the continued focus on quelling Iraq. In all of these developments, feminists and women's organizations have had generally very little to say and have not taken leadership in clarifying the real threats to security in the midst of the racism and human rights abuses against perceived 'enemies' of the United States. This task has fallen on other analysts and human rights advocates, mainly of the objectified enemy group – Middle Easterners and Muslims. The escalation in military responses to terrorism has provided a climate for the United States to have a free hand as a superpower, to adopt military solutions and to offer assistance to other nations in order that they, too, see the world in terms of 'one enemy' – the terrorist. Human rights and non-military concepts of security and women's rights need to be protected through popular resistance to this disturbing precedent which is being accepted by other states as if their own, while the United Nations seems unable to use its powers to curb this view. Women have been largely invisible and their voices not raised strongly enough to question the new international politics except perhaps to note the human rights violations and ethnic prejudices the 'war on terrorism' has unleashed. This response by feminists, however, is inadequate and does not raise sufficient concern by women about the developmental, security, peace or human rights issues that are emerging.

This gap is not just related to the specific repercussions of 11 September. Feminist political analysis of international relations, security and defence is absent from highly sophisticated and insightful feminist analyses of economic development, power imbalances and their implications. The trend of leading feminist analysts to focus on economic developments as the key to women's rights ignores the implications of military power, decision-making,.expenditure and philosophies on human security and development. In the Asia Pacific region, for example, among the many brilliant non-governmental organizations (NGOs) and feminist analysts, political analysis and information-sharing on military/defence developments, spending or new defence technologies are virtually non-existent. Women in many regions remain ignorant of political/military/defence decisions affecting their countries.

Women and armed conflict, as opposed to militarization, is a separate issue that has been raised more prominently in the last few years by such agencies as UNIFEM and the office of the UN Special Rapporteur on Violence Against Women. Some women's organizations have in fact consistently raised women and armed conflict as an issue internationally and regionally, with a focus on violence against women in armed conflicts. Militarization, however, has been viewed as an 'add-on' reference in feminist analyses of globalization. State use of violence as a corollary of the capitalist system for maintaining class interests and the military's role in human rights violations in many countries have long been recognized.

Feminist political analyses of the state must include a specific examination of how, where and in what manner international and national institutions of security and defence are prepared to act and of how to respond to state decisions to use military force to defend economic or political interests. Women must pay close attention to the political, economic and security implications of the military and defence situation in their countries and regions. Globally, there is a need to make military/defence/security developments part of the feminist agenda for change if the women's movement is really about social transformation as it asserts. There exists a pressing need for feminists to demand democratization, transparency and accountability in security decision-making. Furthermore, feminists need to work to redefine notions of security from a feminist perspective and to turn back the use of force by states.

The global media, new information technologies and global misogyny The power of the media to define, mislead and to provide ideological support for domination by groups, states and institutions remains unchanged. The media are able wittingly or unwittingly to advance, legitimize and sustain certain nationalistic, fundamentalist and political agendas that dangerously escalate ethnic prejudices and unthinking public support for state violence and for the suppression of certain groups while forwarding the interests of the powerful. It also contributes to gender stereotypes and negative portrayals of women and girls.

Feminist analyses and efforts to counter the powerful influence of the media, however, are no longer prominent. As a strategy of resistance, feminists no longer counter the media in any high-profile, hard-hitting way. Women, despite their widespread use of the new technologies for their own communications, have not continued to address the 'old-fashioned' issues of gender stereotypes in the media and advertising. Feminist activism on these issues has declined just when the new information technologies, such as the internet, allow unbelievably broad dissemination of the most vile and violent portrayals of women, girls and children. The influence of the media has been treated as a 'been there, done that since the 1970s' issue, to the detriment of young women's conscientization in particular. The pop culture of MTV, for example, is prolific in its perpetuation and dissemination worldwide with no one challenging its imagery or messages, except for the occasional snide remark by an adult critic. Meanwhile, the impact of the global media's portrayals on young men's, women's and children's perceptions of male–female relations and sexuality is incalculable. Feminist analysis of the media needs to be reiterated, not reinvented. Responses to the global media and internet information have to be given priority as the focus of feminist human rights monitoring, critiques and active public resistance. Concerns about censorship, freedom of information and freedom of expression have to be tackled and clarified by feminists in order for the movement to continue responding to the ideological influence of the media on perceptions of women and women's rights.

Finally, we should consider a strategy for the use of the new ICTs to convey women's alternative analysis and information in a concerted way.

Women have not yet used new media, communications technologies, graphic design and public relations methods to counter the daily onslaught of negative media images that are detrimental to women, especially young women. A major priority for the women's movement should be to provide young women and young men with understandings of patriarchy, gender roles and feminism, and to counter negative representations of women in the media which range from sadistically violent to belittling and superficial. The power of the media is undiminished, so while women use new ICTs to communicate among themselves, they must simultaneously develop a strategy to address problems with the media. The use of ICTs to perpetuate gender inequality messages, abuse of women and negative portrayals of women and girls must be considered a feminist issue in this globalized world.

Gender and feminist struggles The shift from tackling women's oppression under patriarchy through feminism, to a focus on gender equality as a development issue, such as gender mainstreaming and gender sensitivity, has been a cause of concern for some feminists because it has depoliticized the struggle for women's rights. Others argue that gender mainstreaming merely returns to the WID approach of 'add women and stir'. By focusing on gender concepts of equality, some perceive a move away from women's resistance to patriarchy and away from feminist concepts of transformation of social institutions to ensure women's rights and empowerment.

The recognition of women's rights and gender issues now reflected in activities for gender-sensitive policies, programmes, projects, research, data collection, services and training sessions, has developed rapidly and gained prominence in governmental institutions, non-governmental organizations and development agencies. Some feminists would argue that these advances and the acceptance of the existence of gender inequalities are outcomes of women's advocacy for gender sensitivity and women's rights in the last decades. For example, in many government institutions, efforts are now made to 'operationalize a gender perspective' into all areas of work, boosted by the UN World Conferences on Women and, more recently, the Beijing Platform for Action.

Governments and development agencies have made commitments to advance gender equality and eliminate discrimination against women. To meet these goals they have undertaken such initiatives as gender analyses, gender mainstreaming, gender budgeting and data collection, and the creation of national machineries for women and gender focal points. Indeed, 'gender work' has many variants and has moved from the early focus in the 1980s on gender planning and removing gender bias in government policies and programmes, to many initiatives to raise awareness of and address the causes and consequences of gender inequality in development outcomes.

This gender equity work, however, has been criticized by some feminists for its ability to co-opt and depoliticize the work of the women's movement. The popularity (and funding) of gender equity concepts has changed the projects and activities of the women's movement, including a new focus on gender research, gender training, advocacy and gender analyses. And while gender equality programmes and analyses can be advanced and progressive, many are superficial and misconstrued concepts of gender. Rather than making an either/or judgement of the shift to 'gender', a new question should be posed: what are the impacts and effects of gender work? If it is perceived as the 'non-feminist' approach to women's rights, an even-handed evaluation of its gains and limitations could be useful and critical.

Centring fundamental feminist principles is one means of ensuring that gender work stays focused on feminist objectives. For example, the APDC regional meetings on gender training concluded that the feminist agenda of social transformation needs to be reiterated and clearly identified in all work for gender equality, including gender training. This way, 'gender work' would be feminist and transformative. Gender work cannot be a technical fix or shortcut to gender equality and it does not evade identifying the central oppressions of women under patriarchy.

Re-evaluating progress in transforming patriarchy: from women's experiences (rather than from UN agreements) One of the greatest influences on women's lives and rights is a basic constant: the strength of patriarchy in all its many forms. Patriarchal institutions and attitudes are powerful and unchanged in their negative impacts upon women across cultures and regions. Simply by glancing at the Asia Pacific region's women's newsletters and information, for example, one is confronted with women sharing their experiences of the many instances of patriarchy and oppression of women in countries, in homes, and in specific local cultural situations.

Concerned feminist activists, especially in the South, have raised the serious threats posed to women by religious fundamentalism and cultural practices. I recall from my twenties that the most difficult first act of feminism for a few of us in a small Pacific regional university was to raise the specifics of culture and women's unequal position, presented by women writers from the two main ethnic groups in Fiji. While I raised the issues of socialization and gender roles generally, friends who raised issues of being an Indo-Fijian or Fijian woman caused outrage. To identify patriarchy in specific national and cultural contexts was truly threatening and a challenge to the status quo. In fact, the most radical feminist words and challenge to patriarchy that I recall from the Pacific more than twenty years ago were uttered by a Cook Islands' woman of middle age at a regional NGO meeting organized by mostly young women for the first UN World Conference on Women in 1975: 'Women clean the pulpit in the church but we cannot speak from it.' I have not heard that challenge again in the Pacific, ever. In the intervening years, Pacific regional meetings moved to focus on preparations for the UN world conferences and women's NGOs have proliferated. We have never come back, however, to raising those fundamental questions and that core understanding by women shared by women across generations of the nature of women's subordination and its relation to patriarchal institutions.

It seems that in sophisticated feminist and gender analyses and choices for action today, the basic foundations of patriarchy and their current impact on women have been taken as given – but at what cost? Violence against women has emerged as a key issue and has been given widespread support at many levels, thanks to women's strategies on violence as a human rights issue internationally, regionally and nationally. At the same time, however, at the personal, local and national levels, too many institutional forms and reinforcements of patriarchy exist that daily cause the death, injury or control of women collectively or individually. These conditions have not been dented at all by gains in international agreements or commitments or by perceived successes in gender mainstreaming. How do we address this disjunction between international gains and lack of progress for women in so many aspects of their lives?

Some issues, such as the influence of the media and information, education and schooling, religious fundamentalism (of many religions), and cultural beliefs and practices, are perennial patriarchal influences that have a daily impact on the lives of women and girls and continue to reinforce male dominance and women's subordination. While the intersectionality of issues and identities affecting women's lives has gained prominence in feminist discourse, particularly before and after the World Conference against Racism, it is not clear that this intellectual acceptance has been borne out in women's action and strategies at all levels. This raises the question, are international actions the main arena for raising these women's rights issues and seeking transformation? Would it be more helpful and a more powerful form of action for the women's movement internationally to support regional and national level struggles, particularly for the most marginalized and powerless women? This solidarity is happening now, using the new information technologies and networking on specific issues, but other global support could be planned and more powerfully executed.

At present, there is a tendency to regard uncritically international agreements and commitments to women's rights or gender equality made at the United Nations world conferences as gains for the women's movement. Conceptual advances, such as recognition of women's rights as human rights, reproductive health and rights, or rape as a war crime, are gains in changing international mind-sets or laws and do push the women's rights agenda forwards. However, only a few of us are able to revel in, learn from and enjoy the increasing international and national recognition of women's rights in human rights and development by these means. We must still be aware of the rhetoric and public recognition of women's rights that is not borne out in the everyday lives of women. Advances at the international level may represent an 'emperor has no clothes factor'. I say this as I believe there is a growing disjunction between what is most widely accepted as progress for women's rights by NGOs and what continues to exist in reality for the majority of the world's women – unchanging patriarchal oppression and widespread poverty. In most societies the less powerful women, and even women with economic means, are no more protected by international women's rights agreements now than they were twenty years ago.

We need instead to examine how perceived gains and advances in agreements, legislation or 'Women's Desks' stand up against what women are experiencing in their everyday lives. Measuring gains in women's lives is not to belittle or dismiss the struggles internationally by women to advance concepts of women's human rights or gender equality; rather this evaluation of the real changes in women's social lives at national and local level is essential in considering future developments in the women's movement.

Furthermore, what have been perceived as gains for women at the international level have to be assessed against the value of feminists' very limited time, energies and resources. At the five-year reviews of the major UN conferences of the last decade, including Rio, Cairo and Beijing, it has been very clear that the Platforms for Action or Charters are not being implemented and governments continue reneging on the necessary political will to fulfil them. This will continue regardless of UN reviews and women's or NGO lobbying. In the light of these results and the continuing marginalization of NGOs and women's voices, should numerous women's NGOs continue to attend most UN meetings and world conferences? Should other strategies be considered, such as sending a consolidated and organized team of skilled advocates representing the women's movement as a whole instead? It seems important that women not spend thousands of dollars attending meetings in large numbers where not much is gained.

Strategies should be evaluated with regard to the limited substance in the reports and advocacy that many women's NGO are bringing to the UN conferences. There is not a great deal of ammunition that women take to such meetings other than very general critical feminist analyses, recommendations on the development changes women want and reiteration of rights issues from a feminist and gender perspective. Our experience of the regional mobilization around the Beijing Platform for Action shows that, with few exceptions, women's groups and organizations are not interested in seriously monitoring government policies or programmes in specific national contexts. There are few alternative, hard-hitting reports by women on national women's rights and development issues presented for the implementation reviews of major UN conferences that are sufficiently detailed in analysis and critiques to counter government reports and complacency. Advocacy and separate NGO statements are also increasingly marginalized in the protracted processes of debate in the UN conference format.

Overall, the earlier rationale for women's participation in international UN and other meetings, which was to change perceptions of human rights and development, should be reconsidered now after the five- and ten-year reviews of such meetings. Monitoring government implementation of international agreements and retaining the language of past commitments while simultaneously holding back the conservative backlash against women's rights are good reasons for involvement. The trend to continue to place major emphasis, internationally and regionally, on women's participation in these UN processes, however, needs major re-evaluation.

Creating an international women's movement? How to improve our mobilizing and organizing

The urgency of the impact of poverty, globalization processes, human rights abuses, lack of democracy and accountability in governments, and the persistent myriad forms of patriarchy and its oppression of women, continue to fuel activist efforts by women. The struggle for women's rights in different arenas and social contexts has led to the proliferation of women's NGOs, to many different paths of action and advocacy for human rights and for changes in the development paradigm. Despite the inspiring and increasingly diverse forms of women's resistance internationally, regionally, nationally and locally, these many activities do not necessarily a movement make. What is meant by 'the women's movement' needs to be analysed by women, especially with respect to its role, strategies and impact on women's rights in the long term. There needs to be clarification as to whether there is a movement at all or whether the women's movement is now being equated, both externally and by feminists, with the collective of women's NGOs and networks, even if they do not act collectively or organize as a movement.

I would argue that the prolific activities by women through NGOs and networks, using the new information technologies for more rapid information-sharing, give the appearance of a movement resonating outwards, although not held together by any globally focused agenda or political strategy. The women's movement lacks a body that can coalesce women's politics and actions into a force to marshal women's power as a movement to press for the fundamental changes constantly repeated in feminist analysis, recommendations and prescriptions for social and economic transformation. At this point in time, there is a risk of the women's movement disappearing into its own many parts, each attached to its own organizational agenda. This so-called 'NGO-ization' trend has led to increased NGO competitiveness and issue-based organizing.

It is by no means clear whether women's NGOs working alone in this manner have the capacity or power to have an impact on the political arena of globalization and patriarchy, or to act on the scale required for achieving feminists' stated goals of social transformation. A question that needs to be asked then is: what are the implications for the women's movement of not acting in the manner of a movement at this critical time, which is characterized by both a concerted resistance to globalization on one hand, and clear evidence of a lack of progress for women against patriarchy on the other?

To act together with power, rather than as organizations and individuals The previous sections of this chapter highlight the timeliness of considering the reassertion of a collective identity, commitment and solidarity for the women's movement. Feminist analyses and advocacy repeatedly stress the need for transformation, empowerment, changing structures in global institutions, alternative economic frameworks and poverty reduction. All of these priorities point to the need for a structure and strategies that will use the strengths of the women's movement to achieve these ends.

Women's interests, while not singular, in many instances need to be pursued in a collective way. There are many other powerful economic and political interests that are organized and clear on their agenda. In contrast, women have achieved great successes in their sensitivity to diversity and difference and have remained reluctant to have a feminist organization as a centre for collective decision-making, political organizing and leadership. They have been reluctant to establish an organization to guide the work of the women's movement as a movement. I would argue that feminists and their organizations need to work and act as a movement to maximize women's power and bring about change worldwide. Clinging to NGO activities and identities for all purposes seems to have reached the limit of its effectiveness.

Practically, we might consider a women's international organization to address inequitable economic, social, political and gender relations, especially for assessing, strategizing and periodically evaluating international feminist advocacy and political action. Considering the demands of feminists for transformative change, and the structures and powers that oppose this change, it is politically naïve of feminists to perceive that change will come about with sporadic NGO and individual mobilization and dispersal. Feminists' fear of managing structures, hierarchy and centralization needs to be re-examined. The alternative is for the women's movement to remain a collection of loosely connected organizations, networking and acting without conscious mobilization and not using methods capable of having an impact on powerful structures. Organizing for more powerful pressure by women for women's rights, gender equality and sustainable development requires consideration of the political methods and mobilization of a women's movement and a central focal point for organizing. In this way, all of the talents and resources of the women's movement could be used in planned actions for change.

Diversity and difference have been celebrated as intrinsic to the development of the women's movement. It is an achievement of the women's movement to incorporate and connect diverse political sectors, identities and issues into the global women's agenda. Presently, the trend is to claim that diversity and difference are integral parts of the women's movement. To recognize diverse positions and interests but also be able to act in a collective, centralized way is the real challenge facing us today.

There is also an urgent need for critical political analysis of feminist assumptions about social change and how it will come about. At present there is an absence of explicit political analysis or theorizing by feminists on how the actions of the women's movement will produce changes for women in the future, economically, socially and politically. How feminists organize to play a leading role as a social movement has also not yet been explicitly analysed, although meetings and discussions of global feminist leadership have been held. The leadership and direction of the women's movement as a whole and its conscious organizing as a serious and powerful force for change need to be articulated and discussed. Furthermore, women need to articulate how they expect change to result from their actions. Making explicit women's theories of social change and what type of methods, organizing and leadership are needed should be the point of departure now for feminist political analysis and evaluation of the strategies, methods, advocacy and organizing of a women's movement.

Finally, there may need to be a reconsideration of how to perceive and use the strengths of a women's movement. Given that while women's rights have been advanced in principle at the international level, women's overall economic and human rights in many of these countries have been little affected by international commitments and ideological advances. What may be needed is to refocus on support from the international women's movement for local and specific advances for women within their own countries.

In terms of reviewing methods of struggle, organizing and building an international women's movement, it is important to turn towards learning from and incorporating the many strategies and talents in mobilization and analysis of feminists working at all levels, particularly at local and national levels. Women in specific situations have far more to offer on the fundamentals that need changing and have a surer understanding of the many interconnected powerful forces that need urgent resistance. A movement must develop which incorporates not just the women that already have a voice at international level, but also pays greater heed to participation of women in the most marginalized and oppressed positions, whose actual experience of oppression must inform feminist political strategizing and analysis.

Concluding remarks

If feminism as an ideology and feminist struggles for women's rights and equitable development are to have a chance as a social movement for transformation, the women's movement needs seriously to develop: (i) a structure; (ii) political will and commitment to collective action; and (iii) measures of providing support and solidarity as a movement to feminist struggles at all levels on diverse issues of importance to women in different social and cultural contexts. The women's movement, if it constitutes itself as such, needs particularly to consider different forms of organizing that have contributed to women's empowerment, such as cooperatives or community-based movements, to review its strategies to advance the agenda of social transformation and to acknowledge if necessary the limited political impact of some feminist interventions and strategies and change them. Organizing women's resistance to patriarchy, globalization and militarization through loose, changing NGO campaigns seems politically naïve and inadequate at this time. If the women's movement is to be more proactive, it is essential that it develops the politics, organizing commitment and solidarity of a social movement that has come a long way and still has a long way to go.

Many struggles, lessons learned, issues and advances at the national and local levels need to be part of the collective force of the women's movement. Many different methods of mobilization, organizing and leadership need to be drawn upon if the women's movement is to reinvent itself as a force to be reckoned with, which is precisely what is needed in facing the globalization agenda, militarization and patriarchy. Will feminists and women's organization leaders commit to acting as a movement in the future? Will they focus on the neglected issues of security and defence, the influence of the global media and new information technology, the politics of gender and pervasive oppressions of patriarchal institutions? It is to be hoped that, as time passes and we all grow older, we will not find, as I did when clearing my office shelves, that the headlines remain the same and nothing has changed.

References

African Information Society-Gender Working Group (1999) *Engendering ICT Policy: Guidelines for Action* (South Africa: African Information Society-Gender Working Group).

Agarwal, B. (2002) 'Are We Not Peasants Too? Land Rights and Women's Claims in India', *SEEDS*, 21: 30 (New York: Population Council).

Agencia Latinoamericana de Information and NOVIB, OXFAM (2001) 'Global Feminism, Plural Leadership', Reflections from an on-line conference on 'Challenges of feminist leadership countering racism, xenophobia and intolerance' (Netherlands: Agencia Latinoamericana de Information and NOVIB, OXFAM).

Amnesty International (1998) *Why are We Still Waiting?: The Struggle for Women's Human Rights* (London: Amnesty International).

Association for Women's Rights in Development (2001) *AWID News*, 15 (1, Winter) (Toronto: Association for Women's Rights in Development).

Bhatt, E. (1992) 'Cooperatives and Empowerment of Women', *PLN Raju Memorial Lecture 1992* (Hyderbad: Samakhya).

Center for Asia-Pacific Women in Politics (2001) *1st Asia Pacific Congress and Training of Women and Men in Media, and Women in Politics, Governance and Decision-making on Transformative Leadership* (Paranaque City: Center for Asia-Pacific Women in Politics, [APWIP]).

Development Alternatives with Women for a New Era (DAWN) (1996) 'Recommendations to the World Bank by the External Gender Consultative Group', *Keeping Informed*, 21 (November) (Sura, Fiji).

— (2002) *DAWN Informs* (March) (Sura, Fiji: Development Alternatives with Women for a New Era).

DAWN and Red de Educacion Popular Entre Mujeres de America Latina y el Caribe (REPEM) (2000) *About Women's Powers and Wisdom: Debates on Political Restructuring and Social Transformation*, English translation of the Report of the Latin American Workshop, Rio de Janeiro, October 1999 (Sura, Fiji: DAWN).

FES – Young Women Leaders Network (2001) *Young Women = New Politics, Expectations and Experiences from Asia and Europe*, Conference proceedings of the FES Regional workshop 'Young Women Leaders', Bangkok, 3–4 November 2001, ed. Gabriele Bruns (Bangkok: Friedrich-Ebert-Stiftung).

Francisco, J. S. and S. E. Marquez-Fong (eds) (2000) *Political Restructuring and Social Transformation: Feminist Critical Essays in Southeast Asia* (Suva, Fiji: DAWN).

Griffen, V. (2000) *Building Partnership for Beijing Implementation and Women's Empowerment* (Kuala Lumpur: Asian and Pacific Development Centre [APDC]).

Griffen, V. and L. Menon (eds) (1999) *Asia-Pacific Post-Beijing Implementation Monitor* (Kuala Lumpur: Asian and Pacific Development Centre [APDC]).

— (2000) *Steps Forward: Initiatives in Beijing Implementation* (Kuala Lumpur: Asian and Pacific Development Centre [APDC]).

Griffen, V. and M. M. Shivdas (eds) (1998) *Asia-Pacific Post-Beijing Implementation Monitor* (Kuala Lumpur: Asian and Pacific Development Centre [APDC]).

Hawkes, S., et al. (2002) 'Reproductive Tract Infections: Prevalence and Risk Factors in Rural Bangladesh', *Bulletin of the World Health Organization* 80 (3): 180–8.

Illo, J. and R. P. Ofreneo (eds) (1999) *Carrying the Burden of the World: Women Reflecting on the Effects of the Crisis on Women and Girls* (Quezon City: Center for Integrative and Development Studies, University of the Philippines).

Isis International (2002) 'Iranian Women vs. Fundamentalism', *We!*, 1 (February). <www.isiswomen.org/pub/we/archive/msg00062.html>

Kanlungan Centre Foundation, Inc. (2002) *TNT (Trends, News and Tidbits)*, 2 (27 November 2001–January 2002) (Quezon City: Kanlungan Centre Foundation, Inc.)

Karl, M. (ed.) (2000) *The Global Knowledge Women's Forum: Transcending the Gender Divide* (Kuala Lumpur: NCWO, UNDP; Manila: APGEN).

Kerr, J. (2001) *International Trends in Gender Equality Work*, Occasional Paper No. 1 (Toronto: Association for Women's Rights in Development).

Khan, N. (2001) 'The Women's Movement in the Future', *Papers from a Panel of the Asia-Pacific Regional NGO Symposium* (Kuala Lumpur: Asian and Pacific Development Centre [APDC]).

'Maternal Mortality – Why Women Need Not Die' (2001) *ARROW's for Change – Women's and Gender Perspectives in Health Policies and Programmes*, 7 (1), (Kuala Lumpur).

Meier, A. (1997) 'Development the Afghan Way', *Choices. The Human Development Magazine*, 6 (1): 10–16.

Mitter, S. (2001) 'Asian Women in the Digital Economy: Policies for Participation', *The Global Knowledge II Women's Forum* (Kuala Lumpur: UNDP Programme).

Mitter, S. and C. Ng (1999) 'Teleworking and Development in Malaysia, Vol. I–III, Sectoral Studies Report', UNV/INTECH Policy Research Project in partnership with MIMOS Bhd. and UNDP (Maastricht: UNV/INTECH).

Mode, P. et al. (1997) 'Summary Minutes of the Conference', Global Feminist

Leadership Development, 22–26 September 1997, Cape Town, South Africa (The Hague: NOVIB).

Mourin, J. and K. P. Nair (1999) 'Women Resist Globalization: Assert Women's Rights!' (1999) an issue forum of the 1998 Asia-Pacific People's Assembly (APPA) (Kuala Lumpur: Tenaganita).

Paidar, P. (2001) 'Gender of Democracy – The Encounter between Feminism and Reformism in Contemporary Iran', *Democracy, Governance and Human Rights Programme Paper Number 6* (Geneva: United Nations Research Institute for Social Development).

Taylor, V. (2000) *Marketisation of Governance: Critical Feminist Perspectives from the South* (Suva, Fiji: Development Alternatives with Women for a New Era [DAWN]).

'The Women's Movement in the Future' (1999) in *Papers from a Panel of the Asia-Pacific Regional NGO Symposium*, 31 August–4 September 1999. Compiled by the Asian and Pacific Development Centre (APDC) (Kuala Lumpur: GAD, Asian Pacific Development Centre [APDC]).

Thomson, S. S. (1995) 'Thai Women in Local Politics', in *Democracy in the Making* (Bangkok: Friedrich Ebert Stiftung and the Gender and Development Research Institute [GDRI]).

Thomson, S. and M. Bhongsvej (1995) *Putting Women's Concerns on the Political Agenda* (Bangkok: Gender and Development Research Institute).

'Why Women? What Politics?' (1995) *Highlights of Regional Congresses of Women in Politics* (Huairou: Global Network of Women in Politics).

Women Environment and Development Organization (2001a) *WEDO News and Views*, 14 (2) (New York: Women Environment and Development Organization).

— (2001b) *WEDO News and Views*, 14 (3) (New York: Women Environment and Development Organization).

'Women and Alternative Leadership' (2002) *In God's Image: Journal of Asian Women's Resource Centre for Culture and Theology* 21 (1, March).

Women in Politics: Voices from the Commonwealth (1999) (London: Commonwealth Secretariat, Gender Affairs Department).

'Women Struggle for Economic Survival and Women's Rights' (1999) *Gabriela Women's Update*, 9 (1), January–March, Manila, Philippines.

'Women's Movement with Everyday Life Struggles' (2000) *Asian Women*, Vol. 2 (Seoul: Research Institute of Asian Women, Sookyung University).

Yasumaru, M. (2001) 'Book Review: Comics for Young Women: Strategies for Stereotypes', *Journal of Asian Women's Studies*, 10: 150–2 (Kokurakita, Japan: Kitakyushu Forum on Asian Women [KFAW]).

11 | Caution! women moving: strategies for organizing feminist visions of the future

SISONKE MSIMANG

Prologue

As I finalized my contribution to this collection, 6 million people in 600 cities around the world were standing up against the impending war with Iraq. It therefore felt like a difficult but very important time to believe in the power of people to defend justice, peace and dignity. Even as I hoped that war would be averted, Bush, Blair and Howard – the Anglo-Saxon male triumvirate that took us into the war – refused to acknowledge the voices of 'the unwilling'. The importance of reflecting on and forging strategies for advancing women's rights therefore seemed ever clearer.

Feminist practice and women's experiences

As a feminist living and working in Africa, I am constantly in search of language that can express the complexities, the nuances and the hurt of women's experiences of poverty and inequality, without being too abstract or resorting to rhetoric. It seems increasingly difficult to find ways of speaking and writing in international fora that do not alienate women who are illiterate and who do not have academic backgrounds. In this chapter I will try to avoid the jargon and the compartmentalization that often defines the development industry and the manner in which development workers often speak and act towards women. This is my first challenge.

I take this challenge seriously because so often governments, NGOs and international institutions focus on isolated issues: economic empowerment, reproductive health, citizenship education, water and sanitation, emergency relief, HIV/AIDS or violence against women. Seldom do they recognize the interconnectedness of these issues in real women's lives. Women, therefore, become like cardboard cutouts, each part of themselves needing a different strategy, programme or action plan. In real life, issues are not so clear-cut.

I remember being twenty-two years old, living in America, and thinking I loved a man deeply. In my mind, he was like hot chocolate on Minnesota mornings, like jazz and sweat in a dark apartment on nights that seemed too cold to survive alone. I wanted to love him. I also wanted to not hurt him because I thought he had already been hurt too much, having spent a lifetime being black and male in America. And when making love turned into a fight about whether or not to use a condom, each and every time, I got tired too quickly, backed down far too easily. With each argument I liked him slightly less but could not name why; I did not yet have the tools with which to argue that his masculinity was putting me at risk. And like the woman-child that I was, my instinct was not to hate him. Despite disliking him, I loved him ever more desperately, the way one does before one is sure of who one is and what pain and betrayal feel like.

After some time I was pregnant and ashamed of myself. I was an African girl living far from home, a citizen of the Third World but elite enough to have a mother with the needed three hundred dollars in a far-away bank account. Had I not had the money, I would not have had the choice. But had I not been a woman, I would not have been pregnant, and, more importantly, I would not have been so afraid of losing his 'love'. Had I not been black, perhaps a protester wouldn't have hissed 'slut' at me under her breath. I don't know. It is hard sometimes to separate the woman from the black. This was my first lesson in the confluence of race, class and gender. There have been many more since, but none as difficult to learn.

As a young, black Third World feminist working on issues of sexual and reproductive health and rights, I am interested in looking at the points at which women's identities as sexual and reproductive beings, as Third World citizens, as brown or black people, and as poor people intersect. The intersections are not always as we would expect them to be. Sometimes they offer windows of opportunity, points where marginalization and privilege intersect. For me, the task ahead for this 'wave' of Third World feminists, of which I consider myself a part, is one of understanding how to construct power bases that are not oppressive. We must come to an understanding of how to extend the meanings of privileges so that we move beyond one's particular ability to obtain an abortion, into the realm of rights for all women, regardless of their intersecting identities.[1]

With this as my starting pointing, my challenge in this chapter was to hazard a guess at where the field of women's rights is going in light of new trends in development. More importantly, I was asked to think about strategies for achieving a gender-just world. As an African, I find it difficult these days to think about development without first thinking about the AIDS pandemic. It is equally as difficult to talk about the future of the continent without making reference to economic globalization and Africa's efforts to step out of the shadows of poverty. Women have a significant stake in ensuring that both these challenges are overcome and I therefore believe they are closely linked to future trends with respect to women's rights around the world.[2]

Moreover, neither HIV/AIDS nor globalization can be addressed without paying some attention to the state of the global women's movement and indeed women's movements all over the world. Their ability (or lack thereof) adequately to address the many challenges facing poor, working-class, disabled, lesbian, and black and brown women across the globe is likely to be tested by the complexity of both of these issues, and the many ways in which they affect women differently depending on where they are located both spatially and geographically in relation to economic, social and political sites of power.

In this chapter, therefore, I will examine globalization with a view to looking at how it threatens a range of women's rights. I will then look at HIV/AIDS, again assessing the ways in which it has already set back girls' and women's basic rights to health, employment, education and security, and what this will mean for a generation of girls who will grow up poor, motherless and unimaginably vulnerable to all types of abuse. Lastly, I will make a case for the reinvigoration of feminist organizing in the global South. I will argue that Third World feminists can equip young women and men with radical visions of futures in which gender, class, race, and sexual hierarchies are eradicated only by cultivating a commitment to honest democracy and to citizen activism.

Globalization

According to Joseph Stiglitz, globalization is 'the closer integration of the countries and peoples of the world which has been brought about by the enormous reduction of costs of transportation and communication, and the breaking down of artificial barriers to the flows of goods, services, capital, knowledge and (to a lesser extent) people across borders'.[3] Stiglitz, like many others, defines globalization as a neutral process. It seems to emanate from nowhere, but affects everyone. In his definition, globalization is seen as a force beyond human control, the next logical, almost natural stage in human development. The idea is that there are a few things wrong with it but, essentially, as John Bellamy Foster asserts, it is as though 'globalization [is a] process that is unfolding from everywhere at once with no centre and no discernible power structure'.[4]

Throughout his latest book, *Globalization and Its Discontents*, Stiglitz describes the World Bank, the International Monetary Fund (IMF) and the World Trade Organization (WTO) as regulators whose policy prescriptions have gone awry. Having once been an insider, Stiglitz is now one of the most prominent critics of the World Bank. In general, however, he has advocated reform of these institutions rather than critiquing the entire process of globalization as a phenomenon that is the manifestation of the latest stage of capitalism.

In contrast, in her most recent offering, *Fences and Windows: Dispatches from the Front Lines of the Globalization Debate*, Naomi Klein refers to globalization as 'part of the continuum of colonisation, centralisation and loss of self-determination that began more than five centuries ago'.[5] Klein's argument is convincing. She demonstrates the extent to which, in a sadly ironic race, the same states whose 'natives' were enslaved and massacred in genocides that paved the way for colonization and imperialism now compete against one another for the attentions of multinational corporations. For the citizens of these states, globalization at a local level has meant the privatization of state functions, decreased employment, decreased social spending and weaker currencies.

The wide-ranging negative impacts of globalization are now well known. For working-class and poor women in particular, globalization has translated into few new employment options. In some parts of the world, including Southeast Asia for example, many women are employed in appalling conditions in factories and in their homes. They are often discouraged from becoming unionized and offered few if any employment benefits, often at minimal pay. At the same time, governments have privatized many state functions, including healthcare, and introduced user-fees for education. Cutbacks in social spending as governments race to prove to investors and institutional lenders that they operate efficiently have made it more difficult than ever for women to feed and clothe their families.

As this account demonstrates, the net result has been a consistent chipping away of the fundamental human rights of women, ranging from education to health to employment. These setbacks are further compounded by women's increased responsibilities towards their children, families and communities. Women's rights to work and protection against employment are also under threat in poor countries such as the Dominican Republic, Jamaica and Lesotho that have established free economic zones. Furthermore, women's right to education cannot be said to exist for the millions of women over fifteen who are illiterate: two-thirds of all illiterate adults are women.[6]

In the past thirty years, feminist efforts to improve women's lives have predominantly focused on improving girls' primary education enrolment rates, teaching women how to read, enhancing access to credit, building women's capacities to run businesses, and working with clinics and hospitals to encourage women to use reproductive health information and services. Another common focus has been to get (mainly elite) women into boardrooms, courthouses, government offices and multilateral agencies. Ironically, although feminist analysis often indicates that it is the institutions within which patriarchy is embedded that need changing, our solutions have primarily helped individual women access power within these institutions. While liberal feminist approaches have succeeded in changing legal systems around the world, seldom have we managed to change institutional cultures in order to advance what Maxine Molyneux called the 'strategic gender interests' of women.[7]

Our two-pronged strategies of 'fixing' local women by inundating them with capacity-building workshops and skills on the one hand, and empowering primarily First World and middle-class women at a global level on the other, will not work for the current crisis of globalization. Globalization calls for a serious rethinking of old strategies, particularly those used by Third World feminists. Often split between our loyalties as women and our loyalties as citizens of Third World nations, it is time that we interrogate what economic development and global processes really mean for our countries.

As Gillian Hart points out in her book, *Disabling Globalization: Places of Power in Post-Apartheid South Africa*:

> The discursive power of globalisation is nowhere more evident than in ... the 'impact model,' that underpins neo-liberal agendas ... Typically framed as the impact of 'the global' on 'the local,' these discourses conjure up inexorable market and technological forces that take shape in the core of the global economy and radiate out from there ... This conflation of 'the global,' with dynamic, technological-economic forces restlessly roving the globe defines its inexorable – and inexorably masculine – character. By the same token, 'the local' appears as a passive, implicitly feminine recipient of global forces whose only option is to appear as alluring as possible. This counter-position and gendering of time and space are thus key components of discourses that naturalise neo-liberalism.[8]

For Third World feminists, whose race and citizenship interests often intersect uncomfortably with their gender and class interests, this analysis is extremely useful. In Hart's description we can see that the economic and sexual hardships that poor brown and black women have had to endure in the name of nation-building and luring global capital are part of a capitalist trajectory of class, race and gender-based exploitation.

So as states fight to make their economies look as alluring as possible to global capital, it is women whose labour is most 'sexy' precisely because it is cheap and can cross conventional boundaries, thereby evading taxes and regulation. In Thailand, the Philippines, Venezuela and Brazil for example, women and children work beyond standard working hours from their homes for starvation wages. Meanwhile, many Southeast Asian women leave their countries to care for the children of richer nations such as Kuwait, Saudi Arabia, Hong Kong and Japan. Their work conditions are unregulated, often leaving them vulnerable to sexual and physical exploitation.[9] These arrangements are representative of the class, race and gender exploitation of globalization.

As Third World feminists, we speak of the strength of local and indigenous women's struggles in fighting for equality at national and community levels, but we often think of our nations as passive in the context of globalization's inexorable march forwards. We need to begin to see the complicity of our states in violating and ignoring the rights of women and poor people in search of the elusive benefits of globalization. We cannot continue to raise our voices against only the World Bank, IMF and WTO. Nor can we continue to confront our own governments' commitments to international human rights agreements such as the Convention on the Elimination of All Forms of Discrimination Again Women without making the links to our countries' choices and actions regarding economic globalization. We cannot accept illusions of passivity in the face of globalization on the part of states.

Activists have begun to question the power of multinational corporations and international institutions that operate at the global level. There remains much to be done, however, to understand the fundamentally conservative connections neoliberals make between Third World patriotism, 'short-term economic hardships' and the inevitability of globalization in its current form. As feminists, we must deepen our analyses.

In order to mobilize for the rights of women, I would argue that Third World feminists (many of whom are elites themselves) must be committed to fight for national and local economic development in ways that do not rely on the exploitation of the labour of poor and working-class women. As we devise ways through which to engage with global and local economies and to support the rights of communities to earn decent incomes, it is critical that we do not endorse programmes that are dependent on the gendered and racialized processes whereby capital is seen as dynamic while poor people are seen only as passive consumers and/or cheap labour.

While we can tinker with and alter the rules by which multilateral agencies regulate the global economy, we must be clear that the global economic system itself is the real problem. The collapse of communism has made it increasingly difficult to imagine societies in which healthcare, education, housing and employment are guaranteed. Without a vision of a different kind of world, however, it is impossible even speak to realistically about human rights and women's rights. As feminists, we must develop this vision in order to build appropriate strategies with respect to globalization.

HIV/AIDS

Today it is clear that HIV/AIDS is an issue of poverty and of gender inequality, but we must additionally be aware that it is also profoundly connected to processes of globalization at a number of levels. HIV thrives in environments of inequality, for example. As a result, the combination of traditionally polygamous communities and exploitative labour practices in Sub-Saharan Africa over the last century has created a perfect breeding ground for the spread of HIV/AIDS in the region. By the time the virus appeared in Southern Africa in the 1980s, extensive rail and road networks facilitated its travel with miners going to visit their families. Homegrown patriarchy made it difficult for women to refuse sex with men they knew had multiple partners. At the same time, the collision of exploitation rooted in colonialism and patriarchy rooted in both European and African cultures has meant that what could have been a public health nuisance has become the worst plague to hit Africa in its history. This is HIV/AIDS in the era of globalization.

Throughout Africa, Structural Adjustment Programmes (SAPs) wreaked havoc on states' capacity to care for their citizens in the 1980s and 1990s. By the early 1990s, the continent had undertaken drastic programmes in order to abide by World Bank-imposed conditions. As part of these austerity measures, currencies were deregulated and their values were decimated in the process, sending food prices soaring. When AIDS took hold in Sub-Saharan Africa in the late 1980s, many African countries were already staggering under the weight of massive debt repayments. The additional burden of structural adjustment contributed to the pandemic by pushing already weakened public health systems to the point of collapse.

By the end of 2000, almost 22 million people had died from AIDS; 13 million children had lost their mother or both of their parents to the disease; more than 40 million people were living with the HIV virus – 90 per cent of them in developing countries, 75 per cent in Sub-Saharan Africa.[10] The implications of these statistics for the lives of women and girls are staggering. In the poorest countries, women are more vulnerable to HIV infection because they have less power to negotiate safer sex with their partners. They are also at increased risk of infection because they are more likely than men to be targets of sexual violence. Women and girls are less likely to know how to prevent transmission because they are less educated. Often, they are discouraged from receiving information related to sex and sexuality precisely because they are female.

Equally worrying is the impact of HIV/AIDS on households. As one woman is quoted as saying: '[w]hen women are sick there is no one to care for them. When men are sick they can be looked after by women.'[11]

HIV/AIDS makes poor households poorer. The income available to families shrinks as breadwinners fall ill, while at the same time hospital and medical expenses mount.[12] For women, AIDS in the family often means not only caring for the same man who probably infected you, but also stopping work in order to do so and thereby jeopardizing the futures of your children. For both boys and girls, but more often for girls, it can mean being taken out of school to care for or supplement the earnings of one or both parents. Already, there are strong indications that children in families where there is no mother are less likely than others to go to school.[13]

The implications of this situation for the future rights of women and girls are devastating. According to one report: '[w]ith AIDS, several of the worst-hit countries, such as South Africa and Botswana, are seeing a reversal of hard-won educational gains, while countries already struggling to achieve EFA (Education for All) goals are being further set back.'[14] The impact of AIDS on teachers is also worth noting. A Zimbabwean study found that '19% of male teachers and almost 29% of female teachers were infected with HIV. Nationwide AIDS-related deaths among South African teachers rose by more than 40% in 2000–2001. The loss of teachers can be especially devastating in rural communities where schools depend heavily on only one or two.'[15]

So not only might we begin to see fewer girls in classrooms, when they do manage to get to school there may be no one to teach them. This loss of potential for girls and women foreshadows the coming orphan crisis. It also tells us a lot about where women's rights are going. Simply put, the rights of women are at risk of being buried just like the thousands of coffins that are pushed into rocky earth every weekend, containing the bodies of young women who were too poor or too scared to insist on condom use. The pandemic is creating a generation of uneducated, extremely vulnerable and dependent young women. The picture is bleak.

Yet there are many things that we do know about how to halt the ravages of HIV/AIDS. We know that girls and women need accurate, detailed information. We know that women and girls need to feel confident, secure and empowered to make decisions about safer sex. We know, too, that behaviour change is a slow process, but that it is possible. Somehow despite this knowledge, however, and despite all the evidence demonstrating that young people with information about their bodies often wait longer to have sex and act more responsibly when they do become sexually active, sexuality education remains limited in many countries, including parts of the United States, and there remain significant barriers to the acquisition of condoms for unmarried women and young people wishing to protect their health.

Perhaps the heart of the issue is the fact that we lack commitment from leaders to eradicate the virus. And worse yet, we do not have a coherent feminist framework for addressing HIV/AIDS. It is a testament primarily to the will and organizational capacities of African women and girls that communities were able to survive the devastation of the early days of the pandemic. And while women have responded in many ways to the devastation HIV/AIDS has wrought in their homes, the question we must ask for both HIV/AIDS and globalization is, what would a feminist response look like? Do we even have a collective vision of what a world free from AIDS and poverty would look like for women? Where does the women's movement even start?

The women's movement(s)

After my abortion, some of the pieces started to come together for me. I physically could no longer be around my boyfriend. He reminded me of what I felt was my own weakness. I blamed myself for not being able to say no to sex when I knew the risks. I had always prided myself on my strength. Somewhat haughtily I reflected that I was not an uneducated little girl who didn't know that if you have sex without condoms you would get pregnant. So I hated him for forcing my body to do his will even when we both knew that I would be the one to bear the consequences of his insistence. I was sick with the knowledge that I had, in the most horrible way possible, put aside my own interests to make him feel good. I knew better.

That semester, feminism began to make sense to me. I read voraciously, needing Audre Lorde and bell hooks, Barbara Smith and Patricia Hill Collins. I hung on every word I read, finally understanding why, for both of us, his need had been more important than my health, my sanity and my body.

The weight and memory of three hundred years of sexualized oppression had taught us both that I was the one who should lick his wounds. My identities as black South African, non-citizen and woman far away from home were not sites of wounds needing care. His masculinity and the racism he had suffered were our preoccupation. There was no room for both of us in the relationship, which, it struck me, was exactly the problem with masculinized and Westernized notions of power: they leave no room for both sides to be fully human.

Finding a community of women – first on paper and then through conversations with women in their teens and twenties who like me had entrusted their bodies to men incapable of loving healthily – was a huge step for me. Initially, I found feminism among friends on campus – a rich collective of African, African-American and Caribbean women. We formed a performance troupe and toured the state, writing, singing and dancing the stories of women's experiences in a range of diasporic contexts. This was my first taste of woman-centred activism. But as I grew and my analysis deepened, these documented experiences explaining other women's realities were not enough for me. I searched for and began to find Third World women whose stories, intellect, analyses and humour inspired and taught me that there was a community within my African context that was both inspirational and supportive.[16]

It must be acknowledged that there are still not enough African feminists who are writing and researching, but that is because so many are occupied with the day-to-day business of supporting other women who are stretched beyond their material, spiritual and emotional means. Yet these readings and the connections I have made between the theories and experiences of other women and my own have to a large extent defined my particular brand of feminism. Today I feel like part of a new wave of Third World women whose writing and activism are beginning to surface within the consciousness of the larger women's movement.

There is no doubt, however, that it is a movement in transition, as are many of the movements for social justice that have defined the last fifty years. There are rifts between women of the North and of the South. There are divisions among older feminists and younger feminists. There are tensions between black feminists and white feminists, and differences of opinion between working-class women and elite women. Yet these divides are almost as old as the movement itself. Feminism has taken on many of the conceptual and practical challenges that have been thrown its way in the last twenty years and has evolved in the process. Most feminists now recognize the fact that women's experiences cannot be universalized. Though seldom acknowledged, the contributions of black and brown women to both the theory and practice of feminism have been tremendous in this regard. For example, see Audre Lorde's *Sister Outsider*, and bell hooks' *Racing Class and Gender*, both of which offer insightful analyses of the ways in which black women face numerous discriminations because of the intersections of their identities.

Strategies for the future

Given the intense challenges posed by globalization and the HIV/AIDS pandemic, it is important that feminist strategies for achieving women's rights in the next few decades are guided by commitments to basic ideals about the notion of what I call 'honest democracy'. The first ideal is a commitment to transparency. Part of the crisis of globalization is that international institutions make decisions affecting ordinary people around the world in a non-transparent way.

Consider that the countries of the global North spend, on average, one billion dollars a day on domestic agricultural subsidies. This is more than six times what they spend on overseas development assistance to developing countries. Consider also that almost 50 per cent of the voting power at the World Bank and IMF is held by seven countries: the United States of America, Japan, France, the United Kingdom, Saudi Arabia, China and the Russian Federation.[17] This demonstrates a huge deficit in terms of transparency. Our strategies for organizing must challenge this status quo.

The second ideal upon which feminist strategies must be based is that of building bridges between global and local activists and their struggles. Our strategies will need to be smarter, working at both local and global levels in ways that are interconnected. Women protesting about poor working conditions should be able to connect with and learn from the activism of women who have risen in other communities organizing around similar issues. Our actions should be grounded in an understanding of the ways in which our problems are connected fundamentally to those of women in other parts of the world. At the same time, we need to develop a consciousness about the extent to which decisions taken by our own governments in our name impact on people in other parts of the world.

These are not difficult connections to make. They simply need to be placed at the forefront of feminist agendas. Using email and the internet, information exchange and swapping stories is possible at a previously unimaginable speed and scale. Ensuring that poor women are not left behind the information and technology revolution, therefore, should be critical to feminist organizing strategies.

The last ideal I want to look at is that of activist citizenship. Feminist actions should be rooted in the firm belief that serious, rigorous citizenship at both national and global levels is increasingly important in this era of globalization. Not only are people's voices important, their knowledge and use of the systems of democracy that are already in place are essential. Where systems exist that are not open and fair, citizen activists will envision new ones and set about building them.[18] We can take inspiration and lessons from the anti-Vietnam War protesters, and also from apartheid, which was torn down by the moral outrage of black South Africans who had the solidarity of people, although not necessarily governments, around the world.

In order to reshape the world, progressive women's organizations will need to scale up their advocacy efforts. Especially in the Third World, the work of NGOs and civil society groups is often inherently political. Yet many cast their services as apolitical because it is often dangerous to confront governments. As governments fail to meet their obligations towards their citizens in terms of basic services, however, and as they relinquish more power to multinational corporations and allow elites to take from official coffers while poor people starve, there is value in openly advocating pro-poor stances. Providing housing for homeless people, for example, is a profoundly political act where the government has made spending choices, such as increasing military budgets, which have resulted in that homelessness.

Women's groups will need to develop advocacy positions that document and demonstrate the effects of government inaction. This requires that feminist organizations both fill practical needs, for example providing termination of pregnancies, while also adopting aggressive positions that require policy-level actions. Organizations that represent the interests of Northern women already combine these two focuses quite effectively. Often when they visit us in developing countries to see how they can help, they end up running the advocacy, pushing the legal systems and determining the articulation of visions for us. What will be needed, especially as we advance the notion of citizen action, are commitments from feminist NGOs based in the global South, from street committees to national organizations, to develop the capacity to do this advocacy themselves.

On the HIV/AIDS front, the challenges are clear: women's inability to negotiate safer sex, lack of access of women and girls to information and reproductive health services, the unfair burden of care that results from caring for the sick and filling in the gaps for those who are too sick to work, the deepening of poverty that results when someone in the house needs medical care, and the crisis of raising and caring for a generation of orphans. Strategies to overcome these challenges are equally clear. Women's organizations across the globe must see the pandemic for what it is, that is, an issue fundamentally related to women's rights and empowerment. In contexts of unequal gender and sexual relations between women and men, efforts to promote condom use for heterosexual women and men will fail. Without eradicating gender inequality, men will not share equally in the added burdens of caring for the sick nor will they do work that is traditionally seen as 'women's work' within their communities.

Within communities badly affected by the pandemic, there is a tendency to deal simply with the fall-out: the orphaned children, the women and men who are already sick, and the economic impacts. Yet the root cause of this pandemic is not the inability to use condoms. It is not even the still unacceptably high numbers of young people who do not have access to condoms. The real issue is that girls and young women do not own their bodies and their voices. They are still largely unable to exercise control over the terms of sexual engagement with the men in their lives, whether it be with their boyfriends, 'sugar daddies', family members who molest them or men on the streets whose violence they have to endure.

The first step, therefore, is framing HIV/AIDS as a human rights issue. This reframing will allow women's organizations to take their governments to task for failing to meet their obligations under international law. Looking at HIV/AIDS as a violation of women's rights to health, inheritance and education, among others, allows feminists to use already existing mechanisms that are recognized and sometimes feared by our governments.

As indicated earlier, women's organizations must build their capacity as advocates for the rights of women. Using documents such as the International Conference on Population and Development (ICPD) Programme of Action and the United Nations General Assembly Special Session on HIV/AIDS (UNGASS) Declaration of Commitment as tools, women can develop blueprints for their own development and empowerment. It is essential that, at every level, women learn how to link demands around their health and their rights to their power as voters. Even women who are illiterate can, as the Americans put it, 'rock the vote' in communities around the world by developing reproductive health and rights agendas and basing their decisions about whom to elect on these platforms.

As devastating as it is, HIV/AIDS also offers feminists an opportunity to reintroduce an issue that is at the heart of feminism: women's unpaid domestic labour. Given the burden of care that falls upon women, and the adverse effect this has on girls' ability to access education and employment, a strong case can be made for introducing legal and community measures to share housework between men and women. In Africa, AIDS has altered the fabric of our societies. We can either retreat further into our old and oppressive ways of coping, or we can build new societies based on mutual respect. AIDS provides us with a chance to start again on this enormous project.

Progressive women politicians can be strong allies in helping to push through legislation to regulate gender relations within the home. Domestic violence laws and policies governing child maintenance have paved the way already, demonstrating that states will protect women in the domestic sphere when they are pushed by women who are angry enough and consistent enough in their demands. In light of the AIDS pandemic, a powerful argument can be made for laws to ensure that men do their share of the house and community work because without everyone's help, there simply will not be enough hands to go around. As speculation about the drought in Southern Africa indicates, the need for more hands is dire: 'HIV is not only contributing to the famine ... but may be a cause of it. Seven million farm-workers have died from the disease in Africa since 1985 ... Agricultural productivity has plummeted, even as the nutritional needs of the sick have become greater than ever.'[19]

With respect to both poverty eradication and HIV/AIDS, it is clear that the only strategies that will work require massive numbers of people working together in solidarity. For decades, the women's movement has espoused the importance of indigenous feminisms and the pluralism of women's voices. These are aspects of the movement that must be re-energized. The feminism of the next few decades must be responsive to and representative of women whose experiences, solutions and interests are rooted in the Third World. In this regard, feminists will need to refer to, draw upon and enrich local and global battles against the interests of global capital.

There is no easy way to conclude these reflections. This seems like such a strange and terrifying time and hence these strategies are all the more urgent. As I write, the world is on the brink of a war that will kill many in order to secure US national interests. On my continent, there are many wars going on, fed by small men with big egos. Each day Africans are maimed and killed by one another, aided and abetted by the guns of the West. I can only hope that the rage of ordinary people, local and global citizens alike, will build from protests against this impending attack on Iraq to a unified statement against any more wars. And I am hoping that their collective attention will turn to the daily violations of women's rights that are carried out in the name of globalization.

I will not wait to see what happens next. I will be one of the many Third World voices screaming for justice, marching for peace and acting for change for women. There is too much to say, and strangely not enough. I will, therefore, conclude with this most hopeful and poignant statement from Indian writer and activist Arundhati Roy:

> A world run by a handful of greedy bankers and C.E.O.s whom nobody elected can't possibly last ... Soviet-style communism failed, not because it was intrinsically evil but because it was flawed. It allowed too few people to usurp too much power. Twenty-first century market-capitalism, American style, will fail for the same reasons. Both are edifices constructed by the human intelligence, undone by human nature ... The time has come, the Walrus said. Perhaps things will become worse and then better. Perhaps there's a small god up in heaven readying herself for us. Another world is not only possible, she's on her way. Maybe many of us won't be here to greet her, but on a quiet day, if I listen very carefully, I can hear her breathing.[20]

Notes

1 For more on the subject of strategies developed by feminist Third World women, see DAWN (1995) 'Markers on the Way: The DAWN Debates on

Alternative Development: DAWN's Platform for the Fourth World Conference on Women' (Beijing: DAWN). <http://www.dawn.org.fj/publications/listofpublications.html>

2 J. B. Foster (2002) 'Monopoly Capital and the New Globalization', *Monthly Review*, 53 (8, January). <http://www.monthlyreview.org/0102jbf.htm>

3 J. Stiglitz (2002) *Globalization and Its Discontents* (London: Penguin Books), p. 3.

4 J. B. Foster (2002) 'Paul Sweezy, Monopoly Capital', in D. Dowd (ed.), *Understanding Capitalism: Critical Analysis from Karl Marx to Amartya Sen* (London: Pluto Press). Taken from Monopoly Capital and the New Globalization, http://www.monthlyreview.org/0102jbf.htm, accessed 4 December 2002.

5 N. Klein (2002) *Fences and Windows: Dispatches from the Front Lines of the Globalization Debate* (London: Flamingo), p. 28.

6 *Education for All: Is the World on Track?* Summary Report (November 2002), p. 61 <http://www.unesco.org/education/efa/monitoring/pdf/Monitoring_2002/EFAGMR1-2_chapter2.pdf>

7 In 1985, Maxine Molyneux wrote a now famous article about the experiences of Nicaraguan women who had participated in the Sandanista revolution. The article ('Mobilization without Emancipation? Women's Interests, the State, and Revolution in Nicaragua', *Feminist Studies*, 11 [2, Summer 1995]: 227–54) made a distinction between practical gender interests and strategic gender interests. She argued that women's movements concerned with basic material issues such as food, water, land, military oppression against their children, and so on, represented 'practical gender interests'. She identified 'strategic gender interests' as those which are explicitly feminist and included strategies for achieving gender equality, including reproductive rights, rights in the family, rights to non-discrimination at work, representation in the state and so on. This framework has been much debated by practitioners and academics alike but the concept remains central to much of gender and development work.

8 G. Hart (2002) *Disabling Globalization: Places of Power in Post-Apartheid South Africa* (Pietermaritzburg: University of Natal Press), p. 27.

9 J. Pyle (2001) 'Sex, Maids, and Export Processing: Gendered Global Production Networks', *International Journal of Politics, Culture and Society*, 15 (1).

10 *AIDS Epidemic Update*, December 2002, UNAIDS. <www.unaids.org>

11 World Bank and World Health Organization (2002) *Dying for Change*, p. 15.

12 *Human Development Report*, 2002, p. 27.

13 *AIDS Epidemic Update*, December 2002, p. 30.

14 World Bank Group (2002) *AIDS Blunts Progress in Education*, 8 May 2002 <http://web.worldbank.org/WBSITE/EXTERNAL/NEWS/0,,contentMDK:20043530~menuPK:34459~pagePK:64003015~piPK:64003012~theSitePK:4607,00.html> Accessed 26 November 2003.

15 UNAIDS, *The Impact of AIDS* (factsheet). Available on UNAIDS website <http://www.unaids.org/barcelona/presskit/factsheets/FSimpact_en.html>

16 These women include Tsitsi Dangaremba, Ata Ama Aidoo, Patricia Mc Fadden, Amina Mama, Ayesha Imam and many others.

17 UNDP (2002) *Human Development Report 2002: Deepening Democracy in a Fragmented World* (Oxford: Oxford University Press), pp. 101–2.

18 For more on feminist visions of democracy, see the work of Mohanty and Alexander. In particular, C. T. Mohanty (1991) 'Cartographies of Struggle: Third World Women and Politics of Feminism', in C. T. Mohanty, A. Russo and L. Torres, *Third World Women and Politics of Feminism* (Bloomington: Indiana University Press).

19 M. Specter (2003) 'The Vaccine', *The New Yorker*, 3 February, pp. 54–65.

20 Transcription of the Arundhati Roy talk called 'Come September', Lensic Performing Arts Center, Santa Fe, New Mexico, 18 September 2002.

12 | International and post-socialist women's rights advocacy: points of convergence and tension

REFLECTIONS FROM ANASTASIA POSADSKAYA-VANDERBECK

Anastasia Posadskaya-Vanderbeck is a leading voice on women's rights and gender and development from the Central and Eastern European region and the newly independent states (CEE/NIS). For fifteen years she has been directing academic and advocacy programmes, during which time she has been instrumental in both raising awareness around women's rights issues within the region and in putting the specific issues of the region on the map of international gender equality work. The region is one of the most marginalized in the international women's movement, but Anastasia's efforts have been instrumental in integrating the region into the international movement.

She has been the director of the Network Women's Program of the Open Society Institute (Soros Foundation) since 1997. In this role, she is responsible for integrating gender equality into programmes in about thirty countries. As a progressive feminist in a donor organization, Anastasia is in a unique position to assist women's organizations and movements in the region to strengthen their reach and relevance; moreover, she is uniquely placed to support their engagement within the international women's movement. As such, she plays a fundamental role in strengthening not only the regional movement, but the international one as well.

We had an opportunity to speak with Anastasia in August and September 2003 about women's rights advocacy in her region and at the global level. The following reflections are from those conversations.

AWID/Mama Cash: *What do you think are the most critical issues that will challenge our efforts for women's rights in the next five to ten years globally?*

Anastasia Posadskaya-Vanderbeck: It seems like there is more or less some agreement, expressed by other contributors to this project, that military proliferation, poverty and fundamentalisms are three very important issues that will affect women's rights. I agree completely with these as priority issues. Another big challenge that I see is the question of how we should be consolidating the global women's movement. One element of this is whether or not the United Nations and its mechanisms and its instruments should still be our focus, or should we change our focus. This issue is especially critical at this time as we consider whether or not there should be a 'Beijing +10'.[1]

In the next five to ten years, the international women's movement will have to deal with the pros and cons of retreating from the UN altogether, or at least of a temporary tactical retreat. This is a critical question given that for the last thirty years the UN has contributed greatly to building the women's movement. It has done so especially through the world conferences on women which brought together women from around the world, creating a space for us to work together and a platform for further organizing and networking. The UN retreat debate is also a critical one since the movement has been pushing the UN to build instruments that are accountable to women's rights – whether in the form of the Beijing Platform for Action or the Convention on the Elimination of All Forms of Discrimination Against Women (CEDAW). Strategic thinking on how best to engage or not engage with the UN, then, is an important challenge.

Others have already identified UN engagement as creating and reinforcing a global feminist elite. Such an elite, on the one hand, is familiar with these instruments and knows how to lobby with them at the international level, but, on the other hand, it sometimes diverts attention from national or local-level advocacy. The financial resources necessary to participate in UN-level conferences are substantial, and the skills and capacity necessary to engage in the processes, including a good grasp of English, are very demanding. As well, the demanding nature of UN advocacy can take away from regional, national and local advocacy, result in burn-out in those who try to keep up with the demands, and produce a disjuncture in terms of being able to translate international commitments into community realities.

A third argument that is put forward as a reason to retreat from the UN is that it has become a toothless institution. We can lobby as much as we want at the UN, we can put all our efforts into UN mechanisms, but it will not really affect the reality of women's lives, especially at the local level.

Another argument is that the UN is not only weak, but it is so dominated by all these wars and by the United States and its current right-wing administration, that it is dangerous to continue to focus on UN advocacy. Ironically, it is also argued that those institutions with more power and force, such as the World Bank, the World Trade Organization and the International Monetary Fund, which are also dominated by the USA, should be targeted instead because of their influence and impact. They are seen to be the institutions that really influence the politics and policies of governments, as opposed to policies being self-defined domestically. This is an important factor to consider, especially in terms of the current right-wing US administration's potential longer-term influence on all of these institutions. Even if the American people succeed in bringing in a different administration, we cannot simply return to focusing on the UN because the repercussions of current US policies on the international financial institutions will be felt for some time to come.

To complicate matters further, it seems that while existing UN mechanisms or regional mechanisms are being weakened, new mechanisms are being introduced. For example, the Millennium Development Goals (MDGs) are now being used at the United Nations, in international financial institutions and in governments. They have components of gender equality and education for all, but they are still insufficient. Not only are they insufficient in and of themselves for women's rights, but as they increasingly become a focus for development programming, gender advocates may have an ever-more difficult time in creating effective strategies for women's rights. As a mechanism for development, the MDGs are non-transparent and it is difficult to understand how they should really be used.

I am on the MDG task force for education and gender equality, and in this role I still have many questions about applying the MDGs. I wonder, how does this whole thing work? What will be the outcome? What will be the possibilities for real change within the MDG framework? And most importantly, how can women's movements around the world mobilize themselves around the MDGs and translate them into a strategic advocacy tool? I still have no answer for that. I do not think they are very transformable, at least right now. Also, despite the emphasis that has been placed on the MDGs by the World Bank and the UN, they have been overshadowed by the current global climate, including the 'war on terror'.

So it seems to me that we will have to be very strategic about even a temporary tactical retreat from UN engagement because of how it may affect national, local and regional women's movements. Despite all of the criticism, the UN has been very important to the gains we have made to date. As I see it, the challenge is not about substantive women's rights issues, but rather about the ways we achieve women's rights protections.

AWID/Mama Cash: *Do you see a way of challenging the elitist nature of UN advocacy activities?*

AP-V: We need to involve the voices of grassroots women, poor women. Exactly how this is going to happen is the problem; I know how difficult it is in practice. There are women in my region who are supporting others to get online and join email discussions, for example, but frankly, there is not much real participation taking place. People are simply too busy.

Regardless of the criticisms raised against them, an important way to overcome this lack of participation is through conferences, despite barriers to access. For those women who are able to come, conferences can reach grassroots women in a face-to-face and more meaningful way than e-based discussion. In a way, in spite of all the difficulties of being a part of these events and organizing them, I do think they have unequivocal value as venues for women to come together. We have to cherish these spaces because there are so few of them.

AWID/Mama Cash: *What impact do you think retreating from the UN would have on your region?*

AP-V: From my experience in the post-socialist region, I believe that it would be very dangerous to devalue in any way the binding, though sometimes ignored and unenforceable, gender equality mechanisms of the United Nations. Very often, the international commitments that were made by governments in the region are the only framework which gender advocates have learned to use and around which advocacy can be shaped. I think this is an essential point: retreating from using UN mechanisms could actually *disempower* women from these countries who have already been empowered by learning about CEDAW, Beijing processes and Cairo. If we say, 'OK, now forget about the UN, let's work with international financial institutions', it would require substantial time and resources to develop new advocacy strategies, time and resources that are simply not available.

And initially these new approaches would be even more elitist than the existing UN-focused ones, until they eventually reach grassroots women. In this sense, I think that it would be prudent that any new strategies we develop are not put forth as a substitution for UN advocacy but rather build on the achievements of the past and reinforce our work at the UN. This is especially true for the post-socialist region. I also feel that sophisticated and savvy women's movements, who are able to maintain accountability efforts at the UN, will contribute to overcoming the ever-expanding challenges and barriers to gender equality presented by poverty, fundamentalisms and militarization. If this is the case, then a full abandonment of the UN as a site for advocacy could hinder broader efforts for women's rights.

AWID/Mama Cash: *How is the current global climate affecting women's rights?*

AP-V: I think it is important to develop a very good analysis of how this 'war on terror' has started a chain reaction of increasing military budgets and military–industrial complexes and the social consequences of that, not only in this country but all over the world. The 'war on terror' will affect women's lives in so many ways and it seems to me that both the gains made by the rights agenda and also the development agenda are being jeopardized, in the USA and elsewhere. This will have a tremendous impact. Already, it has reduced the resources available for the gender equality and women's rights agenda. Under these circumstances, it will be a struggle to protect the gains already made for gender equality, let alone advance them further.

What is ironic is that on the surface it would appear that these gains are being advanced, and that the message of gender equality and women's rights has really been integrated into both government and non-governmental organizations around the world. This seems to be one of the unintended consequences of mainstreaming gender equality and women's empowerment, which is the cooptation and manipulation of women's rights for the non-related goals of both governments and non-governmental institutions. This is very thoughtful manipulation. It is being created by people who have a good understanding of gender equality and who are able to present a partial commitment to women's rights in a way that seems to be a full commitment. This is a big threat.

An obvious example of this manipulation is the way that the women's rights agenda was adopted as a form of justification for the invasion of Afghanistan. It had been known for many years that the Taliban was oppressing women, but it was only after 6 October 2001, when military action began in Afghanistan, that the film *Behind the Veil* was shown countless times on CNN. Similarly, only recently was there a mainstream article on domestic violence in Iraq. Excuse me, but this is exactly what is happening in every other country, it is not just Iraq. Yet domestic violence was represented as something unique to Saddam Hussein's regime. Of course it is an important issue, but the timing of this coverage in the media is very suspect. I expect that this type of manipulation has existed for some time, but I believe that it is becoming increasingly more sophisticated and that we need to be especially vigilant to ensure that the agenda of women's rights protection is not used to advance other kinds of oppression.

Development institutions have also coopted the women's rights agenda. Let's face it, who knows how many institutions have cancelled their women's programmes by saying 'We now do mainstreaming', without real expertise or mechanisms to implement or demonstrate this mainstreaming. Gender mainstreaming, in fact, has sometimes completely curtailed work on women's rights. I do not want to name organizations, but even within my own organization we always have to be vigilant. When someone tells me they will be mainstreaming and therefore closing down their women's programme, I always want to look very closely at what exactly they want to achieve and why, at what is happening in the projects and at what will be the result for women's rights. I believe that this kind of careful monitoring helps to reduce the manipulation of gender mainstreaming.

AWID/Mama Cash: *What particular issues are affecting your region?*

AP-V: Let me take a historical perspective here. Once the transition from socialist systems began there was a real backlash against gender equality because gender equality had been part of the official political agenda and rhetoric in the socialist time. The beginning of the transition was very challenging for women's movements and we had to distinguish ourselves from coopted policies on gender equality that were part of socialism. Initially, when the transition began, we couldn't speak of gender equality because it represented the old rhetoric of socialism, and the social change processes that were taking place rejected anything from what it was like under socialism. That was so tough. It was difficult to be understood as not demanding more of the past but to be understood as part of the larger agenda of social change of which gender equality was still an essential part.

From the beginning of the 1990s we argued that democracy without women is no democracy. We were involved in the Beijing conference and we had a small caucus for the post-socialist countries, but I think that our presence was marginalized. Still, I think it was an important landmark for raising awareness among our own region and the rest of the world. There were and are very big challenges in post-socialist countries including access for women to employment and to education. We also managed to put the cultural and political transformations and their impacts on women on to the agenda. The political change that had been taking place had not been accounted for in any international framework, but we were able to bring attention to this both at national and international levels.

The current changes taking place within the region are based very much on the divisions between states caused by accession to the European Union. Unfortunately, in a region that already has many divisions and conflicts both within and between states, the EU accession process has only deepened these divides. The war on terror has also affected the region a lot. There are private negotiations taking place, country by country, with the USA, and some countries are trying to use the tensions between the European Union and the USA to their advantage. This just shows how building political alliances and divisions is very complicated, and it is so far removed from women's rights and gender equality agendas.

For the EU accession countries I think that what the women's movement has managed to do is to put gender equality on to the agenda. This has been accomplished, with our support, by monitoring the Programme on Equal Opportunities for Women and Men and the (EOWM) European accession process. It is amazing how low a priority gender equality is within the negotiation process and also how ignorant the accession countries and the EU are about gender issues. In the coming years, I think there is a need to reinforce the need for monitoring equal opportunities and not to allow it to be a paper-only exercise, without any real force. I also think that one of the roles for women from accession countries will be to enforce the work of Western feminists within the European Union, the European Women's Lobby, and help them push the European Union to prioritize gender equality issues and really delivering on them.

I also believe that reproductive rights will be a very big part of this chapter in history. Reproductive rights are at risk in numerous countries, including Russia, Poland, Slovakia, Hungary and the Czech Republic. Specifically, for example, in Russia there has been a change in the laws around abortion. Where previously there were twelve so-called 'social reasons' for permitting abortion, now there is just one: rape. The countries that join the EU now will be on different ground and there will be more opportunities to fight for reproductive rights.

AWID/Mama Cash: *So if those are the issues, then what about the strategies?*

AP-V: What can I say? Other contributors to this project have rightly pointed out some important neglected areas such as preparing new leadership of the women's movement. Also, there is the necessity of ensuring that strategies are built from the bottom up and are informed by grassroots women's organizations. If we fail to engage with women in poor communities, they will be more vulnerable to the forces of fundamentalisms and other coopting factors.

These are things that have already been mentioned. What I think is dangerous in this discussion of creating new visions and strategies is losing sight of or failing to build upon the gains we have already made. I think women's movements are learning movements and there is a very rich volume of experience that already exists. My concern is that sometimes when working towards new strategies, we critique the past overly harshly. Our new strategies may start from a new place and move in a completely different direction than past work. I think that new directions make sense at certain times, but I also think that keeping a focus on the achievements previously gained and making sure that they continue to work is useful and necessary, especially with respect to women's rights instruments.

It is essential to maintain our focus on particular strategies to ensure that we achieve sustainable impact before shifting priorities. This is true in the area of violence against women, for example. As someone who works in a donor organization, I know that there is a certain feeling of 'How long can we focus on this issue area?', and 'How long can we provide resources for this work?' But despite this feeling on the part of donors, we continue to have more and more recorded violence, in many places and of different types. I think that maintaining the commitments of both advocates on the one hand and funding agencies on the other hand is fundamental. Only when we can see a reduction and ultimately an end to violence against women can we stop working on this issue. I do not know when this time will come, but the example highlights the need to deepen our impact as a strategy, rather than shifting our time and resources to a new issue.

This is true for gender mainstreaming too. Initially, there was such excitement and commitment to gender mainstreaming and its ability to change not only our organizations but society at large. As I discussed earlier, this has sometimes failed and the mainstreaming agenda has been manipulated. Regardless of these setbacks, and as much as I am critical and sometimes sceptical about mainstreaming, I believe it would be premature to turn around and stop mainstreaming. What is needed, instead, is to uphold the values behind mainstreaming and have a critical analysis of its implementation. From this analysis we can identify lessons from successes and failures. The strategy is about continuing with mainstreaming as a strategy but with a critical and reflective edge, rather than moving on to an entirely new strategy.

Thinking about the whole conversation we had around the UN and its instruments, I also believe that we should strengthen the instruments of women's rights and ensure that those who violate women's rights are held to account. For example, CEDAW is applicable in our region and it is a powerful instrument that we use and will continue to use. However, some of its mechanisms are still very bureaucratic, non-transparent and not given any priority. We should push for these mechanisms to have more weight and force, and for them to be transformed into a reliable means of achieving women's rights. This is something we should be working more on.

One way we can be doing this is to review UN mechanisms and instruments in non-UN alternative spaces. In this sense, I think the role of the NGO-sponsored forums really could be strengthened. An international women's gathering could become a landmark UN review event. In this way, we could let governments know that the UN human rights review processes are not quiet, elite processes with only select participants who have access to provide either scheduled reporting or critique in some ways. Instead, the whole process of reviewing state accountability could lie with civil society and women's groups. Governments would then know that they are going to be watched whether they want it or not, whether there is a Beijing+10 or not. We need to find a way to keep women's rights issues as a global priority even in the absence of another world conference on women. Collective effort is needed on these issues, too, because they affect resource issues: the stronger and more crucial our alternative spaces are, the more support we will receive.

I believe that a lot of collective thinking is still needed to develop the details of our strategies. That is the strength of the women's movement – committed women and men coming together and strategizing together, not alone. For example, today we had a great brainstorming session via telephone with our Budapest office; as a group we completely redefined the agenda of the meeting. It was very exciting because we all owned it, by the end of our conversation we were grasping on to something entirely new. I am limited in terms of what I can do inside my own head. Wouldn't it be wonderful to have this sort of dialogue like we are doing here as a small group brainstorming session?

As I talk of this collective thinking, however, a big void in the women's movement emerges. We miss out on so many voices. I am concerned that China, for example, is not present as much as it should be in the global women's movement. We are talking about more than a billion people. We should always be concerned about the inclusiveness of the global women's movement and why some voices are less present than others.

AWID/Mama Cash: *What about regional strategies?*

AP-V: Returning to my region, there are a couple of points I'd like to make. First, over the last ten years, three main types of institutions of social change within the women's movement have emerged: women's information centres, anti-violence networks in general and crisis centres and shelters in particular, and Gender Studies and Women's Studies programmes. Each of these exists in separate institutions and some have already started to network nationally, regionally and globally. However, the region's women's movement will not survive the next ten years unless these institutions are strengthened and sustained. Sustainability of these independent voices and the places where they are nurtured is absolutely crucial.

One way of sustaining these independent voices is by strengthening the quality of feminist research, especially policy-oriented research. In our region, there has been an expansion of Gender Studies centres. They are raising awareness about gender and women's issues. From an international perspective, however, if we look closely into the quality of the research and the ethics of the research, it is not very high. We absolutely need to increase our efforts to ensure that the feminist research coming out of the region is rigorous and of a high quality. This could be accomplished through stricter peer reviews or through the creation of associations that can provide such internal controls. Feminist research is a fundamental resource for a strong women's movement. Without reliable research, the case for gender equality is weakened. This has already been identified as a priority within the Open Society Network. We need to measure impact by the quantity of new policy papers and reviews, but also by the quality of this work.

Of course the region, and the women's movement, will face the challenge of economic and political independence. Without independence, and independent voices, there will be no movement, so this is a strategy. Within my institution we are going to focus in the next three years on the institutions of change. This is part of our strategy to strengthen and maintain the women's movement.

Another strategy for this region is to identify the impacts of recent legal reforms. There are a number of laws on equal rights and opportunities for women and men, on violence against women, on parity and political participation. Depending on the stage of legal reforms, the movement will have to undertake different steps. If a law has not been passed, the movement will have to work to get it passed. If a law has been passed, the movement will need to work to see it implemented beyond words on paper. And if a law is being enforced, they will need to monitor its enforcement. This goes really across the region; otherwise law reform is unfinished business.

Another thing that we will have to strategize on are reproductive rights. There is increasing pressure on these rights and they are being politicized in a number of counties, including Russia, Slovakia, Croatia, Hungary, Lithuania and possibly the Czech Republic. The movement will have to prepare much more than it has to date for the reproductive rights struggle. In terms of strategies, some are already in place. For example, ASWRA (the Association for Women's Reproductive Rights of Central Western Europe) now has plans to advance to Russia and Central Asia. International connections are absolutely important in this work and a high level of expertise is crucial.

Finally, it is also vital for the region to maintain connections with the rest of the world. This is especially the case for the more marginal countries within the region such as in Central Asia. Without these connections, the strength of independent civil society may be lost or smothered by the 'governmental NGOs', which in fact have a large presence in the spectrum of the so-called 'non-governmental organizations' in the region. This notion of connections returns to the earlier point I made about the necessity of the women's movement to be inclusive. We have always to be concerned with who is present and whose voices are included in the venues where international agendas are being formulated.

AWID/Mama Cash: *In conclusion, do you have any big vision for the future that you want to share?*

AP-V: Personally, I feel that these are tough times and more tough times are coming. It is easy to be frustrated. It takes so much effort to gain such little achievement. We can see that women's work worldwide is making a difference – speech by speech, little by little – and with only minimal, but well-used, resources.

But then you look at mainstream politics, and how it is changing the lives of people globally. With vast amounts of money, bomb by bomb ... the work of destruction, unfortunately, has so many resources behind it. It is easy to be frustrated, but, at the same time, we cannot stop fighting. Women's rights work is an absolute priority. Those who devote their lives to this work are unstoppable and unshakeable, and will one day make this world a better place for all, not just for some. So that is my hope and my vision: keep optimism and keeping the feeling of solidarity. I know that we can change things for the better, in spite of all the odds of the current time.

Note

1 'Beijing+10' refers to the ten-year follow-up review to the Fourth World Conference on Women, which took place in Beijing, China, 4–15 September 1995.

13 | Gender equality advocates speak: feminist issues and strategies in the future

RHONDA LEESON

Design a political and social system in which women function effectively. Hundreds of years of women's oppression are not fixed by various campaigns and stopgap solutions. We need to architect our society so that it is a place where women and men can live. (AWID survey participant)

Over the past thirty to forty years, gender equality advocates and feminists around the world have fought to gain greater rights in society and to eliminate patriarchy. While the challenges women face and strategies they employ have differed across time and across cultures, the goals of gender equality and rights for all have stayed at the centre of the work. The impacts of globalization, fundamentalist movements, economic disparities and new technologies, however, have all increased the trials of women as well as altering the methods we use to address them. And these changes are only accelerating.

What is the future of feminism, then, and how do we get there? What are the goals of the gender equality struggle? How can we be proactive in making the world look the way we want it to? The Association of Women's Rights in Development (AWID) and Mama Cash wanted to address these questions and the challenges of the future head-on.[1] As an international network of researchers and activists, business people and policy-makers, development workers and activists, AWID's membership encompasses more than 4,500 people, half of whom are located in the global South and Eastern Europe. This highly diverse membership, active in women's rights work with an immeasurable degree of experience, was an ideal group to poll about critical issues and innovative strategies to guarantee women's rights into the future. We wanted to draw on that experience and explore it, giving us an opportunity to compare their responses with the ideas of the contributing authors. And we wanted to learn what people doing this work think are the important issues and strategies that need to be pursued at this time, as well as what approaches need to be employed for the future. The membership was therefore invited to share their opinions with us, in the form of a questionnaire.

The questions posed to the AWID members took two forms: open-ended questions to identify the most important issues and strategies for gender equality work, both now and in the future; and classification questions to rank a wide range of the issues and strategies that have been utilized in this field. The actual survey and the complete questions can be found at the end of this chapter. Responses were as comprehensive and varied as the participants, so only the most noteworthy answers are examined here. What follows is a discussion of the responses, highlighting the most important challenges and approaches for the future of feminism according to the AWID membership. Sites of overlap and of contradiction with the authors in this book will also be integrated throughout this chapter.

> Intensify efforts to build practical gender equity promotion approaches into all development-related programs, without exception. Far too little has been done to get out of theory and get things translated into practical guidelines. (AWID survey participant)

The questionnaire, and the people who answered

We asked and they answered. One hundred and forty-four AWID members completed our questionnaire, which included questions on what they felt would or should be the critical issues and strategies in the immediate and near future. The diverse set of critical reflections we received allowed us to extend the reach of our analysis and provided substantial fodder for thought. The questionnaire respondents were diverse. Of the 144, 65 per cent completed the questionnaire in English, 24 per cent in Spanish and 10 per cent in French. Respondents reported being from forty-six different countries, including 51 per cent from developing countries.[2] As a result, this survey has a far more global perspective than is often present in this type of feminist work.

The diversity of respondents was not only in terms of geography and language, but was also reflected in the information they provided about their work for gender equality, their experience and their age. For example, an astounding 80 per cent of those who answered this question have been involved in gender equality/women's rights work for more than five years. Interestingly, most of those who responded in Spanish had been involved in women's movements for more than fifteen years, while the French-speaking respondents were almost equally divided between those who had been involved for less than five years and those who had more than fifteen years' experience in the struggle for gender equality. In terms of the focus of their gender work, most identified themselves as working at the national level, with 51 per cent of the group doing some national-level work and 21 per cent focusing exclusively at this level. Another 16 per cent stated that they focus at the global level, 13 per cent local and 10 per cent regional. This demonstrates that, in terms of their perspectives, this group of respondents truly had a diverse set of experiences to draw on.

In terms of age, this was also a diverse group with respondents representing the full range of gender equality advocates and women's rights activists. Sixty-five per cent of those who gave their age were between twenty-five and forty-four years of age. Only eight women over the age of sixty responded to the question on age, or at least identified themselves as being within the 'over 60' category. More surprisingly perhaps, only four respondents identified themselves as less than twenty-five years of age. There are several possible explanations for this disappointing level of responses from younger women. Given that the future of the movement may depend on fresh ideas from dynamic young leaders, their lack of input into collaborative dialogues such as this is a concern. Interestingly, attracting young women to the movement and fostering their leadership is a priority that has been identified by Criquillion, Kerr and Adeleye-Fayemi in this volume and is now a priority of several international feminist networks. It is this revitalization of the global women's movements that is the focus of both the contributors to this volume, and the impetus behind the AWID questionnaire that we are presenting here.

Issues we should be addressing now

The AWID membership questionnaire first asked respondents to identify the most important issue in the world currently, with regard to gender equality and social transformation. Although many issues were raised as areas needing attention, three main categories were evident. 'Empowerment of women', 'economics and financial resources' and 'education' emerged as the most frequently cited challenges currently facing gender equality worldwide.

Empowerment of women

> I believe that the greatest need for change is at the individual, family, and community level. We need to help women and men examine and rethink their various roles, beliefs and values. (AWID questionnaire participant)

More respondents considered empowerment of and development for women the most important issue that was raised. While it may seem obvious and overly simplistic to some, empowerment is a vital concern when it comes to achieving gender equality. Social transformation will occur on a global scale only when it is demanded by large segments of the population, including both women and men; but the demand will come only through the empowerment of women – efforts that must occur at all levels in society. As one Spanish participant noted, it is important to make people aware that male dominance is not a problem from the past, but instead is an on-going struggle that affects our interpersonal relationships every day. And because achieving empowerment is the first step in the process of realizing gender equality, it affects every other issue that our survey participants highlighted.

Economics and financial resources

> I would work on financial independence. It is not the root or cause of many problems experienced by women, but the lack of accessible financial resources often means women feel they are stuck in dangerous situations or locations. (AWID questionnaire participant)

A second matter raised by AWID questionnaire participants as a current issue facing gender equality globally is that of economics and financial resources. This broad category had numerous related issues within it. Included among these are: access to, and increase of, resources for women; changing decision-making structures to accommodate women; training on employment skills; women's property rights; and recognizing, improving and giving access to women's work. What all of these issues have in common is giving women more economic control. By improving women's access and control over finances, women will gain independence in other areas and can work towards a better quality of life for both themselves and their families. As many of the participants stressed, improving a woman's financial stability will benefit society as a whole, helping to create social transformation.

While the contributing authors to this book were also concerned with economics, it was manifest mainly within the issue of poverty, especially poverty of women as a consequence of globalization. Facio, Adeleye-Fayemi and Dhanraj, Misra and Batliwala all focused on this aspect of economic concerns. Kerr and Bracke, on the other hand, wrote about the links between poverty and women's movements, with regard to the impact poverty has on women's rights.

Education

> From my own experience working in women's projects, achieving gender equality and social transformation requires a great educational effort in order to transform the domestic environment where women and men coexist. (AWID questionnaire participant)

The need to improve education for women and girls was another issue voiced by questionnaire respondents as most important for gender equality at this time. In fact, education is mentioned throughout the responses as both an issue of concern and a strategy for achieving change, both now and into the future. Access to, and provision of, education are clearly seen as the means through which gender equality will be achieved around the world. The empowerment of women discussed earlier in this section will not be possible without improving access to education. Economic stability and financial control will likewise require education in order to be successful. Because of the impacts education can have in all other areas of a woman's life, it is not surprising that it is so frequently mentioned here. Thus, while getting gender equality into education programmes was discussed by many of the survey participants, it is the access to education in the first place that continues to be a vital concern for many equality advocates.

Given the importance of education to participants around the world, it is notable that few of the contributing authors focused on it. Education was not as specifically important to them as it was to the AWID members taking part in the questionnaire. The only mentions of education by the authors were in relation to other topics, and as more of a strategy than an issue needing to be addressed. Msimang, for example, includes education, along with healthcare, housing and employment, as one of the services guaranteed in her vision of a different kind of world that must be struggled for.

Intersectionality One significant issue several of the contributors to this volume raised, but which was discussed by only a few of the participants, involves the relations between women of colour and white women, as well as the intersectionality framework.[3] As a theory and a tool of analysis, intersectionality is gaining broader acceptance and understanding within the feminist and development fields: Griffen, Criquillion and Kerr all included discussions of this theory in their chapters. For Kerr and Criquillion, the intersections of identity and the potential to use diversity to our advantage are presented as benefits to global feminism; they see these efforts as work that must be nurtured and improved. For Griffen, though, the focus is more on the impacts these actions and strategies will have on the ability and efforts of women to transform patriarchy. For these authors, intersectionality is seen more as a strategy than an issue, but it is equally important to both discussions. As one of the few respondents to address this, an English-speaking participant wrote:

> I think the women's movements need to be integrating issues, not working on just one. This means building an analysis about power that challenges social and economic injustice, control over women's lives and bodies, and

environmental degradation, in the context of a uni-polar, militarized and increasingly undemocratic world. It means keeping intersections of race/ethnicity, class, gender, national origin, sexual orientation and other identities present in all of our analysis. We need to create spaces where this kind of integrated analysis can emerge.

It is this need for integrated analysis that intersectionality can provide, and it is the reason behind the theory's popular growth. Thus while empowerment, economic issues and education are the gender equality challenges that are of concern to respondents right now, intersectionality provides options for advocacy work in the future, and points to the need to work together more justly and more effectively.

Challenges into the future

The second question posed in the AWID questionnaire reflected a forward-thinking perspective. Participants were asked to identify what the single most important challenge to gender equality and women's rights work will be in five to ten years. As expected, we were given a wide variety of answers. But it was the strength of the global woman's movement that elicited the most responses to this question; more specifically, participants were concerned with women's collective strategies and actions, and with fragmentation in the movement. The recognition that we will need to work collectively to achieve our goals, especially with regard to globalization, economic disparities, armed conflicts and changing patriarchal institutions, was clearly expressed in several of the responses. These answers reflect the necessity of collective action strategies in feminist movements to apply international pressure on governments, corporations, non-governmental organizations and the public at large, in order to achieve success on other gender equality issues. And while many respondents noted that the global backlash against feminism continues, this was seen as a challenge to be overcome, not one to diminish the work.

This collective action strategy is not without its detractors, however. As often as respondents noted the need for collective action, fragmentations within the global women's movement were issues of concern for other participants. For example, 'we need to make sure that women of colour are not perpetually relegated to inferior positions in the gender work relative to white women' (AWID questionnaire participant). As with the earlier discussion on intersectionality, these fragmentations of the global women's movement have resulted from ignoring some women and from homogenizing feminist issues. As a challenge to the future of gender equality, then, fragmentation will require advocates to, in the words of one participant, 'develop a nuanced response that does not feed ethnic or racial stereotypes or fear-mongering'.

These issues were also of great concern for the contributors to this collection. The feminist movement generally, and women's collective strategies and actions were areas discussed by many of the authors. Facio and Adeleye-Fayemi both emphasized the lack of clarity in the feminist movement while Griffen and Bracke focused on the depoliticization of the struggle. Posadskaya-Vanderbeck, however, was concerned with maintaining the empowerment of women at the grassroots level. At the same time, Kerr acknowledged fragmentation in global women's movements in her discussion, as she identified a weakness in the movements regarding the inability to address the diversity of women's identities.

One issue addressed by the contributing authors more than the participants related to conflict and militarization in the future. While only seven participants raised conflict and militarization as an issue, this may possibly reflect the more national or local focus of the respondents that I highlighted earlier. And the attention to this issue on the part of the authors may have occurred because several of them were writing their chapters during the 2003 US-led invasion of Iraq, and shortly after the incursion into Afghanistan. The focus both for Adeleye-Fayemi and for Dhanraj, Misra and Batliwala was the increasing feminization of poverty that is associated with conflicts and wars. Griffen, on the other hand, considered the lack of response from the feminist movement on issues of security decision-making and military developments to be a concern, and expressed the need to put these issues on the feminist agenda in the future. And for Francisco, the manipulation by some governments of the 'War on Terror' agenda to impose oppressive measures internally was the primary threat. Some of the questionnaire respondents also included conflict as an issue in which a global women's movement could play a strong role, which again demonstrates why it will be so important in the near future to have an active, inclusive and vocal women's movement that can take on gender equality issues requiring collective action and global resistance.

Ranking multiple issues on their importance to the movement(s) To analyse further the issues of concern for the future of gender equality work globally, survey participants were also asked to rank fifteen issues according to whether they have been over-, appropriately or under-emphasized. While the responses were wide-ranging, with language variations, there were some notable trends among the results. Strikingly, not one issue was identified as 'over-emphasized' by a majority of the respondents. In addition, only one, namely the 'growth of fundamentalisms', was considered appropriately emphasized by the majority. There was a difference in the Spanish-speaking and French-speaking answers to the 'growth of fundamentalisms', however. The French-speaking women split their answers between appropriately and under-emphasized, while the Spanish-speaking results were generally equal between all three.

Another two categories were closely divided in responses. 'The HIV/AIDS pandemic' and the 'lack of democratic governments' were both split between the appropriately and under-emphasized columns, with respondents from all three language groups typically following this pattern. HIV/AIDS was also raised as a specific concern by Adeleye-Fayemi, Kerr and Msimang, with the latter clearly linking the future of gender equality and women's/human rights to the impact HIV/AIDS is having in South Africa.

Most participants considered the remaining twelve issues to be under-emphasized by gender equality advocates today. Again, generally, the language breakdown of the responses coincided with this result, with only three exceptions. For each of these, 'increasing US dominance', 'right-wing challenge to reproductive rights' and 'negative effects of trade and investment, as well as foreign debt', the Spanish-speaking replies were closely divided between appropriately and under-emphasized.

What is the relevance of these results? While the structure of this questionnaire allowed for only single responses on what respondents considered to be the most important challenges, this section allowed them to express their opinion on several issues of concern for women's rights. From the results, it is clear that, outside of regional variations on some of these topics, gender equality advocates around the globe believe much more work is simultaneously required on a multitude of issues. These issues highlight our goals for the future of women's rights; how we achieve these goals is where we look next.

Strategies to change the present

Multiple challenges need multiple strategies: no single solution can possibly solve all problems. Thus, while it is important to discuss the current and future issues facing the global women's movement, this is not the whole picture. It is equally important to determine what strategies will need to be pursued in order to achieve these goals. Through the AWID membership questionnaire, we wanted to gather the opinions of gender equity advocates on the strategies they used and considered most effective. In this section, the survey asked participants, given unlimited resources, what strategy they would consider most important to pursue in order to achieve gender equality globally. The strategies our respondents considered most important in current work come from several different frameworks.

The two most frequently cited strategies fall under 'education and advocacy' work and 'global networking' campaigns.

Education and advocacy

> I would carry out conversations with women and men. These discussion workshops would be aimed at diverse groups (media, college students, children, public servants), in which personal reflections would include gender, and the repercussions of male dominance on interactions between and among women and men. (AWID questionnaire participant)

As I discussed earlier, education and advocacy are as important issues of concern as they are strategies to address other issues. Respondents listed education over all others as the best strategy for the future of global gender equality. Education as a strategy shifts the focus from a matter of access to schools into a matter of the content that the students will be taught. Thus, education is used as the tool through which gender equality issues are addressed, and through which advocacy can occur. The two roles of 'education as issue' and 'education as strategy' reinforce each other. As one Spanish-speaking participant stated: 'This is a strategy of promotion and generation of attitudes in favour of equality [through both] the formal and informal education systems.'

Global networking

> My strategy would involve networking, and building spaces, circles, groups and communities of women who are learning how to live differently. I would support spaces from which an articulation may be possible between politics and life, between thought and lifestyle. (AWID questionnaire participant)

Networking, or creating links between gender equality advocates and women's groups in the form of a global women's movement, has already been discussed here as an issue of importance for the future. As with education, however, networking is equally important as a strategy through which gender equality can be advanced.

Other strategies within the global mobilization realm were raised also. As one English-speaking contributor noted:

> We're good at creating institutions, doing advocacy, and providing direct services. We're good at research and analysis. We are not good at movement building and identifying strategic points of intervention that challenge power ... While women's autonomous organizing is important, women

need to focus more on shaping the agenda of actors in the global justice movement.

Networking among women's groups and gender advocates was mentioned by several of the authors, including Afkhami, Posadskaya-Vanderbeck, Francisco, Msimang, Griffen and Dhanraj, Misra and Batliwala. For both Msimang and Griffen, this networking took the form of building bridges between global and local efforts, while for Dhanraj, Misra and Batliwala, the emphasis was focused more on strengthening the base of women's movements. In Afkhami's chapter, however, her attention on networking focused on leadership, and the need for these leaders to work in dialogical communication with others.

Tactics for creating our ideal future

While education and global networking campaigns are presented as current strategies for effecting gender equality, future strategies for this work are less clear. Questionnaire participants were asked what strategy they consider will be most important to gender equality work in five to ten years' time. The opinions of the participants were as varied as the contributors throughout this volume, but two key themes were notable. Mass mobilization, and the use of ICTs and the media had similar numbers of responses, and came through as main strategies for the future as identified by these AWID participants.

Mass mobilization

> When a new generation of women realize that the rights they have inherited are not permanent and awaken to defend them it will unleash a force which will be very positive for gender equality. (AWID questionnaire participant)

One strategy not often raised by participants is related to mass mobilization. As a strategy, mass mobilization is presented by these respondents as getting more women in positions of leadership, and in creating institutional change to promote equality. With regard to the former, an English-speaking participant wrote about 'increasing significantly the numbers of women in political and appointive decision-making positions and building links between them on key political and economic issues'. As to the latter, one Spanish-speaking contributor suggested we work for 'change and institutional development of the public powers in structure, practices and agents in order to create an institutional culture of equality'.

Activist citizenship, as a reflection of mass mobilization, was incorporated into many of the chapters in this volume. Afkhami, Bracke, Msimang, Criquillion and Adeleye-Fayemi all consider this an important aspect of the future of global feminist work. Criquillion and Afkhami, for example, emphasize the need to have direct representation and participation of women in the political sphere, while Bracke challenges women's movements to politicize. The reconstruction of the women's movement locally, nationally and globally, as another form of mass mobilization, was likewise a very great concern for Msimang, Facio and Dhanraj, Misra and Batliwala. In the latter chapter, these women address the need to reclaim women from fundamentalist organizations. Msimang urges women's rights advocates to refer to, draw upon and enrich local and global battles; and, in the same vein, Facio calls for a return to the mutual support and consciousness-raising actions from the 1960s and 1970s, through the development of a feminist spirituality.

Use of ICTs and the media

> We need recognition of the different waves of the women's movement and of a common base, projecting the building of equality through the use of popular culture and new forms of communication media. (AWID questionnaire participant)

One possibility for achieving mass mobilization in the future is through the use of information and communication technologies (ICTs) and the media. While some respondents did raise these communication techniques as issues, most did not include them as a strategy for the future. One English-speaking contributor who did propose this stated that 'communication is critical, and in particular communication strategies that will reach women in *their* environments – to address, counter and create a balance within their relationships – in the home, community, and work environment'. Communication within the area of media and ICTs was a focus for some of the authors in this collection as well, including Griffen, Criquillion, Msimang, Afkhami and Francisco. In their discussions, Msimang and Afkhami both recognize the tremendous need to ensure poor women and women in the less developed world have access to ICTs. Criquillion's suggestion was to utilize traditional media and ICTs strategically to influence public opinion on women's realities and interests. For Francisco, it was the potential to use ICTs to link up internationally and to share information that she saw as being useful and having great potential into the future.

Rating the strategies of the global feminist movement Throughout this section of the survey, then, strategies for achieving global gender equality both now and in the future were identified. As in the issues section, survey participants were also asked to rank fourteen strategies based on whether they were effective, somewhat effective or ineffective. Of the fourteen, none was ranked mainly as ineffective. 'Making international financial institutions accountable to women' was given high rankings in all three categories, demonstrating a lack of consensus on this issue globally, as all three language groups were similarly divided. While 'Working with parliamentarians and governments to implement international and national commitments' had numerous votes for 'effective', it was the only one of these issues where 'somewhat effective' was the main response.

This split in category responses was much closer in another four strategies, namely: 'using the United Nations system more effectively'; 'peace building and defence policy'; 'tackling the media'; and 'using human rights approaches'. For the first of these, 'using the UN System', the English-speaking and Spanish-speaking responses were more evenly divided between all three than were the French-speaking. Likewise, 'peace-building and defence policy' had similar results in English-speaking for all three. The other eight were all dominated by 'effective' answers. Unlike the first set of ranking questions, however, the results for these eight were much more diverse, with varying opinions on the effectiveness of these strategies across the board.

Again, what do all of these results tell us about the future of women's rights globally? There is less consistency in this strategy section, and more diversity in terms of language results. Clearly, the strategies for achieving gender equality are considered as diverse as the issues. As one participant noted: 'I think it will depend on where and when this strategy will be used. The strategies will have to be created and adapted to the audience receiving the message.'

Some concluding thoughts

Throughout the responses on this AWID membership questionnaire, education and networking were raised over and over, as issues needing to be addressed and as strategies to accomplish this. We did not expect consensus in deciding any one issue was most pressing, nor agreement on the ideal strategy for achieving gender equality on a global scale. And as the variety of opinions make evident, there are many issues and strategies prevalent in the women's rights movement that demand serious attention. But according to our diverse and global membership, it is evident that both education and networking will play vital roles in the future of the struggle.

As for the contributors to this volume, for the most part their chapters end on a positive note. While they recognize that there is much work to be done, and that this work will often be difficult, there is also hope for a future that is free of exploitation, hatred and oppression. The AWID questionnaire ends in the same tone: not by looking forward, however, as the contributors have done in this volume, but by looking back. Participants were asked, 'what was your proudest moment working in the gender equality/women's right's movement?' Many of the strengths and the goals of the feminist movement over the past several decades can be summed up in their responses, which reflect why we persist in this work. Beyond merely recounting accomplishments, almost all of the moments that were recalled by the respondents signalled their passion and their lifelong commitment to the work, providing inspiring expressions of their pride in the past, and their hope for the future.

For many of these respondents, the struggle for women's rights requires the sacrifice of time, of other work and, sometimes, of health and personal safety. But their personal connection to this work is strengthened when it is obvious that this vital work is having an impact, such as the comment 'every time a woman tells me that the program I founded changed her life' demonstrates. For other participants, their proudest moment came in the achievement of goals their organizations had been striving to realize. Within this vein, one participant wrote about the time 'when the bills promoting women's rights that we have been working hard to promote have been passed into national laws'. Similarly, a Spanish-speaking respondent in the same tone noted that 'when I was Minister of Women's Rights in my country, the National Council of Women was created as the national institution for public policies related to women'. For these participants, then, the results of their efforts have meant a fundamental change for women's rights in their nation. And I will leave the final word here to a contributor participant who had pride in the women's rights movement as a whole:

> When I was a young feminist I walked in demonstrations in the main streets of so many cities proclaiming my vision of a future. I thought [I] was radical and idealistic – 20 years later cabinet ministers take those visions as starting points for policy. I'm proud to be part of a movement that transformed a social paradigm. (AWID questionnaire participant)

Survey questions

Issues

1. If you had the time and the unlimited resources, what would be the most important issue that you would work on to promote gender equality and social transformation globally? (*Limit your answer to 30 words.*)

2. In five to ten years' time, what do you think the most important challenge will be for gender equality work globally? (*Limit your answer to 30 words.*)

Strategies

1. If you had the time and unlimited resources, what would be the most important strategy that you would pursue to promote gender equality globally? (*Limit your answer to 30 words.*)

2. In five to ten years' time, what do you think the most important strategy will be for gender equality work globally? (*Limit your answer to 30 words.*)

3. Below are some of the major problems that need to be addressed in order to promote gender equality globally. Rate all 15 items as Over-emphasized, Appropriately Emphasized or Under-emphasized by gender equality advocates today.

a) Growth of fundamentalisms
b) Increasing economic disparities
c) The HIV/AIDS pandemic
d) Increasing global conflicts and militarization
e) Lack of democratic governments
f) Male-biased media
g) Depletion/privatization of natural resources
h) Lack of corporate accountability
i) Lack of gender sensitivity and accountability of international financial institutions
j) The negative impact of new technologies
k) Negative effects of trade and investment, as well as foreign debt
l) Increasing US dominance
m) Right-wing challenge to reproductive rights
n) Racism
o) Lack of effective mechanisms for women's human rights protection
p) Undervaluing of women's work
q) Other (*Please specify.*)
r) Other (*Please specify.*)

4. Below is a list of some of the major strategies that are being used globally to promote gender equality. Rank all items as Effective, Somewhat Effective or Ineffective, in addressing future challenges to gender equality.

a) Building mass grassroots social movements committed to women's rights
b) Making international financial institutions accountable to women
c) Using the United Nations system more effectively
d) Working with parliamentarians and governments to implement international and national commitments

e) Promoting feminist leadership development and getting feminists into positions of power
f) Using popular culture and new forms of media to transform public consciousness
g) Undertaking thorough research to bolster the rationale for gender-equitable development
h) Peace-building and defence policy
i) Tackling the media
j) Using human rights approaches
k) Mobilizing more financial resources for women's rights/gender equality
l) Working strategically with other social movements and constituencies
m) Analysing achievements of the past
n) Demystifying the economy
o) Other (*Please specify.*)
p) Other (*Please specify.*)

Personal information:

(Please note that all this information will be held as confidential.)

1. Country (of residence)
2. What issues do you work on primarily?
3. What level do you work at primarily?
   Global; Regional; National; Local; Don't know/not sure
4. Into which of the following ranges does your age fall?
   Under 18; 18–24; 25–34; 35–44; 45–60; Over 60
5. How long have you been a member of AWID?
   Less than one year; 1–2 years; 3–5 years; 6–10 years; More than 10 years; Not a member, Don't know/not sure
6. How long have you been involved in gender equality/women's rights issues?
   Less than 2 years; 2 to 5 years; 5 to 15 years; 15 or more years; Don't know/not sure

Conclusion (optional)

What was your proudest moment working in the gender equality/women's right's movement?

Notes

1 For more information on AWID and Mama Cash, including their visions, goals and projects, please visit <www.awid.org and www.mamacash.nl>

2 Not all women who completed the survey identified which country they are from, but from the majority who did, 70 per cent of the French-speaking respondents were from Africa and 75 per cent of the Spanish-speaking were from Latin America. While not definitive, the French-speaking and Spanish-speaking results can therefore be considered at least partially reflective of these regions.

3 Intersectionality is a framework of analysis dealing with the oppressions and privileges that result from people's various identities (including gender, race, class, ethnicity, sexual orientation, religion, education and ability, among others), and how the oppressions people experience because of these identities fundamentally change depending on where and how they intersect. An intersectional approach looks at how to recognize hierarchies and power relationships that exist between people so that we can move beyond them, with the ultimate goal being the elimination of discrimination from society.

Editors and contributors

The Editors

Joanna Kerr is the Executive Director of AWID. Previously she managed the gender programme at the North–South Institute, a Canadian think tank, for almost 7 years. She holds an MA in Gender and Development from the Institute of Development Studies, University of Sussex, UK. Her publications include *Ours by Right: Women's Rights as Human Rights* (Zed Books, 1993), *Gender and Jobs in China's New Economy* (with Julie Delahanty, 1996), *The Gender Dimensions of Economic Reforms in Africa* (edited with Lynn Brown, 1997), and *Demanding Dignity: Women Confronting Economic Reforms in Africa* (edited with Dzodzi Tsikata, 2000)

Ellen Sprenger is a consultant based in Toronto, Canada, specializing in social change fundraising, future-oriented strategic planning and overall organizational change management. Ellen was the Executive Director of Mama Cash between 2001 and 2004. She also worked for Novib–Oxfam Netherlands (1992–2001) as a senior policy adviser on gender equality and as quality and control manager. Ellen has worked with activists, practitioners and researchers in different countries in Europe, Africa, Asia, the Middle East and Latin America as well as in North America. She is co-author of *Gender and Organizational Change: Bridging the Gap between Policy and Practice* (Royal Tropical Institute, 1997). Ellen holds an MA in International Development and an MBA.

Alison Symington is Research Manager at AWID. Her work focuses on issues of globalization, trade policy, human rights accountability, international institutions and women's economic and social rights protection. She holds a law degree from the University of Toronto and a Masters of Law in International Legal Studies from New York University. She has held several research positions based in the University of Toronto, looking at issues of international women's rights, the use of international and comparative law in domestic jurisdictions, the politics of trade negotiations, and the citizenship and nationality rights of women and children.

The Contributors

Bisi Adeleye-Fayemi is the Executive Director and a co-founder of the African Women's Development Fund, the first Africa-wide grant-making initiative for African women's organisations. Prior to her current position, she was for ten years (1991–2001) the Director of Akina Mama wa Afrika (AMwA), an international development organization for African women based in the UK. While at AMwA, she set up the African Women's Leadership Institute, a regional training and networking forum which has trained women all over Africa. She has an MA in History from the University of Ife, Nigeria and an MA in Gender Studies from Middlesex University, UK. She has experience in feminist organizational development, and training expertise in leadership development and resource mobilization.

Mahnaz Afkhami is the founding president of Women's Learning Partnership, Executive Director of the Foundation for Iranian Studies, and former Minister of State for Women's Affairs in Iran. Formerly she was President of the Sisterhood is Global Institute. She has been a leading advocate for women's rights internationally for more than three decades. She has written and lectured extensively on women's human rights, women in leadership, and women, civil society, and democracy. Among her publications are *Women and the Law in Iran* (1993), *Women in Exile* (1994), *Faith and Freedom: Women's Human Rights in the Muslim World* (1995), *Claiming our Rights: A Manual for Women's Human Rights Education in Muslim Societies* (1996), *Muslim Women and the Politics of Participation* (1997), and *Safe and Secure: Eliminating Violence Against Women and Girls in Muslim Societies* (1998), Leading to Choices: a leadership handbook for women (2001), and *Toward a Compassionate Society* (2002).

Srilatha Batliwala has worked as a Program Officer in the Governance and Civil Society Unit of the Ford Foundation in New York, handling programmes related to strengthening international civil society and the non-profit sector in the US. She has also been a Fellow and head of the Women's Policy Research and Advocacy (WOPRA) Unit of the National Institute of Advanced Studies, Bangalore, India, where she co-ordinated a study of the status of women in 1,200 rural households in Karnataka state. Her major achievements include setting up and implementing the famous Mahila Samkhya, a federal programme for women's empowerment, which was instrumental in organizing over 30,000 poor rural women into collectives which fought for changes in their social, legal and political status. She is also a founder and co-director of SPARC, an NGO working with urban pavement and slum dwellers. Her publications include *Status of Rural Women in Karnataka* and *Women's Empowerment in South Asia – Concepts and Practices.* Ms. Batliwala holds a Master's Degree in Social Work from the Tata Institute of Social Science, Bombay.

Sarah Bracke is a feminist researcher and activist based in Brussels. For a number of years she has been working on the question of women's involvement in so-called religious fundamentalist movements in Europe, and has recently started to work on possible feminist responses to the securitarian discourses that are currently so popular. She is involved in several feminist groups, such as AFOK (Autonoom Feministisch OnderzoeksKollektief, Belgium), Femi (Netherlands) and a European transnational network of women's studies students and researchers: the NextGENDERation network. Within NextGENDERation, she's involved in a working group on globalization and feminist resistance that organizes a number of activities at the European Social Fora.

Ana Criquillion is a feminist and activist in the women's movement in Nicaragua. She is the co-founder and president of the Fundación Puntos de Encuentro, a Nicaraguan NGO founded in 1990 to promote women's and young people's rights. She was the founder of the first women's secretariat in trade unions in Nicaragua, held the first Chair in Women's Studies at the University of Managua, and she has been part of the co-ordination team of 'Entre Mujeres' in Latin America, a North–South Dialogue project. Ana was also the national co-ordinator of the Nicaraguan delegation to the Fourth UN Conference on Women in Beijing. She is the author of several publications on gender, international aid and capacity building.

Deepa Dhanraj is the Executive Director of D&N Production, based in Bangalore, India. She has been actively involved in the women's movement in India since 1980 and has directed many award-winning documentaries focusing on the empowerment of the poor and marginalized women. Her films include *The Legacy of Malthus*, which challenges the theory that overpopulation is responsible for poverty and environmental destruction; *Something Like a War*, a historical overview of India's coercive family planning programme and its effects on women; and *Sudesha*, a portrait of a village activist in the Chipko Forest Conservation Movement in the foothills of the Himalaya. She has also directed training films and participated in workshops and seminars on political participation, health and education.

Alda Facio is a jurist, writer and international expert on women's human rights, gender violence and gender analysis. She is one of the founders and the first director of the Women's Caucus for Gender Justice in the International Criminal Court (ICC), and since 1990 has been the Director of the Women, Gender and Justice Program at the United Nations Latin

American Institute for Crime Prevention (ILANUD), based in Costa Rica. She is a facilitator in training on the Convention on the Elimination of Discrimination Against Women (CEDAW), held once a year in New York for participants from reporting countries, and in training in other countries for NGOs and government officials who will be reporting in the near future. She has written a book on how to write 'shadow reports' to the Committee on the Elimination of Violence Against Women, and is currently writing a manual for judges on how to apply it. She also participated as a government delegate in the drafting of the Optional Protocol to CEDAW and at the Rome Conference which adopted the Statute of the ICC. She has written law proposals on violence against women and measures to eliminate discrimination against women for various Latin American legislatures, and she has taught at graduate level in several universities on gender-sensitive perspectives and written extensively on subjects relating to women's human rights.

Josefa (Gigi) Francisco is the Executive Director of the Women and Gender Institute of Miriam College Foundation in Quezon City, Philippines. She is a full-time faculty member in the International Studies Department and holds a graduate degree in Asian Studies from the University of the Philippines. She is the South-east Asia regional co-ordinator for DAWN and also regional co-ordinator of the Gender and Trade Network for Asia. Her numerous publications include *Globalization and Patriarchy in Symbiosis: The Asian Financial Crisi* (with Gita Sen, 2000), *Literacy Packet on Trade Intensification in Asia: What it means to women's work* (2001), and *Gender Gap Toolkit for Social Investigation* (2002).

Vanessa Griffin was co-ordinator of the Gender and Development Program of the Asian and Pacific Development Centre from 1995 to 2002. Previously, she was a lecturer in History and Politics at the University of the South Pacific in Suva, Fiji. She was also a founding member in the 1970s of Pacific Women's Resource Center. She has worked in the health sector in Papua New Guinea, and has been a writer and editor on gender and development issues in the Asia and Pacific region since the first UN International Women's Conference in 1975 in Mexico City.

Rhonda Leeson is a young feminist researcher and anti-oppression activist living in Toronto, Canada. A recent graduate, she holds an MA in Anthropology and International Development from the University of Guelph, with a focus on intersectionality and women's organizations in South Africa. Her grassroots activism centres on eliminating sexual violence against women and children. As a freelance consultant, she provides research support to AWID.

Geetanjali Misra is currently the Executive Director of Creating Resources for Empowerment and Action (CREA) and has worked at the activist, grant-making and policy levels on issues of sexuality, reproductive health, human rights and violence against women. Previously, she was the Sexuality and Reproductive Health Program Officer at the Ford Foundation, where she worked on HIV/AIDS, sexuality, violence against women and research and advocacy relating to reproductive freedom. She is the co-founder of SAKHI for South Asian women in New York, a non-profit organization committed to ending violence against women of South Asian origin.

Sisonke Msimang is currently the Co-ordinator of the Regional Secretariat of the Youth Against AIDS Network (YAAN). YAAN is a youth-run and managed organization focused on co-ordinating and strengthening the efforts of youth activists in the fight against AIDS in Africa. Prior to joining YAAN, Sisonke worked for the HIV/AIDS and Human Rights Programme of the United Nations Development Fund for Women (UNIFEM) in New York. Before this, she was a consultant working with a number of NGOs and international agencies focusing on reproductive health, HIV/AIDS and gender. She has also worked for the United Nations Population Fund (UNFPA) as a Programme Officer, and at the African Gender Institute as a researcher and a trainer.

Anastasia Posadskaya-Vanderbeck has fifteen years of experience directing academic and advocacy programmes focusing on women's rights. Since 1997, she has served as a Director of the Network Women's Programme of the Open Society Institute (Soros Foundation), with the mandate to integrate women's rights in the international work of the foundation. In this capacity she is responsible for development, monitoring and implementation of international programmes in about 30 countries. She has been a member of the Millennium Development Goals Task Force on Education and Gender Equality since 2002, and was on the International Planning Committee of the 9th AWID Forum in Guadalajara (2001–2003). In 1999–2000 she was awarded the Julian and Virginia Cornell Distinguished Visiting Professorship by Swarthmore College, USA. She co-edited *Women in Russia: New Era in Russian Feminism* (1994) and *A Revolution of Their Own: Voices of Women in Russian History* (with Barbara Alpern Engel, 1998), and is the author of about 40 articles in the academic and popular press.

Index